Trialogue

Jews, Christians, & Muslims in Dialogue

Leonard Swidler
Khalid Duran
Reuven Firestone

TRIALOGUE

JEWS, CHRISTIANS, AND MUSLIMS IN DIALOGUE

Twenty-Third Publications
A Division of Bayard
One Montauk Avenue, Suite 200
New London, CT 06320
(860) 437-3012 or (800) 321-0411
www.23rdpublications.com

ISBN 978-1-58595-587-9
Library of Congress Catalog Card Number: 2006920451
Printed in the U.S.A.

Contents

Appendices

Endnotes

Index

INTRODUCTION

The Cosmic Dance of Dialogue

Dialogue—the mutually beneficial interaction of differing components—is at the very heart of the Universe, of which we humans are the highest expression. It's there in the basic interaction of *Matter and Energy* (in Einstein's unforgettable formula: $E=mc^2$—Energy equals mass times the square of the speed of light), in the creative interaction of *Protons and Electrons* in every atom, in the vital symbiosis of *Body and Spirit* in every human, in the creative dialogue between *Woman and Man*, and in the dynamic relationship between *Individual and Society*. Thus, the very essence of our humanity is dialogical, and a fulfilled human life is the highest expression of the "Cosmic Dance of Dialogue."

In the early millennia of the history of humanity, as we spread outward from our starting point in central Africa, the forces of Divergence were dominant. However, because we live on a globe, in our frenetic divergence we eventually began to encounter each other more and more frequently. Now the forces of stunning Convergence are becoming increasingly dominant.

In the past, during the age of divergence, we could live in isolation from each other; we could ignore each other. Now, in the age of convergence, we are forced to live in one world. We increasingly live in a global village. We cannot ignore the other, the different. Too often in the past we have tried to make over the other into a likeness of ourselves, often by violence. But this is the very opposite of dialogue. This egocentric arrogance is in fundamental opposition to the Cosmic Dance of Dialogue. It is not creative; it is destructive.

Hence, we humans today have a stark choice: dialogue or death!

Dialogues of the Head, Hands, and Heart

For us humans there are three main dimensions to dialogue—the mutually beneficial interaction among those who are different—corresponding to the structure of our humanness: dialogue of the head, dialogue of the hands, and dialogue of the heart.

The Cognitive or Intellectual: Seeking the Truth

In the dialogue of the head, we mentally reach out to the other to learn from those who think differently from us. We try to understand how they see the world and why they act as they do. This dialogue of the head is vital, for how we see and understand the world and life determines how we act toward ourselves, toward other persons, and toward the world around us.

The Illative or Ethical: Seeking the Good

In the dialogue of the hands, we join together with others to work to make the world a better place in which we all must live together. Since we can no longer live separately in this one world, we must work jointly to make it not just a house but a home for all of us.

The Affective or Aesthetic: Seeking the Beautiful

In the dialogue of the heart, we share in the expressions of the emotions of those different from us. Because we humans are body and spirit, or rather body-spirit, we give bodily-spiritual expression in all the arts to our multifarious responses to our encounters with life: joy, sorrow, gratitude, anger, and most of all, love. All the world delights in beauty, wherein we find the familiar that avoids sameness, and wherein we find diversity that avoids distastefulness.

Wholeness and Holiness: Seeking the One

We humans cannot live a divided life for long. If we are to even survive, let alone flourish, we must "get it all together." We must live a "whole" life. Indeed, this is what the religions of the Western tradition mean when they say that we humans should be "holy." Literally, to be holy means to be whole. Hence, in our human dance of dialogue, we must "get it all together," we must be whole and holy. We must dance together the dialogue of the head, the dialogue of the hands, and the dialogue of the heart

For Reflection and Discussion

1. Business leaders used to emphasize the spirit of competition as driving their enterprise. Now they are more likely to exalt cooperation and team work as the way to success. Before reading further in this book, what is your assessment of the spirit of cooperation and dialogue among religions today?
2. The authors envision the universe as a "Cosmic Dance" and suggest that dialogue among religions is a way of participating in that dance. What other images, positive and negative, might describe interaction among religions?
3. Sometimes while dancing, we step on each other's feet. How important is it to have a sense of humor while engaging in dialogue? Give examples.
4. The authors give us a stark challenge: dialogue or death! What is your response to this challenge?

PART ONE

The Importance of Dialogue

LEONARD SWIDLER

CHAPTER ONE

What Is Dialogue?

Today when we speak of dialogue between religions or ideologies, we mean something quite definite, namely, a two-way communication between persons; one-way lecturing or speaking is obviously not dialogue. However, there are many different kinds of two-way communication, for example, fighting, wrangling, debating, etc. Clearly none of these are dialogue. On the other extreme is the communication between persons who hold precisely the same views on a particular subject. We also do not mean this when we use the term dialogue; rather, we might call that something like encouragement, reinforcement—but certainly not dialogue. Now if we look at these two opposite kinds of two-way communication which are *not* meant by the word dialogue, we can learn quite precisely what we do in fact mean when we use the term dialogue.

Looking at the last example first—the principle underlying "reinforcement" is the assumption that both sides have a total grasp on the truth of the subject and hence simply need to be supported in their commitment to it. Since this example and the principle underlying it are excluded from the meaning of dialogue, clearly dialogue must include the notion that neither side has a total grasp of the truth of the subject, but that both need to seek further.

The principle underlying "debating" in the second example is the assumption that one side has all the truth concerning the subject and that the other side needs to be informed or convinced of it. Since that example also and its principle are excluded from the meaning of dialogue, this clearly implies that dialogue means that no one side has a monopoly on the truth on the subject, but both need to seek further.

It may turn out in some instances, of course, that after a more or less extensive dialogue, it is learned that the two sides in fact agree completely on the subject discussed. Naturally, such a discovery does not mean that the encounter was a non-dialogue, but rather that the dialogue was the means of learning the new truth that both sides agreed on the subject. To continue from that point on, however, to speak only about the area of agreement, would then be to move from dialogue to reinforcement.

Hence, to express at least the initial part of the meaning of dialogue positively: dialogue is a two-way communication between persons who hold significantly differing views on a subject, with the purpose of learning more truth about the subject from one another.

This analysis may seem obvious and hence superfluous. But we believe not. Dialogue has become a faddish term and is sometimes, like charity, used to cover a multitude of sins. Sometimes, for example, it is used by those who are quite convinced that they have all the truth on a subject, but feel that in today's climate with "dialogue" in vogue, a less aggressive style will be more effective in communicating to the "ignorant" the truth that they already possess in full. Therefore, while their encounters with others still rely on the older non-dialogue principle—that they have all the truth on a subject—their less importuning approach will now be called "dialogue." This type of use would appear to be merely an opportunistic manipulation of the term dialogue.

Maybe some of those people, however, truly believe that they are engaging in dialogue when they employ such a "soft sell" approach and encourage their interlocutors to also express their own views on the subject—even though it is known ahead of time, of course, that they are false—for such a "dialogue" may well make the ignorant person more open to receiving the truth that the one side knows it already has. In that situation, the "truth-holders" simply had a basic misunderstanding of the term dialogue and mistakenly called their convert-making "dialogue." Therefore, the above clarification is important.

In this context, we are speaking about a particular kind of dialogue, namely interreligious dialogue in the broadest sense, that is, dialogue on a religious subject by persons who understand themselves to be in different religious traditions and communities. If religion is understood as an explanation of the ultimate meaning of life and how to live accordingly, that would include all such systems, even though they customarily would not be called religions, but rather, ideologies, such as, atheistic Humanism and Marxism. Hence, it is more accurate to speak of both interreligious and interideological dialogue.

Why Dialogue Arose

One can, of course, justifiably point to a number of recent developments that have contributed to the rise of dialogue, for example, growth in mass education, communications, and travel, a world economy, threatening global destruction. Nevertheless, a major underlying cause is a paradigm shift in the West in how we perceive and describe the world. A paradigm is simply the model, the cluster of assumptions, on whose basis phenomena are perceived and explained, for example, the geocentric paradigm for explaining the movements of the planets. A shift to another paradigm—as to the heliocentric—will have a major impact. Such a paradigm shift has occurred and is still occurring in the Western understanding of truth statements, which has made dialogue not just possible, but necessary.

Whereas the understanding of truth in the West was largely absolute, static, monologic, or exclusive up to the nineteenth century, it has subsequently become de-absolutized, dynamic, and dialogic—in a word relational. This relatively new view of truth came about in at least six different but closely related ways.

1. Until the nineteenth century in Europe, truth (a statement about reality) was conceived in an absolute, static, exclusivistic either-or manner. It was believed that if a statement was true at one time, it would remain true, and not only in the sense of statements about empirical facts but also in the sense of statements about the meanings of things. Such is a classicist or absolutist view of truth.

2. Then, in the nineteenth century, scholars came to perceive all statements about the meaning of something as being partially products of their historical circumstances. Only by placing truth statements in their historical situations, their historical *Sitz im Leben*, could they be properly understood. A text could be understood only in context. Therefore, all statements about the meaning of things were seen to be de-absolutized in terms of time. Such is a historical view of truth.

3. Later on it was noted that we ask questions so as to obtain the knowledge and truth according to which we want to live. This is a praxis or intentional view of truth, that is, a statement has to be understood in relationship to the action-oriented intention of the thinker.

4. Early in the twentieth century, Karl Mannheim developed what he called the sociology of knowledge, which points out that every statement about truth and meaning is perspectival because all reality is perceived and spoken of from the cultural, class, sexual, and so forth, perspective of the perceiver. Such is a perspectival view of truth.
5. A number of thinkers, and most especially Ludwig Wittgenstein, have discovered something of the limitations of human language. Every description of reality is necessarily only partial, for although reality can be seen from an almost limitless number of perspectives, human language can express things from only one perspective at once. This partial and limited quality of all language is necessarily greatly intensified when one attempts to speak of the transcendent, which by definition "goes-beyond." Such is a language-limited view of truth.
6. The contemporary discipline of hermeneutics stresses that all knowledge is interpreted knowledge. This means that in all knowledge "I" come to know something; the object comes into me in a certain way, namely, through the lens that I use to perceive it. As Thomas Aquinas wrote, "Things known are in the knower according to the mode of the knower."[1] Such is an interpretative view of truth.
7. Further yet, reality can "speak" to me only with the language that I give it. The "answers" that I receive back from reality will always be in the language, the thought categories, of the questions I put to it. If and when the answers I receive are sometimes confused and unsatisfying, I probably need to learn to speak a more appropriate language when I put questions to reality. For example, if I ask the question: "How heavy is green?" of course I will receive a nonsense answer. Or if I ask questions about living things in mechanical categories, I will receive confusing and unsatisfying answers. I will likewise receive confusing and unsatisfying answers to questions about human sexuality if I use categories that are solely physical-biological. Witness the absurdity of the answer that birth control is forbidden by the natural law—the question falsely assumes that the nature of humanity is merely physical-biological. Such an understanding of truth is a dialogic understanding.[2]

In brief, our understanding of truth and reality has been undergoing a radical shift. The new paradigm understands all statements about reality, especially about the meaning of things, to be historical, praxial or intentional, perspectival, language-limited or partial, interpretive, and dialogic. Our understanding of truth statements, in short, has become "de-absolutized"—it has become "relational." All statements about reality are now seen to be related to the historical context, praxis intentionality, perspective, etc., of the speaker, and in that sense are no longer "absolute." Therefore, if my perception and description of the world is true only in a limited sense, that is, only as seen from my place in the world, if I wish to expand my grasp of reality, I need to learn from others what they know of reality that they can perceive from their place in the world that I cannot see from mine. That, however, can happen only through dialogue.

Seven Views of "Truth"

1. **Classicist/absolutist:** Truth is static, unchanging, absolute, and universal. (What was true in Africa in 1000 BCE is true in North America in 2007.)
2. **Historical:** Truth claims are time-bound; awareness of what is true changes through history.
3. **Praxis/intentional:** The intentions and goals of truth-seekers influence what they identify as truth.
4. **Perspectival:** All truth claims reflect the unique perspectives of people: their culture, class, race, sex, etc.
5. **Language-limited:** Words used to describe truth are necessarily partial; our language limits our conversations about truth.
6. **Interpretive:** Everyone filters "the truth" and interprets it; no statements about truth exist apart from such interpretation.
7. **Dialogic:** Since truth claims are limited and perspectival, truth-seeking happens best when people engage in open dialogue with others who together seek closer approximations of the truth.

For Reflection and Discussion

1. In light of these seven views of truth, how would you describe your own approach to truth-seeking?
2. Is dialogue, in your opinion, a rejection of "truth" or a doorway into truth?
3. How would you define dialogue in your own words?

Who Should Dialogue

One important question is, who can, who should, engage in interreligious, interideological dialogue? There is clearly a fundamental communal aspect to such a dialogue. For example, if a person is neither a Lutheran nor a Jew, he or she could not engage in a specifically Lutheran-Jewish dialogue. Likewise, persons not belonging to any religious or ideological community could not, of course, engage in interreligious, interideological dialogue. They might of course engage in meaningful religious or ideological dialogue, but it simply would not be interreligious, interideological, between religions or ideologies.

Who then would qualify as a member of a religious community? If the question is of the official representation of a community at a dialogue, the clear answer is those who are appointed by the appropriate official body in that community: the congregation, Bet Din, roshi, bishop, Central Committee or whatever. However, if it is not a case of official representation, general reputation is usually the criteria. Some persons' qualifications, however, can be challenged by elements within a community, even very important official elements. The Vatican Congregation for the Doctrine of the Faith, for example, has declared that Professors Hans Küng, Charles Curran, and Roger Haight are no longer to be considered Catholic theologians. In all three cases, however, hundreds of Catholic theologians subsequently stated publicly in writing that they were indeed still Catholic theologians.

In the end, however, it seems best to follow the principle that each person should decide for himself or herself whether or not they are members of a religious community. Extraordinary cases may at rare times present initial anomalies, but they inevitably will resolve themselves. Furthermore, it *is* important to be aware that, especially in the initial stages of any interreligious, interideological dialogue, it is very likely that the literally ec-centric members of religious, ideological communities will be the ones who will have the interest and ability to enter into dialogue. The more centrist persons will do so only after the dialogue has been proved safe for the mainline, official elements to venture into.

It is important to note that interreligious, interideological dialogue is not limited to official representatives of communities. Actually the great majority of the vast amount of such dialogue, particularly in the past four decades, has not been carried on by official representatives, although that too has been happening with increasing frequency.

What is needed then is 1) an openness to learn from the other, 2) knowledge of one's own tradition, and 3) a similarly disposed and knowledgeable dialogue partner from the other tradition. This can happen on almost any level of knowledge and education. The key is the openness to learn from the other. Naturally no one's knowledge of his or her own tradition can ever be complete; each person must continually learn more about it. One merely needs to realize that one's knowledge is in fact limited and know where to turn to gain the information needed. It is also important, however, that the dialogue partners be more or less equal in knowledge of their own traditions. The larger the asymmetry is, the less the communication will be two-way or dialogic.

Hence, it is important that interreligious, interideological dialogue *not* be limited to official representatives or even to the experts in the various traditions, although they both have their irreplaceable roles to play in the dialogue. Dialogue should involve every level of religious and ideological communities, all the way down to the "persons in the pews." Only in this way will the religious, ideological communities learn from one another and come to understand one another as they truly are.

The Catholic bishops of the world expressed this insight very clearly and vigorously at the Second Vatican Council (1962–65) when they "exhorted *all the Catholic faithful* to recognize the signs of the times and to take an active and intelligent part in the work of ecumenism [dialogue among the Christian churches, and in an extended understanding, dialogue among the religions and ideologies, as is made clear by other Vatican II documents and the establishment of permanent Vatican Secretariats for dialogue with non-Christians and with non-Believers]." Not being content with this exhortation, the bishops went on to say that, "in ecumenical work, [all] Catholics must…make the *first approaches* toward them [non-Catholics]." In case there were some opaque minds or recalcitrant wills out there, the bishops once more made it clear that ecumenism [interreligious, interideological dialogue] "involves the whole Church, faithful and clergy alike. It extends to everyone, according to the talent of each" (Vatican II, *Decree on Ecumenism*, 4,5). Certainly this insight is not to be limited to the one billion-plus Catholics in the world—and the further billions they directly or indirectly influence—massive and important as that group may be.

However, what about the challenge of those who charge that "dialogists" are really elitists because they define dialogue in such a liberal manner that only like-minded liberals can join in? In fact, only those who have a "de-absolutized" understanding of truth will be able or even want to enter into dialogue. Put in other words, only those who understand all truth statements, that is, all statements about reality, to be always limited in a variety of ways and in that sense not absolute (the word comes from the Latin *ab-solvere*, "un-limited"), can enter into dialogue. This, however, is no elitist discrimination against "absolutists" or fundamentalists by not allowing them to engage in dialogue. Such a charge would simply be another case of not understanding what dialogue is: a two-way communication so that both sides can learn. If one partner grants that it has something to learn from the other, that admission presupposes that the first partner has only a limited—a de-absolutized—grasp of truth concerning the subject. If one partner thinks that it has an absolute grasp of the truth concerning the subject, it obviously believes that it has nothing to learn from the other, and hence the encounter will not be a dialogue but some kind of attempt at one-way teaching or a debate. Thus the partner with the absolutized view of truth will not only not be able to engage in dialogue, it will very much not want to—unless it falls into the category either of harboring the earlier described misunderstanding of the meaning of dialogue or the intention of an opportunistic manipulation of the term.

For Reflection and Discussion

1. The authors point out that beginning in particular with Vatican Council II (1962–65), Catholic leaders have been strong advocates of interreligious dialogue. How clearly and forcefully has that message been communicated to you from your religious leaders?
2. In your experience, how clearly has the call to engage in interreligious dialogue filtered down to the average member of your religious community?
3. Do you feel that you know your own tradition well enough to dialogue about it? Why or why not?
4. What might motivate someone to reject dialogue? How would you address his or her concerns?

Kinds of Dialogue

In the question of what constitutes interreligious, interideological dialogue, it is important to notice that we normally mean a two-way communication in ideas and words. At times, however, we give the term an extended meaning of

Interreligious dialogue leads to...

1. New information about others
2. Expanded understanding of ourselves
3. Changes in attitudes and perspective
4. Behavioral change

joint action or collaboration and joint prayer or sharing of the spiritual or depth dimension of our tradition. While the intellectual and verbal communication is indeed the primary meaning of dialogue, if the results therefrom do not spill over into the other two areas of action and spirituality, it will have proved sterile. Beyond that it can lead toward a kind of schizophrenia and even hypocrisy.

On the positive side, serious involvement in joint action and/or spirituality will tend to challenge previously-held intellectual positions and lead to dialogue in the cognitive field. Catholic and Protestant clergy, for example, who found themselves together in the Nazi Concentration Camp in Dachau because of joint resistance to Nazi actions began to ask each other why they did what they did and through dialogue were surprised to learn that they held many more positions in common than positions that separated them. In fact these encounters and others like them fostered the *Una Sancta* Movement in Germany, which in turn was the engine that moved the Catholic Church in the Second Vatican Council officially to embrace ecumenism and interreligious dialogue after many centuries of vigorous official rejection.[3]

Because religion is not something just of the head and the hands, but also of the heart—of the whole human being—our encounter with our partner must also eventually include the depth or spiritual dimension. This spiritual or depth dimension engages our emotions, our imagination, our intuitive consciousness. If we do not come to know each other in this deepest dimension of ourselves, our dialogue will remain relatively superficial. The technique called by John Dunne "crossing over" can be of help here. Through it we focus on a central image, metaphor, from our partner's spiritual life and let it work on our imagination, our emotions, evoking whatever responses it may, leading us to different feelings. We then return to our own inner world enriched, expanded, with a deeper sympathy for and sensitivity to our partner's inner world. Within the context of this expanded inner dimension, we will be prompted to look thereafter for new cognitive articulations adequate to reflect it, and we will be prompted to express our new awareness and understanding of our partner's religious reality in appropriate action.

Encountering our partner on merely one or two levels will indeed be authentic dialogue, but given the integrative and comprehensive nature of religion and ideology, it is only natural that we be led from dialogue on one level to the others. Only with dialogue in this full fashion on all three levels will our interreligious, interideological dialogue be complete.

Goals of Dialogue

The general goal of dialogue is for each side to learn and to change accordingly. Naturally if each side comes to the encounter primarily to learn from the other, the other side must teach, and thus both learning and teaching occur. We know, however, that if each side comes primarily to teach, both sides will tend to close up and as a result neither teaching nor learning takes place.

We naturally gradually learn more and more about our partners in the dialogue and in the process also shuck off the misinformation about them we may have had. However, we also learn something more, something even closer to home. Our dialogue partner likewise becomes for us something of a mirror in which we perceive ourselves in ways we otherwise could not. In the very process of responding to the questions of our partners we look into our inner selves and into our traditions in ways that we perhaps never would have, and thus come to know ourselves as we could not have outside the dialogue.

In addition, in listening to our partners' descriptions of their perceptions of us, we learn much about "how we are in the world." Because no one is simply in himself or herself, but is always in relationship to others, "how we are in the world," how we relate to and impact others, is in fact part of our reality, is part of us. As an example, it is only by being in dialogue with another culture that we really come to know our own. I became aware of my particular American culture, for example, only as I lived in Europe for a number of years. I became conscious of American culture as such with its similarities to and differences from the European only in the mirror of my dialogue partner of European culture.

This expanded knowledge of ourselves and of the other that we gain in dialogue cannot, of course, remain ineffective in our lives. As our self-understanding and understanding of those persons and things around us change, so too must our attitude toward ourselves and others change, and thus our behavior as well. Once again, to the extent that this inner and outer change, this transformation, does not take place, to that extent we tend toward schizophrenia and hypocrisy. Whether one wants to speak of dialogue and then of the subsequent transformation as "beyond dialogue," as John Cobb does in his book *Beyond Dialogue*, or speak of transformation as an integral part of the continuing dialogue process, as Klaus Klostermeier does (*Journal of Ecumenical Studies*, 21, 4 [Fall, 1984], pp. 755–59), need not detain us here. What is important is to see that the chain of dialogue-knowledge-change must not be broken. If the final link, change, falls away, the authenticity of the second, knowledge, and the first, dialogue, are called into question. To repeat: The goal of dialogue is for "each side to learn and change accordingly."

There are likewise communal goals in interreligious, interideological dialogue. Some of these will be special to the situation of the particular dialogue partners. Several Christian churches, for example, may enter into dialogue with the goal of structural union. Such union goals, however, will be something particular to religious communities *within* one religion, that is, within Christianity, within Buddhism, within Islam, etc. Dialogue *between* different religions and ideologies will not have this structural union goal. Rather, it will seek first of all to know the dialogue partners as accurately as possible and try to understand them as sympathetically as possible. Dialogue will seek to learn what the partners' commonalities and differences are.

There is a simple technique to learn where the authentic commonalities and differences are between two religions or ideologies: Attempt to agree with the dialogue partner as far as possible on a subject without violating one's own integrity; where one can go no further, that is where the authentic difference is and what has been shared up until that point are commonalities. Experience informs us that very often our true differences lie elsewhere than we had believed before the dialogue.

One communal goal in looking to learn the commonalities and differences two religions hold is to bridge over antipathies and misunderstandings—to draw closer together in thought, feeling, and action on the basis of commonalities held. This goal, however, can be reached only if another principle is also observed: interreligious, interideological dialogue must be a two-sided dialogue—across the communal divide and within it. We need to be in regular dialogue with our fellow religionists, sharing with them the results of our interreligious, interideological dialogue so they too can enhance their understanding of what is held in common and where the differences truly are. Only thus can both communities grow in knowledge and inner and outer transformation and thereby bridge antipathies and draw closer. Further, if this two-sided dialogue is not maintained, the individual dialogue partners alone will grow in knowledge and experience the resultant transformation, thus slowly moving away from their unchanging community, thereby becoming a third reality, a *tertium quid*—hardly the intended integrative goal of dialogue.

It is important to learn as fully as possible the things we share in common with our dialogue partners, which most often will be much more extensive than we could have anticipated beforehand; we will thus be drawn together in greater harmony. It is also important that we learn more comprehensively what our differences are. Such differences may be 1) complementary, as for example, emphasis on the prophetic rather than the mystical, 2) analogous, as for example, the notion of God in the Semitic religions and of *Sunyata* in Mahayana Buddhism, or 3) contradictory, where the acceptance of one entails the rejection of the other, as for example, the Judeo-Christian notion of the inviolable dignity of each individual person and the now largely disappeared Hindu custom of *suttee*, widow burning. The issue of the third category of differences will be discussed below, but here we can note that the differences in the first two categories are not simply to be perceived and acknowledged; they should in fact be cherished and celebrated both for their own sakes and because by discerning them we have extended our own understanding of reality and how to live accordingly—the primary goal of dialogue.

For Reflection and Discussion

1. Education implies openness to growth and change. Otherwise, what's the point of investing time and money in it? Is the same true of engaging in interreligious dialogue?
2. Should people who enter into dialogue expect their beliefs, viewpoints, and knowledge to change?
3. How do you feel about that prospect in your own dialogue?

The Means of Dialogue

A great variety of means and techniques of dialogue have been successfully used and doubtless some are yet to be developed. The overall guiding principle in this issue, however, should be to use our creative imaginations and our sensitivity for persons. Techniques that have already been utilized range from joint lectures and dialogues by experts from different traditions that are listened to by large audiences on one extreme, to personal conversations between rank and file individuals from different traditions on the other. Whenever something more formal than a personal conversation is planned, all the traditions to be engaged in the dialogue should be involved in its initial planning. This is particularly true when different communities first begin to encounter one another. Then dialogue on the potential dialogue itself becomes an essential part of the dialogic encounter.

In the first encounters between communities, the most difficult points of differences should not be tackled. Rather, those subjects which show promise of highlighting commonalities should be treated first so that mutual trust between the partners can be established and developed. Without mutual trust, there will be no dialogue.

Vital to the development of this needed mutual trust is that each partner come to the dialogue with total sincerity and honesty. My partners in dialogue wish to learn to know me and my tradition as we truly are; this is impossible if I am not totally sincere and honest. The same is true for my dialogue partners; I cannot learn to know them and their traditions truly if they are not completely sincere and honest. We must simultaneously presume total sincerity and honesty in our partners as well as practice these virtues ourselves, otherwise there will be no trust.

Care must also be taken in dialogue to compare our ideals with our partner's ideals and our practices with our partner's practices. By comparing our ideals with our partner's practices we will always "win," but of course we will learn nothing—a total defeat of the purpose of dialogue.

Each partner in the dialogue must define himself or herself; only a Muslim, for example, can know from the inside what is means to be a Muslim, and this self-understanding will change, grow, expand, deepen as the dialogue develops, and can be accurately described only by the one experiencing the living, growing religious reality. Each partner needs to come to the dialogue with no fixed assumptions as to where the authentic differences between the traditions are, but only after following the partner with sympathy and agreement as far as one can without violating one's own integrity will the true point of difference be determined. Of course, only equals can engage in full authentic dialogue; the degree of equality will determine the degree of two-way communication, that is, the degree of dialogue experienced. A "safe space" may have to be provided for an "unequal" partner to be able to engage in dialogue.

An indispensable major means of dialogue is a self-critical attitude toward ourselves and our tradition. If we are not willing to look self-critically at our own and *our tradition's* position on a subject, the implication clearly is that we have nothing to learn from our partner. If that is the case, we are not interested in dialogue—whose primary purpose is to learn from our partner. To be certain, we come to the dialogue as a Buddhist, as a Christian, as a Marxist, etc., with sincerity, honesty, and integrity. Self-criticism, however, does not mean a lack of sincerity, honesty, integrity. Indeed, a lack of self-criticism will mean there is no valid sincerity, no real honesty, no authentic integrity.

Finally, the most fundamental means to dialogue is having a correct understanding of dialogue, which is a two-way communication so that both partners can learn from each other, and change accordingly. If this basic goal is kept fixed in view and acted on with imagination, creative and fruitful dialogue—and a growing transformation of each participant's life and that of their communities—will follow. (See Chapter Two: The Dialogue Decalogue.)

The Subject of Dialogue

We have already spoken about first choosing subjects that promise to yield a high degree of common ground so as to establish and develop mutual trust. Let's now look at the three main areas of dialogue: the cognitive, the active, and the spiritual.

In some ways the last, the spiritual area, would seem to be the most attractive, at least to those with a more interior, mystical, psychological bent. Moreover it offers a greater degree of commonality. The mystics appear to all meet together on a high level of unity with the Ultimate Reality no matter how it is described, including even in the more philosophical systems like Neoplatonism. The greatest of the Muslim Sufis, Jewish Kabbalists, Hindu Bhaktas, Christian Mystics, Buddhist Bodhisattvas, and Platonist philosophers all seem to be at one in their striving for and experience of unity with the One, which in the West is called God, *Theos.* At times the image is projected of God being the peak of the mountain that all humans are climbing by way of different paths. Each one has a different *Way* (*hodos* in Christian Greek; *halakhah* in

Jewish Hebrew; *shar'ia* in Muslim Arabic; *marga* in Hindu Sanskrit; *magga* in Buddhist Pali; *tao* in Chinese Taoism) to reach *Theos*, but all are centered on the one goal. Such an interpretation of religion or ideology is called theocentric.

Attractive as is theocentrism, one must be cautious not to wave the varying understandings of God aside as if they were without importance. They can make a significant difference in human self-understanding, and hence how we behave toward ourselves, each other, the world around us, and the Ultimate Source. Moreover, a theocentric approach has the disadvantage of excluding non-theists from the dialogue. This would exclude not only atheistic Humanists and Marxists, but also non-theistic Theravada Buddhists, who do not deny the existence of God but rather understand ultimate reality in a non-theistic, non-personal manner (theism posits a "personal" God, *Theos*). One alternative way to include these partners in the dialogue, even in this area of "spirituality," is to speak of the search for ultimate meaning in life, for "salvation" (*salus* in Latin, meaning a salutary, whole, holy life; similarly, *soteria* in Greek), as what all humans have in common in the "spiritual" area, theists and non-theists alike. As a result, we can speak of a soteriocentrism.

In the active area dialogue has to take place in a fundamental way on the underlying principles for action which motivate each tradition. Once again, many similarities will be found, but also differences, which will prove significant in determining the communities' differing stands on various issues of personal and social ethics. It is only by carefully and sensitively locating those underlying ethical principles for ethical decision-making that later misunderstandings and unwarranted frustrations in specific ethical issues can be avoided. Then specific ethical matters, such as sexual ethics, social ethics, ecological ethics, medical ethics, can become the focus of interreligious, interideological dialogue—and ultimately joint action where it has been found congruent with each tradition's principles and warranted in the concrete circumstances.

It is, however, in the cognitive area where the range of possible subjects is greatest. It is almost unlimited—remembering the caution that the less difficult topics be chosen first and the more difficult later. However, every dialogue group should be encouraged to follow creatively its own inner instincts and interests. Some groups, of course, will start with more particular concrete matters and then be gradually drawn to discuss the underlying issues and principles. Others will begin with more fundamental matters and eventually be drawn to reflect on more and more concrete implications of the basic principles already discovered. In any case, if proper preparation and sensitivity are provided, no subject should *a priori* be declared off-limits.

Encouragement can be drawn here from the Vatican Curia (for some, an unexpected source). The Secretariat for Dialogue with Unbelievers wrote that even "doctrinal dialogue should be initiated with courage and sincerity, with the greatest freedom and with reverence." It then went further to make a statement that is mind-jarring in its liberality: "Doctrinal discussion requires perceptiveness, both in honestly setting out one's own opinion and in recognizing the truth everywhere, even if the truth demolishes one so that one is forced to reconsider one's own position, in theory and in practice, at least in part." The Secretariat then stressed that "in discussion the truth will prevail by no other means than by the truth itself. Therefore, the liberty of the participants must be ensured by law and reverenced in practice."[4] These are emphatic words—which should be applicable not only to the Catholics of the world but in general.

When to Dialogue—and When Not to

In principle, of course, we ought to be open to dialogue with all possible partners on all possible subjects. Normally this principle should be followed today and doubtless for many years to come because the world's religions and ideologies have stored up so much misinformation about and hostility toward one another that it is almost impossible for us to know ahead of time what our potential partner is truly like on any given subject. We normally need first of all to enter into sincere dialogue with every potential partner, at least until we learn where our true differences lie.

In this matter of differences, however, we have to be very careful in the distinctions we need to make. As pointed out above, in the process of the dialogue we will often learn that what we thought were real differences in fact turn out to be only apparent differences; different words or misunderstandings have merely hidden commonly shared positions. When we enter dialogue we have to allow for the possibility that we will ultimately learn that on some matters we will find not a commonality but an authentic difference. As mentioned, these authentic differences can be of three kinds: complementary, analogous, or contradictory. Complementary authentic differences will of course be true differences, but not such that only one could be valid. We know from our experience that the complementary differences will usually far outnumber the contradictory. Learning of these authentic but complementary differences will not only enhance our knowledge but also may very well lead to the desire to adapt one or more of our partner's complementary differences for ourselves. As the very term suggests, the differences somehow complete each other. As the Chinese Taoist saying puts it: *Xiang fan xiang cheng* (contraries complete each other).

Just as we must constantly be extremely cautious about "fixing" our differences *a priori* lest in acting precipitously we misplace them, so too, we must not too easily and quickly place our true differences in the contradictory category. Perhaps, for example, Hindu *moksha*, Zen Buddhist *satori*, Christian "freedom of the children of God," and Marxist "communist state" could be understood as different but nevertheless analogous descriptions of true human liberation. In speaking of true but analogous differences in beliefs or values here, we are no longer talking about discerning teachings or practices in our partners' tradition which we might then wish to appropriate for our own tradition. That does and should happen, but then we are speaking either of something which the two traditions ultimately held in common and was perhaps atrophied or suppressed in one, or of something which is an authentic but complementary difference. If this difference, however, is perceived as analogous rather than complementary or contradictory, it will be seen to operate within the total organic structure of the other religion-ideology and to fulfill its function properly only within it. It would not be able to have the same function, i.e., relationship to the other parts in our total organic structure, and hence would not be understood to be in direct opposition, in contradiction to the "differing" element within our structure. These real but analogous differences in beliefs or values should be seen not as in conflict with one another, but as parallel in function, and in that sense analogous.

Yet, at times we can find contradictory truth claims, value claims, presented by different religious-deological traditions. That happens, of course, only when they cannot be seen as somehow ultimately different expressions of the same thing (a commonality) or as complementary or analogous. When it happens, even though it be relatively rare, a profound and unavoidable problem faces the two communities: What should be their attitude and behavior toward each other? Should they remain in dialogue, tolerate each other, ignore each other, or oppose each other? This problem is especially pressing in matters of value judgments. What, for example, should the Christian (or Jew, Muslim, Marxist) have done in face of the now largely, but unfortunately not entirely, suppressed Hindu tradition of widow burning (*suttee*)? Should he or she try to learn its value, tolerate it, ignore it, oppose it (in what manner)? Or the Nazi tenet of killing all Jews? These are relatively clear issues, but what of a religion-ideology that approves slavery, as Christianity, Judaism, and Islam did until only a little over a century ago? Maybe that is clear enough today, but what of sexism—or only a little sexism? Or the claim that only through capitalism—or socialism—human liberation can be gained? Making a decision on the proper stance becomes less and less clear-cut.

Eventually it was clear to most non-Hindus in the nineteenth century that the proper attitude was not dialogue with Hinduism on *suttee*, but opposition. But apparently it was not so clear to all non-Nazis that opposition to Jewish genocide was the right stance to take. Furthermore, it took Christians almost two thousand years to come to that conclusion concerning slavery. Many religions and ideologies today stand in the midst of a battle over sexism, some even refusing to admit the existence of the issue. Lastly, no argument need be made to point out the controversial nature of the contemporary capitalism-socialism issue.

Obviously, important contradictory differences between religions-ideologies do exist and at times warrant not dialogue but opposition. Individually we also make critical judgments on the acceptability of positions within our own traditions and rather frequently within our personal lives. But certainly this exercise of our critical faculties is not to be limited to ourselves and our traditions; this perhaps most human of faculties should be made available to all—with all the proper constraints and concerns for dialogue already detailed at length. Of course, it must first be determined on what grounds we can judge whether a religious-ideological difference is in fact contradictory, and then, if it is, whether it is of sufficient importance and nature to warrant active opposition.

Full Human Life

Because all religions-ideologies are attempts to explain the meaning of human life and how to live accordingly, those doctrines and customs which are perceived as hostile to human life are not complementary or analogous but contradictory, and opposition to them should be proportional to the extent they threaten life. An authentically full human life then must be the measure against which all elements of all religions-ideologies are tested as we make judgments about whether they are in harmony, complementarity, analogy, or contradiction, and then act accordingly.

Since human beings are by nature historical beings, what it means to be fully human is evolving. At bottom everything human flows from what would seem to be acceptable to all as a description of the minimally essential human structure, that is, being an animal who can think abstractly and make free decisions. Only gradually has humanity come to the contemporary position where claims are made in favor of "human rights," that things are due to all humans specifically because they are human. This position, in fact, has not always and everywhere been held. Indeed, it was for the most part hardly conceived until recently.

Only a little over a hundred years ago, for example, slavery was still widely accepted and even vigorously defended and practiced by high Christian churchmen, not to speak of Jewish and Muslim slave traders. And yet this radical violation of human rights has today been largely eliminated both in practice and law. Today no thinker or public leader would contemplate justifying slavery, at least in its directly named form of the past (see the *Universal Declaration of Human Rights* by the United Nations in 1948; art. 4). Here we have an obvious example of the historical evolution of the understanding of what it means to be fully human, i.e., that human beings are by nature radically free.

However, the human right to private property (*Universal Declaration* art. 17: "Everyone has the right to own property alone"), perhaps first publicly acknowledged in the West in seventeenth-century John Locke's phrase, "life, liberty and property," had been unthinkable until the requisite previous development of control over matter. The same is true of the twentieth-century claim to the right to work (*Universal Declaration*, art. 23):

> The development of this new control over nature—first over external nature and increasingly also over human nature—...has made possible entirely new dimensions of human self-development, and its apparently illimitable expansion leads to the expectation, at least in the developed countries, that it can release a sufficient potential so that everyone can participate in them—and consequently has a right to participate therein.[5]

Here are clear examples of the historical evolution of the understanding—if not always the practical realization—of what is means to be fully human in terms of the expansion of the basic capabilities of humanity.

What fundamentally was acknowledged in the twentieth century as the foundation of being human is that human beings ought to be autonomous in their decisions—such decisions being directed by their own reason and limited only by the same rights of others: "All human beings are born free and equal in dignity and rights. They are endowed with reason and conscience and should act toward one another in a spirit of brotherhood" (*Universal Declaration*, art. 1). In the ethical sphere, this autonomy, which Thomas Aquinas recognized already in the thirteenth century,[6] expanded into the social, political spheres in the eighteenth century. This is expressed in the slogan of the French Revolution: Liberty, Equality, Fraternity (contemporary consciousness of sexist language would lead to a substitute like "Solidarity" for "Fraternity"). With the term "Liberty" is understood all the personal and civil rights; with the term "Equality" is understood the political rights of participation in public decision-making; with the term "Solidarity" is understood (in an expanded twentieth-century sense) the social rights.

Though frequently resistant in the past, and too often still in the present, the great religious communities of the world have often and in a variety of ways expressed a growing awareness of and commitment to similar notions of what it means to be fully human. Through dialogue, humanity is painfully creeping toward a consensus on what is involved in an authentically full human life. The 1948 United Nations' *Universal Declaration of Human Rights* was an important step in that direction. Of course, much more consensus needs to be attained if interreligious, interideological dialogue is to reach its full potential. Toward that end the Global Ethic Movement was launched.[7]

Conclusion

The conclusion from these reflections, I believe, is clear: Interreligious, interideological dialogue is absolutely necessary in our contemporary world. Every religion and ideology can certainly make claim to the official statements from the Catholic Church about the necessity of dialogue, starting with Pope Paul VI in his first encyclical:

> Dialogue is *demanded* nowadays....It is *demanded* by the dynamic course of action which is changing the face of modern society. It is *demanded* by the pluralism of society, and by the maturity man has reached in this day and age. Be he religious or not, his secular education has enabled him to think and speak, and to conduct a dialogue with dignity. (*Ecclesiam suam*, no. 78)

To this the Vatican Curia later added:

> All Christians should do their best to promote dialogue between men of every class as a duty of fraternal charity suited to our progressive and adult age....The willingness to engage in dialogue is the measure and the strength of that general renewal which must be carried out in the Church (read: in every religion and ideology). (*Humanae personae dignitatem*, August 28, 1968, no. 1)

For Reflection and Discussion

1. Describe a significant encounter you have had with another religion or with a member of another religion. Explore the impact the encounter had on you. Was it positive or negative? Did it influence your ongoing perception of the entire religion and its members? Did you feel angry or threatened? Were you intrigued and interested to learn more? Did the other seem strange and baffling?
2. Have you had an experience of interreligious dialogue already? If so, what was the experience like?
3. Make a list of questions you have about each of the Abrahamic religions—Judaism, Christianity, and Islam. Add to this list as you read through this book. Which question in particular is most important for you right now?

CHAPTER TWO

The Dialogue Decalogue[1]

Dialogue is a conversation on a common subject between two or more persons with differing views, the primary purpose of which is for each participant to learn from the other(s) so that they can change and grow. This very definition of dialogue embodies the first commandment of dialogue.

In the religious-ideological sphere in the past, we came together to discuss with those differing with us, for example, Catholics with Protestants, either to defeat an opponent or to learn about an opponent so as to deal more effectively with him or her, or at best to negotiate with him or her. If we faced one another at all, it was in confrontation—sometimes more openly polemically, sometimes more subtly so, but always with the ultimate goal of defeating the other, because we were convinced that we alone had the absolute truth.

But dialogue is *not* debate. In dialogue each partner must listen to the other as openly and sympathetically as they can in an attempt to understand the other's position as precisely and as much from within, as possible. Such an attitude automatically includes the assumption that at any point we might find the partner's position so persuasive that if we would act with integrity we would have to change, and change can be disturbing.

We are here, of course, speaking of a specific kind of dialogue, an interreligious, interideological dialogue. To have such, it is not sufficient that the dialogue partners discuss a religious-ideological subject, that is, the meaning of life and how to live accordingly. Rather, they must come to the dialogue as persons somehow significantly identified with a religious or ideological community. If I were neither a Christian nor a Marxist, for example, I could not participate as a partner in Christian-Marxist dialogue, though I might listen in, ask some questions for information, and make some helpful comments.

It is obvious that interreligious, interideological dialogue is something new under the sun. We could not conceive of it let alone do it in the past. How, then, can we effectively engage in this new thing? The following are some basic ground rules or "commandments" of interreligious, interideological dialogue that must be observed if dialogue is actually to take place. These are not theoretical rules, or commandments given from on high, but ones that have been learned from hard experience.

First Commandment The primary purpose of dialogue is to learn, that is, to change and grow in the perception and understanding of reality, and then to act accordingly. The very fact that I learn that my dialogue partner believes "this" rather than "that" proportionally changes my attitude toward him or her; and a change in my attitude is a significant change in me. We enter into dialogue so we can learn, change, and grow, not so we can force change on the other, as one hopes to do in debate—a hope realized in inverse proportion to the frequency and ferocity with which debate is entered into. On the other hand, because in dialogue each partner comes with the intention of learning and changing himself or herself, one's partner in fact will also change. Thus the goal of debate, and much more, is accomplished far more effectively by dialogue.

Second Commandment Interreligious, interideological dialogue must be a two-sided project—within each religious or ideological community and between religious or ideological communities. Because of the corporate nature of interreligious dialogue, and since the primary goal of dialogue is that partners learn and change themselves, it is also necessary that each participant enter into dialogue not only with a partner across the faith line—the Lutheran with the Anglican, for example—but also with his co-religionists, with other Lutherans, to share with them the fruits of the interreligious dialogue. Only thus can the whole community eventually learn and change, moving toward an ever more perceptive insight into reality.

Third Commandment Each participant must come to the dialogue with complete honesty and sincerity. It should be made clear in what direction the major and minor thrusts of the tradition move, what the future shifts might be, and, if necessary, where the participant has difficulties with her own tradition. False fronts have no place in dialogue.

Conversely, each participant must assume a similar complete honesty and sincerity in the other partners. Not only will the absence of sincerity prevent dialogue from happening, but the absence of the assumption of the partner's sincerity will do so as well. In brief: no trust, no dialogue.

Fourth Commandment In interreligious, interideological dialogue we must not compare our ideals with our partner's practice, but our ideals with our partner's ideals, our practice with our partner's practice.

Fifth Commandment Each participant must define himself. Only the Jew, for example, can define what it means to be a Jew. The rest can only describe what it looks like from the outside. Moreover, because dialogue is a dynamic medium, as each participant learns, he will change and hence continually deepen, expand, and modify his self-definition as a Jew—being careful to remain in constant dialogue with other Jews. Thus it is mandatory that each dialogue partner define what it means to be an authentic member of his own tradition.

Conversely, the one interpreted must be able to recognize herself in the interpretation. This is the golden rule of interreligious hermeneutics, as has been often reiterated by the "apostle of interreligious dialogue," Raimundo Panikkar. For the sake of understanding, each dialogue participant will naturally attempt to express for herself what she thinks is the meaning of the partner's statement, but the partner must be able to recognize herself in that expression. The advocate of "a world theology," Wilfred Cantwell Smith, would add that the expression must also be verifiable by critical observers who are not involved.

Sixth Commandment Each participant must come to the dialogue with no hard-and-fast assumptions as to where the points of disagreement are. Each partner should not only listen to the other partner with openness and sympathy but also attempt to agree with the dialogue partner as far as is possible while still maintaining integrity with his own tradition. Where he absolutely can agree no further without violating his own integrity, precisely there is the real point of disagreement—which most often turns out to be different from the point of disagreement that was assumed ahead of time.

Seventh Commandment Dialogue can take place only between equals or *par cum pari*, as Vatican II put it. Each must come to learn from the other. Therefore, if, for example, the Muslim views Hinduism as inferior, or if the Hindu views Islam as inferior, there will be no dialogue. If authentic interreligious, interideological dialogue between Muslims and Hindus is to occur, both the Muslim and the Hindu must come mainly to learn from the other; only then will it be "equal with equal," *par cum pari*. This rule also indicates that there can be no such thing as a one-way dialogue. For example, Jewish-Christian discussions begun in the 1960s were mainly only prolegomena to interreligious dialogue. Understandably and properly, the Jews came to these exchanges only to teach Christians, and the Christians came mainly to learn. If authentic interreligious dialogue between Christians and Jews is to occur, the Jews must also come mainly to learn; only then will it too be *par cum pari.*

Eighth Commandment Dialogue can take place only on the basis of mutual trust. Although interreligious, interideological dialogue must occur with some kind of corporate dimension, that is, the participants must be involved as members of a religious or ideological community—for example, as Marxists or Taoists—it is also fundamentally true that it is only *persons* who can enter into dialogue. A dialogue among persons can be built only on personal trust. Hence it is wise not to tackle the most difficult problems in the beginning, but rather to approach first those issues most likely to provide some common ground, thereby establishing the basis of human trust. Gradually, as this personal trust deepens and expands, the more thorny matters can be undertaken. As in learning, we move from the known to the unknown, so in dialogue we proceed from commonly held matters—which, given our mutual ignorance resulting from centuries of hostility will take us quite some time to discover fully—to discuss matters of disagreement.

Ninth Commandment Persons entering into interreligious, interideological dialogue must be at least minimally self-critical of both themselves and their own religious or ideological traditions. A lack of such self-criticism implies that one's own tradition already has all the correct answers. Such an attitude makes dialogue not only unnecessary but even impossible since we enter into dialogue primarily so *we* can learn—which obviously is impossible if our tradition has never made a misstep, if it has all the right answers. To be sure, in interreligious, interideological dialogue one must stand within a religious or ideological tradition with integrity and conviction, but such integrity and conviction must include, not exclude, a healthy self-criticism. Without it there can be no dialogue—and indeed no integrity.

Tenth Commandment Each participant eventually must attempt to experience the partner's religion or ideology from within. A religion or ideology is not merely something of the head but also of the spirit, heart, and whole being, individual and communal. John Dunne speaks of "passing over" into another's religious or ideological experience and then coming back enlightened, broadened, and deepened. While retaining our own religious integrity, we need to find ways of experiencing something of the emotional and spiritual power of the symbols and cultural vehicles of our partner's religion—and then come back to our own enriched and expanded, having experienced at least a little of the affective side of our partner's experience.

Interreligious, interideological dialogue operates in three areas: the practical, where we collaborate to help humanity; the depth or spiritual dimension where we attempt to experience the partner's religion or ideology from within; the cognitive, where we seek understanding and truth. Interreligious, interideological dialogue also has three phases. In the first phase we unlearn misinformation about one another and begin to know one another as we truly are. In phase two we begin to discern values in the partner's tradition and wish to appropriate them into our own tradition. For example, in the Buddhist-Christian dialogue, Christians might learn a greater appreciation of the meditative tradition, and Buddhists might learn a greater appreciation of the prophetic, social justice tradition. (Both values are traditionally though not exclusively associated with the other's community.) If we are serious, persistent, and sensitive enough in the dialogue, we may at times enter into phase three. Here we together begin to explore new areas of reality, of meaning, and of truth, of which neither partner had even been aware before. We are brought face to face with this new, as-yet-unknown-to-us dimension of reality only because of questions, insights, and probings produced in the dialogue. We may thus dare to say that patiently pursued dialogue can become an instrument of new revelation, a further unveiling of reality—on which we must then act.

There is something radically different about phase one on the one hand and phases two and three on the other. In the latter we do not simply add on quantitatively another "truth" or value from the partner's tradition. Instead, as we assimilate it within our own religious self-understanding, it will proportionately transform our self-understanding. Since our dialogue partner will be in a similar position, we will then be able to witness authentically to those elements of deep value in our own tradition that our partner's tradition may well be able to assimilate with self-transforming profit. All this of course will have to be done with complete integrity on each side, each partner remaining authentically true to the vital core of his or her own religious tradition. However, in significant ways that vital core will be perceived and experienced differently under the influence of the dialogue, but if the dialogue is carried on with both integrity and openness, the result will be that, for example, the Jew will be even more authentically Jewish and the Christian even more authentically Christian, not despite the dialogue but because of it. There can be no talk of a syncretism here, for syncretism means amalgamating various elements of different religions into some kind of a (con)fused whole without concern for the integrity of the religions involved—which is not the case with authentic dialogue.

For Reflection and Discussion

1. Imagine a Jew, a Muslim, a Catholic, and a Protestant wanting to engage in interreligious dialogue on one or more of the following topics: understanding of God, forms of worship, the origins and role of Scripture, authority within the community, how members of one religion view others.
2. In what specific ways can the "Dialogue Decalogue" be applied to this exchange? Is there any item of the "Decalogue" that you particularly agree with? Why is this so?
3. Is there any item of the "Decalogue" that you particularly disagree with? Why?

CHAPTER THREE

Seven Stages of Deep-Dialogue/Critical-Thinking

The following are seven stages of Deep-Dialogue/Critical-Thinking that a person can go through if he or she persists in the project.[1]

Stage One

Radical Encountering of Difference

(*Self Faces the Other*)

This first encounter comes with a certain shock, with a realization of an other, a different way of life, a different worldview, an alien other that resists, interrupts, or disrupts my settled patterns of interpretation. With this primal encounter there is a new realization that my habits of mind cannot make sense of this other. This radical encounter with difference—a different world, a different way of making sense of and experiencing the world—is disconcerting, sometimes threatening, and evokes a vulnerability to this alien presence. I have a new sense of de-limitation and I feel challenged to change, to revise my way of relating to this other. I realize now that my habit of translating the other into *my* pattern of "minding," of appropriating the other to *my* worldview, is dysfunctional. I am forced toward a *self-critical-thinking*. So I face a sudden silence, pause, opening—an open horizon of uncertainty and risk. I must make a decision to move forward or draw back.

Stage Two

Crossing Over, Letting Go, and Entering the World of the Other

(*Self Transformed through Empathy*)

After the initial shock and realization that I now face an alien world, a worldview very different from my own, I feel challenged to inquire, investigate, engage, and enter this new world—to engage in *critical-thinking.* As I open my self to this other I realize that I need to stand back and distance myself from my former habits and patterns of minding the world. I begin to realize that this other world organizes and processes the world very differently from my way. I realize that I must learn new habits and ways of interpretation to make sense of this different world. I must learn a "new language." Indeed, I must translate myself into a different form of life that sees the world differently. This involves a bracketing of my prejudices.

Stage Three

Inhabiting and Experiencing the World of the Other (*Self Transformed into the Other*)

I begin to feel a new and deep empathy for my new habitat; I want to let myself go—free myself to enter, experiment, learn, and grow in this new way of being—to embrace *critical-thinking.* I hold on to my prior views as much as I can, but I advance in a conservative fashion. Still, I experience an excitement in discovering and inhabiting a new and different worldview. I have a new realization of an other, an alternative reality and form of life. But in the end I realize this is not my home.

Stage Four

Crossing Back with Expanded Vision (*Self Returns Home with New Knowledge*)

I now cross back, return, to my own world, bringing back new knowledge of how to think and act (*critical-thinking*)—and may even wish to adopt/adapt some of it for myself. As a result of this primary encounter with the world of the other, I now realize that there are other ways of understanding reality. I am therefore open to rethinking how I see myself, others, and the world. I encounter myself and culture anew, with a newly opened mind. My encounter with radical difference now challenges my former identity, and everything begins to appear in a new light. There now begins a dramatic deepening of my sense of myself, my identity, my ethnicity, my life-world, my religion, my culture. There is no return to my former unilateral way of thinking.

Stage Five

The Dialogical/Critical Awakening: A Radical Paradigm Shift (*Self Inwardly Transformed*)

As a result of this new encounter with self, when I cross back from my deep encounter with an other, I begin to experience a profound shift in all aspects of my world—in my inner experience, in my encounter with others, in my relating to the world. I begin to realize that my encounter with the other has shaken the foundation of my former worldview, my former identity. Now that I am mindful of the living reality of other worlds, other perspectives, I can no longer return to my former identity and forget this living presence of the other. Indeed, I now begin to realize that there are many other worlds, other forms of life, other perspectives that surround me. I now open myself to a plurality of other worlds and perspectives, and this irrevocably changes my sense of self. I feel transformed to a deeper sense of relation and connection with my ecology. I feel more deeply rooted in this experience of relationality and community. I now see that my true identity is essentially connected with this expansive network of relations with others. This is the ignition of the dialogical/critical awakening.

Stage Six

The Global Awakening: The Paradigm Shift Matures (*Self Related to Self, Others, the World*)

In my transformed dialogical/critical awakening, I discover a deeper common ground between the multiple worlds and perspectives that surround me. I have a new sense that self and others are inseparably bound in an interrelational web. I realize that multiplicity and diversity enriches my self and my world. I now see that all worlds are situated in a common ground of reality and that radical differences are nevertheless situated in a field of unity. I experience three related dimensions of global dialogical/critical awakening:

1. An ever-deepening discovery of self: I become aware of a deep inner dialogue within myself. I discover a rich multiplicity and diversity of perspectives within my own inner world. In this inner dialogue I feel increasingly more deeply rooted and grounded in my world. My identity is enriched with multiplicity and I experience a more potent sense of

my uniqueness as I celebrate my expanded world of relationality with others and with the ecology.

2. A dynamic dialogue opens with others in my community. As my new inner dialogue and critical thinking evolves, I find myself in a new, transformed relation with others who share my world, tradition, religion, culture. This new phase of relations with my peers can be disorienting and disconcerting, for as I now dramatically grow in my identity, I find myself in an estranged distance from many of my peers, even as I discover a deeper affinity and embrace of my community, my *polis.* I face a new turbulence—miscommunication and misunderstanding with my colleagues—and a challenging and dramatic dialogue unfolds in my *polis.*
3. A global awakening emerges in all aspects of my life. As this inner and outer dialogue/critical-thinking matures, I realize that my understanding of my world enters a new "global" light. I realize that I am surrounded with many worldviews. I enter a global horizon and a global consciousness in which interreligious, intercultural, interideological, interdisciplinary, interpersonal dialogues abound in all directions. I now have a new globalized sense of reality—a dialogical domain in which multiple alternative worlds are situated in dynamic ever-deepening relations. With this understanding comes a new attitude to life and to ethics.

Stage Seven

Personal and Global Transforming of Life and Behavior
(*Self Lives and Acts in a New Global Dialogical Consciousness*)

As this paradigm shift in my life matures, I realize that there is a deep change in all aspects of my life—a new moral consciousness and a new practice. As my new dialogical/critical consciousness becomes a habit of life, I find that my behavior and my disposition to self and other has blossomed. I feel a new sense of communion with myself, with others, and with the ecology. I realize that the deepest care for myself essentially involves my care for others and for the environment. I have a deeper sense of belonging to my world, to my community, and with this a boundless sense of responsibility in all of my conduct. I now realize that I am transformed in the deepest habits of mind and behavior. I find a deeper sense of self-realization, fulfillment, and meaning in my life and my relations with others and the world around me.

For Reflection and Discussion

1. If you have already engaged in interreligious dialogue, even on an elementary level, did you experience the seven stages of deep-dialogue/critical thinking to any degree? Explain the dynamics of your experience.
2. If you have never engaged in interreligious dialogue, how do you feel about the possibility of entering into these seven stages?
3. How would you describe the relationship between critical thinking and interreligious dialogue?

CHAPTER FOUR

Trialogue

Why should Jews, Christians, and Muslims enter into dialogue with one another? There are many reasons, which will be alluded to in the following pages, but I would like to start with a positive reason, namely the many things these three Abrahamic religions have in common.

Things Held in Common

1. They all come from the same Hebraic roots and claim Abraham as their originating ancestor: their historical, cultural, and religious traditions all flow out of one original source, an *Urquelle.*

2. All three traditions are religions of ethical monotheism, that is they all claim there is one, loving, just, creator God who is the source, sustainer, and goal of all reality and that all human beings, as images of God, are expected to live in love and justice. In other words, belief in the one God has ethical consequences concerning oneself, other persons, and the world. This is a *common* heritage of the three Abrahamic religions, which is by no means shared by all elements of the other major world religions.

3. The three traditions are all historical religions, that is they believe that God acts through human history, that God communicates through historical events, through particular human persons, preeminently Moses, Jesus, and Muhammad. Historical events, like the exodus, Crucifixion, and *hijrah,* and human persons do not at all play the same central role in many other world religions, as, for example, Hinduism and Taoism.

4. Judaism, Christianity, and Islam are all religions of revelation, that is believers are persuaded that God has communicated, has revealed, something of God's own self and will in special ways through particular persons, but for the

edification, for the salvation—or said in another way, for the humanization, which is also the divinization—of all humankind. In all three religions this revelation has two special vehicles: prophets and Scriptures.

a. Clearly in Judaism the men prophets Isaiah, Amos, Hosea, Jeremiah, and the women prophets Miriam, Huldah, etc. are outstanding mouthpieces of Yahweh (*pro-phetes*, "one who speaks for another"), and the greatest of all the prophets in Judaism is Moses. For Christianity, Moses and the other prophets are God's spokespersons—but also included among the Christian prophets are a number of persons named either in the Christian Scriptures or in early Christian writings, such as Anna (Lk 2:36–8), and the two daughters of Philip (Eusebius, *Eccl. Hist.* III.31). For Christians, Jesus came to be viewed as a prophet and as something beyond a prophet as well. For Islam all these Jewish and Christian prophets are also authentic prophets, God's revealing voice in the world, and to that list they add Muhammad, the Seal of the Prophets.

b. For these three faiths God's special revelation is also communicated in "The Book," the Bible. For Jews the Holy Scriptures are the Hebrew Bible. For Christians, it is the Hebrew Bible and the New Testament, and for Muslims it is those two plus the Al-Qur'an, considered by them to be corrective and supplemental to earlier Scriptures. For Muslims, Jews and Christians share with them the special name "People of the Book."

There are many more things that the three Abrahamic faiths have in common, such as the importance of covenant, of law, and faith, of the community (witness in the three traditions the central role of the terms "people," "church," and "*ummah*," respectively). But just looking at the list of commonalities already briefly spelled out will provide us with an initial set of fundamental reasons why it is imperative for Jews, Christians, and Muslims to engage in serious, ongoing dialogue.

First, if Jews, Christians, and Muslims believe that there is only one, loving, just God in whose image they are and whose will they try to follow, they need to face the question of why there are three different ways of doing that. Obviously this question can be faced only in dialogue.

Second, if Jews, Christians, and Muslims believe that God acts through human history, that God communicates through historical events and particular human persons, they need to face the question of whether all religiously significant historical events and persons are limited to their own histories. Put colloquially: Do Jews, Christians, and Muslims really believe that they have God in their own historical boxes, or that by their own principles God transcends all limitations, including even their sacred historical events and persons?

Third, if Jews, Christians, and Muslims believe that God communicates, reveals, God's self to humans not only through things, events, and human persons in general, but also in special ways through particular events and persons, they are going to have to face the question of whether God's will as delivered through God's spokespersons, i.e., prophets, and the recording in writing of their teachings and kindred material in what is known as Holy Scriptures, is limited to their own prophets and Scriptures. Concretely, Jews will have to reflect on whether Jesus and the writings of his first Jewish followers have something to say about God's will for humankind to non-Christians (and themselves?). Jews and Christians will have to reflect on whether the prophet Muhammad and his "recitation," i.e., "Al-Qur'an," have something to say about God's will for humankind to non-Muslims. Muslims will have to ask themselves whether the continued existence through the centuries of Judaism and Christianity does not embody a message of God to themselves?

Obviously these questions and others of serious importance to the ultimate meaning of life can be addressed only in dialogue among Jews, Christians, and Muslims.

Once this is recognized, however, it also immediately becomes clear that all the questions just listed, that challenge the absoluteness and exclusivity of the three Abrahamic traditions' claims about having all the truth, about God being found only in the boxes of their history, prophets, scriptures, and revelation, also apply to the non-Abrahamic religions and ideologies, such as Hinduism, Buddhism and Humanism.

Praxis

Pragmatically one cannot engage in dialogue with all possible partners at the same time. All the goals of one dialogue with a certain set of partners can never be fulfilled by another set of dialogue partners. For example, the goal of working toward denominational unity between the Lutheran Church in America and the American Lutheran Church would never have been accomplished if Catholics had been full partners in that dialogue with Lutherans. Or again, Jews and Christians have certain items on their mutual theological agenda, e.g., the Jewish claim that the Messiah has not yet come, that will not be adequately addressed if Muslims are added as full partners. And so it goes with each addition or new mix of dialogue partners.

There is a special urgency about the need for Christians to dialogue among themselves to work toward the goal of some kind of effective, visible Christian unity. The absurdity and scandal of there being hundreds of separate churches all claiming "one foundation, which is Jesus Christ," is patent. The need for intra-Jewish dialogue I will leave to my Jewish sisters and brothers to inform me about. However, for Christians, dialogue with Jews has an extraordinarily high priority which cannot be displaced. Where it has not been both initiated and continued, it needs to be undertaken with all possible speed and perseverance. This is true even for those Christian communities where there exists no Jewish community. Christians will always have difficulty in knowing themselves fully if they do not in some way engage in significant dialogue with the adherents of the religion of Jesus, namely, Judaism.

There is something like—though not precisely—a relationship of parent and offspring that compels Jews and Christians to enter into dialogue with Muslims. There are today all the external reasons for Jewish-Christian dialogue with Islam that flow from the reality of the earth now being a global village and the unavoidable symbiotic relationship between the Judeo-Christian industrialized West and the partly oil-rich, relatively non-industrialized Islamic world.

Expectations from the Trialogue

A special word of caution to Jews and Christians entering into dialogue with Muslims is in order. They will be starting such a venture with several disadvantages: 1) the heritage of colonialism, 2) ignorance about Islam, 3) distorted image of Muslims, and 4) culture gap, and then something special about Islamist terror.

1. The Heritage of Colonialism

The vast majority of Muslims trained in Islamics are non-Westerners, which means they very likely come from a country that was until recently a colony of the West. Many Muslims are still traumatized by Western colonialism and frequently identify Christianity, and to a lesser extent, Judaism, with the West. Jewish and Christian dialogue partners need to be aware of this and move to defuse the problem.

2. Ignorance about Islam

Jews and Christians will need to make a special effort to learn about Islam beyond what was required for them intelligently to engage in the Jewish-Christian dialogue, for in the latter they usually knew at least a little about the partner's religion. With Islam, they will likely be starting with a negative attitude resulting from sheer ignorance and massive misinformation.

3. Distorted Image of Muslims

Most often the current Western image of a Muslim is a gross distortion of Islam. Indeed, it is frequently that of some kind of inhuman monster. But the Ayatollah Khomeni or Osama bin Laden distortion of Islam is no more representative of Islam than the Rev. Ian Paisley of Northern Ireland is of Christianity in general or Richard Nixon was of the pacifist Quaker tradition, or the Jewish murderer of Israeli Prime Minister Yitzak Rabin is of Judaism. More about this follows.

4. Culture Gap

Most difficult of all is the fact that a huge cultural gap exists between the great majority of Muslims and precisely those Jews and Christians who are open to dialogue. In brief: Islam as a whole has not yet really experienced the "Enlightenment" and come to terms with it, as has much of the Judeo-Christian tradition, although obviously not all of it. Only a minority of Muslim Islamics scholars will share the de-absolutized understanding of truth described above, which means that many efforts at dialogue with Muslims will in fact be prolegomena to true interreligious dialogue. Frequently such attempts will be not unlike "dialogue" with many Orthodox Jews or evangelical Christians—or with Roman Catholics before Vatican II.

But the prolegomena must be traversed in order to reach authentic dialogue. Surely the words of the Vatican and Pope Paul VI apply to all Christians and Jews, who "must assuredly be concerned for their separated brethren…making the first approaches toward them.…Dialogue is *demanded* nowadays…by the pluralism of society and by the maturity man has reached in this day and age."[1] It is toward that end all Christians and Jews must strive, first among themselves, then with one another, and then with their quasi offspring, Islam.

For Reflection and Discussion

1. How might people in a colonized nation view their colonizers?
2. How might people in a colonizing nation view the colonized?
3. What impact might a history of colonization have on interreligious dialogue?
4. In particular, what effect do you think it has had on dialogue with Muslims?

Encouragement from Past Trialogues

Starting in 1978 and on through 1984, a semi-annual national scholars Trialogue was held at the Kennedy Institute of Ethics of Georgetown University in Washington, D.C.[2] It provided a learning experience that enabled the International Scholars Annual Trialogue (ISAT) to be launched in 1989. ISAT consisted of nine scholars of each tradition coming from countries scattered around the world. The point to having the same scholars each time was that progress could be made, building on previous shared work. The effects of such a long-term "fundamental research and dialogue" approach to the interrelationship among the three "Semitic" religions might be difficult to predict. We do know, however, that the long-term "fundamental research and dialogue" approach to the interrelationship between Protestantism and Catholicism in Germany in the 1950s had a profoundly positive effect on the revolutionary changes that Protestant-Catholic relations have undergone since the early 1960s.[3] One cannot guarantee such positive results in the much more complex Jewish-Christian-Muslim relationship, but one can guarantee that without such a "fundamental research and dialogue" approach in a long-term manner, positive developments in their relationship will *not* come about.

By the third meeting, personal trust had been built and amazing results began to emerge, but not easily. "We are at an impasse. Each of our traditions, Judaism, Christianity, Islam, has at its core a central 'absolute,' which is non-negotiable and blocks the possibility of genuine dialogue: The Chosen People/Promised Land, The Christ, The Al-Qur'an." Thus the situation was described at the end of the third ISAT and consequently it was decided to make those three "absolutes" the focus of intense research: Nine papers were prepared on the respective "absolutes" as found in each tradition's Scriptures, history, and contemporary thought.

These papers were the basis of the dialogue in January of 1992 at Emory University in Atlanta. By then a deep trust among the participants had developed that allowed them to be self-critical even in front of the "outsiders," and to accept the constructive critiques offered by them. "We have long since passed the stage of 'ecumenical politeness,'" remarked Pinchas Lapide, a Jewish participant from Germany/Israel, "and can now proceed to remove both the beam from our own eye and the speck from our brother's or sister's."

The Chosen People with their intimate connection to the Promised Land has been understood by Jews on one extreme to mean that the Jewish people are uniquely privileged by God and that the Holy Land (stretching from the Nile to the Euphrates, i.e, from the heart of Egypt to the heart of Iraq) has been eternally committed by God to their complete possession.

More commonly the Chosen People concept has been understood to mean that the Jews, now scattered in the "diaspora," have been chosen to make known to the nations God's ethical laws (Ten Commandments, etc.). Some Jews even spoke of living in the Holy Land without necessarily having sovereignty.

In modern times the idea of the Chosen People has been quasi-rejected by some Jews, as reflected in the humorous verse: "How odd of God to choose the Jews," and even directly repudiated by others, e.g., Mordecai Kaplan and the Reconstructionists. Even Zionism is understood by some Jews to mean that the state in the Holy Land should include fully non-Jews as well as Jews. Clearly the Chosen People/Promised Land is only a "relative absolute," given to constant reinterpretation and negotiation.

Concerning the Christian non-negotiable "absolute," Jesus the Christ, the variation in interpretation over the centuries has been as great. The first followers of Jesus experienced him as a great teacher and spokesperson or prophet of God: a "rabbi" and "nabi." Some of his followers also saw him as the "Messiah," that is, the "anointed one of God" who would expel the hated occupiers of the Holy Land, reestablish the kingdom of Israel, and bring peace throughout the world. Because of his execution, however, Jesus was not perceived by most Jews thereafter as the Messiah, but for the Gentile followers the Hebrew "Messiah" was greatly spiritualized into the Greek *Christos*, "Christ."

The largely metaphorically-oriented Semitic thought pattern (and hence language) of the New Testament was later increasingly understood by the then mostly Hellenistic followers of Jesus as if it were Greek abstract metaphysical language—thus in the early ecumenical councils claiming divinity as well as humanity for Jesus.

This meant that Jesus the Christ was "absolute"; all truth and goodness was to be found in him. Thus, there was no point to dialogue with non-Christians, since they could communicate no truth or value which the Christians did not already possess in their founder, Christ.

Today there are many committed Christian scholars who are convinced of the rightness of the view of the first followers of Jesus: Jesus is experienced as a great teacher and model of how to live an authentic human, indeed, "divine" life; moreover, Jesus was divine for he was totally open to and permeated by all reality, including Ultimate Reality, God. However, because Jesus' humanity was filled with divinity does not mean that divinity did not also permeate other beings, including other religious figures.

Clearly the non-negotiable "absolute," the Christ, has been interpreted not only in the traditionally exclusivistic absolute manner, but also both in initial and contemporary Christianity in a "relatively absolute" manner, that is, as absolutely the best teacher and model of life for Christians who also provides a model for all humans, divinity "enfleshed" without excluding the possibility of other religious figures being teachers and models of life as well, also "enfleshing" divinity in themselves.[4]

For traditional Islam (the term means "to submit" to God), its non-negotiable "absolute," the Al-Qur'an, is the very word of God dictated verbatim to Muhammad by the angel Gabriel, correcting the previous revelations of God found in the Bible, but distorted there by the Jews and Christians. Thus, not to follow the Al-Qur'an is not to follow God's correct word, not "to submit" to God.

In contemporary Islam an increasing number of scholars and educated laity understand the Al-Qur'an as God's message, and therefore absolute, but necessarily communicated to limited humans in a human, and therefore limited, language. The Al-Qur'an itself makes clear that God does not expect all people to follow the religion of Islam, that so long as people follow their consciences they will be blessed. Thus Islam's "non-negotiable absolute" likewise is also often understood in a non-absolute way.

A general major conclusion of the intense discussions of this Trialogue was that it is obvious that each of the three "non-negotiable absolutes" have been subject to an immense amount of interpretation and "negotiation" within each tradition. Hence, they do not block dialogue, though they make it difficult at times—but also enriching!

For Reflection and Discussion

1. The above description of Trialogue reflects a de-absolutized understanding of language and interpretation applied to key statements of belief in Judaism, Christianity, and Islam. In your opinion, what is the goal of deep dialogue in regard to absolutist claims held by many members of various religions?
2. Is dialogue necessarily de-absolutizing? Why or why not?
3. Do you think that deep dialogue tends to result in a loss of faith, a clarification of faith, or a deepening of faith? For what reasons?

PART TWO

Preparing for Dialogue: Judaism

REUVEN FIRESTONE

CHAPTER FIVE

The Way that New Religions Emerge

All believers in the "Abrahamic" religions—those expressions of the spirit belonging to the three families of religion known as Judaism, Christianity, and Islam—derive their entire spiritual existence from the same deity, however that deity is called and experienced. In all these formulations of monotheism, God is at the center, and God is always worshiped as a loving and compassionate being. These religions represent, at the very least, billions of believers, located in every corner of the world.

Monotheism began as a *unifying* system. Conceptually, it removed the universe and all its many different peoples from the fractious and uncertain rule of often bickering and limited deities and placed them under the mercy and grace of the One Great God.[1] And yet from the earliest annals of religious history, when monotheists have gotten together, we observe them bickering, arguing, and even fighting and killing one another over *which* understanding of the One Great God is true. If only one is true, then it is presumed that all others are therefore false. These conflicts can be observed not only *between* discrete expressions of monotheism, but also *within* each system.

Jews fought not only their common pagan Roman enemy in the failed war of liberation against the Roman Empire in CE 66 (and which ended in the final and absolute destruction of the Jerusalem Temple). They also fought each other at that time, quarreling and even warring over differences that ranged from divergences in beliefs to differences over political positions. The Jews were not alone with their internal disputes.

Christians argued with one another for centuries over the meaning of Christ and over the authority to interpret revelation. Factions developed from earliest times, but the worst was the terrible human destruction in Europe during the sixteenth century. Islam, too, was torn by factions and fighting, not only over the leadership of the community, but also over such theological issues as the nature of God and whether the Al-Qur'an was a creation of God or coexistent with God. In all three sets of internal fighting, believers *within* each system killed one another over the meanings and expectations associated with God.

Distinguishing terms...

Henotheism: I and my community worship one God: other people have their own God or Gods.

Monotheism: There is one God of all people; no other God or Gods exist.

The story of that profound tension between unity and conflict within and between expressions of monotheism begins with the very *emergence* of monotheism. It seems to have taken monotheism quite a while to be accepted as a belief system in the long history of humanity. Scholars of the ancient Near East generally place its origins among the ancient Israelites. But there is still controversy over exactly when and where the first expressions of monotheism emerged. There is the Egyptian pharaoh, Akhenaten who, among his fascinating innovations in art, government, and religion, seems to reflect, at the very least, a kind of henotheism, a word that describes the exclusive worship of one God while not denying the existence of other Gods.[2] Some consider Akhenaten to have been a true monotheist.[3] But like many ancient religions, the religion of Akhenaten did not endure.

Indeed, as current scholarship is engaged in chronicling the early history of Israelite monotheism, it is also uncovering expressions of monotheism that, like the religion of Akhenaten, did not survive the vicissitudes of history. Much later than the Egyptian experiment, during the period of emerging Christianity and Rabbinic Judaism, many Greco-Romans held religious beliefs that although generally labeled negatively as pagan or superstition by Christians, included competing expressions of monotheism that were arising at the same time.[4] And although less well known, the Al-Qur'an refers to pre-Islamic *hanifs*, those who turn their faces away from idolatry to the One God.[5]

What happened to these other expressions of monotheism? They have virtually disappeared from history and can be reconstructed only through references in Jewish, Christian, and Muslim writings that condemned them, or by putting together the remnants of their texts and religious artifacts discovered in archaeological digs. Why have such monotheistic religious systems been forgotten?

For Reflection and Discussion

1. Does henotheism exist today under the guise of monotheism for some people? (That is, do they believe that their understanding of God is the God different from other people's God?)
2. Should the monotheism shared by Judaism, Christianity, and Islam be a source of unity and shared vision? How do you explain those times when it isn't?
3. How has monotheism been a source in history of argument between monotheistic religions?

New Religions Are Threatening

For those of us who find great comfort and warmth in the compassion of God, it is hard to imagine that our religion could be perceived as threatening. But as we know, each expression of the three families of monotheism began with revelation, and revelation always marks a *new beginning* and a new dispensation. Each revealed scripture notes the existence of earlier religions, and each also notes that those earlier religions opposed the new revelation, its message, and the leadership and organization of the new faith.

The pattern is really quite simple. Religion seems to have existed since the beginning of human consciousness. According to human history as taught by the Bible and Al-Qur'an, despite direct communication between God and humanity through Adam and Eve, Cain and Abel, and Noah and his family, consistent belief in a singular God did not catch on. When monotheism finally succeeded among the ancient Israelites, they immediately found themselves opposed by all the established religious communities with whom they came into contact. The story of these relationships is always told in the Bible from the perspective of the Israelites, so we don't know the perspective of the Egyptians, the Canaanites, and all the other peoples the Israelites met in their early historical journeys. But we know from the Bible that the Israelites needed constantly to remain steadfast against the temptations of idolatry.[6] At the same time that the Israelites were threatened by the appeal of idolatry among the established religions of the land, the established religions felt threatened by the attraction of emerging biblical monotheism.

New religious movements seem never to have ceased in human history. We know something about how establishment religions react to new religious movements from observing the emergence of new religions in our own time. In virtually every case, whether it be the Baha'is and the Ahmadiyya in parts of the world dominated religiously by Islam or the Latter-day Saints (Mormon) Church and the many religious groups we define as "cults" in the Christianity-dominated world even in our own generations, emerging religious movements shake up the establishment religions. In response, the establishment religions inevitably label new religious movements as false religions or heresies.

For our purpose of trying to understand how religions interact with one another, it makes no difference whether these religious movements are true expressions of the divine will or not. They are used only as models that we can observe today. By considering how we think of new religious movements in our own day, we can better imagine what happened in ancient history during the emergence of Judaism, Christianity, and Islam.

Establishment religions always try to foil the success of new religious movements. Sometimes establishment religions absorb them until they disappear as discrete entities. When this does not work or if a new movement is too dissimilar to be absorbed, the established religions try to discredit it or destroy it in other ways. Emerging Judaism, Christianity, and Islam were all threatened and attacked by the establishment religions of their day. This is clear from their own Scriptures, which condemn the attacks of the establishment and even go on the offensive against the establishment themselves. Here are only a few examples.

> When the Israelites were in Shittim, the people profaned themselves by whoring with the Moabite women, who invited them to the sacrifices offered to their gods. The Israelites ate the sacrificial food and prostrated themselves before the gods of Moab; they joined in the worship of Baal of Peor. This aroused the anger of the Lord, who said to Moses, "Take all the leaders of the people and hurl them down to their death before the Lord in the full light of day, that the fury of my anger may turn away from Israel." Moses gave this order to the Israelite leaders: "Each of you put to death those of his tribe who have joined in the worship of the Baal of Peor." The Lord said to Moses, "Make the Midianites suffer as they made you suffer with their wiles, and strike them down." (Numbers 25)

> Then the Pharisees went away and agreed on a plan to trap [Jesus] in argument. They sent some of their followers to him, together with

> members of Herod's party. "Teacher," they said, "we know you are a sincere man; you teach in all sincerity the way of life that God requires, courting no man's favor whoever he may be. Give us your ruling on this: Are we or are we not permitted to pay taxes to the Roman emperor?" Jesus was aware of their malicious intention and said, "You hypocrites! Why are you trying to catch me out?" (Matthew 22)

> Many of the People of the Book[7] would like to render you again unbelievers after your having believed, because of envy on their part after the truth has become clear to them. But forgive and be indulgent until God gives His command, for God is the Power over everything...and [the people of the Book] say, no one enters the Garden unless he be a Jew or a Christian. These are their own beliefs. Say [to them, Muhammad], "Bring your proof [of this] if you are truthful!" (Qur'an 2:109–11)

These new religions, then, through the authority of their own beloved scriptures, defend themselves. They first argue against the verbal attacks of their accusers, but they eventually engage in the attack themselves. If a new religious movement becomes successful, it eventually becomes an "established" religion itself. And it can then feel threatened by the newer generations of religious movements. We observe this cycle in all of our Scriptures. Scripture is polemical, meaning that it is argumentative. It argues, not only against other religions that existed before it, but also against certain contrary factions even *within* the community.

> The Lord spoke to Moses, "Hurry down, for your people, whom you brought out of the land of Egypt, have acted basely. They have been quick to turn aside from the way that I enjoined upon them. They have made themselves a molten calf and bowed low to it and sacrificed to it, saying: 'This is your God, O Israel, who brought you out of the land of Egypt!'" (Exodus 32:7–8)

> Beloved, believe not every spirit....Every spirit that confesses that Jesus Christ has come in the flesh is of God. And every spirit that does not confess that Jesus Christ has come in the flesh is not of God. And this is that spirit of antichrist....We are of God; he that knows God, hears us. He that is not of God, does not hear us. (1 John 4:1, 2, 6)

> When the dissenters[8] come to you [Muhammad], they say, "We bear witness that you are indeed God's messenger." And God knows that

> you are indeed His messenger, and God bears witness that the dissenters are indeed speaking falsely. They make their faith a pretext so that they may turn [people] from the way of God. They are engaged in evil. This is because they believed and then disbelieved. It is sealed on their hearts and they do not understand. They are the enemy, so beware of them. God confound them! How they are perverted! (Qur'an 63:1–4).

Polemics must be understood as part of the process of religious formation. It has often been observed that the development of an individual and independent identity is impossible without positioning it in relation to something different. It has also been observed that the uniqueness of the one, unfortunately, is often constructed by defining it comparatively with an "other," which inevitably defines the "other" negatively. Polemics are a basic part of monotheistic scripture, and arguments and accusations are found in the many layers of religious literatures that exist outside the canon of our respective Scriptures as well. The Talmud and related literatures of Judaism, Patristic literature of Christianity, and the Hadith of Islam all include significant polemics against other religions and against factions within the religious systems as well.

In order to survive, religions need to be resilient. For reasons that we can only guess, the lost forms of monotheism described above were not as successful as Judaism, Christianity, and Islam in the face of the religious competition of their times. But what is too often forgotten is the fact that every case of religious polemic occurs within a specific and limited historical context. Scriptural polemic inevitably records the tension and arguments of specific events and times early on in religious formation. Continuing to apply them to the current age is simply an error and misunderstanding of the role and meaning of scriptural polemics.

Condemnation and Context

The biblical condemnation of Canaanite worship was leveled against their specific practices and not against such highly spiritual forms of multitheisms, such as some forms of Hinduism. Even the worst New Testament condemnations of Pharisees and rabbis applied to their own specific historical situation in Roman Judea, not to Jews in general. In fact, most of those who supported Jesus were Jews themselves, so any such attacks were not attacks against Judaism. And the Qur'anic arguments against Jews, Christians, Muslim dissenters, and polytheists represented disputes only in the context of seventh century Arabia. They were not intended to apply to Jews and Christians, for example, living in other times and other places. No case of scriptural polemics was intended to apply to our current world. Unfortunately, religious leaders and their followers have too often mistakenly taken scriptural arguments and condemnations out of their specific contexts and applied them universally. This has resulted not only in the humiliation of the "other," but also the degradation of the self.

Our Scriptures all contain deep universal statements about the human condition, about the meaning of God and God's relationship to humanity, and about how to live a moral and ethical life. These ideas and teachings are universal and are timeless. But our Scriptures also contain material that is historical and time-bound. These references do not apply to situations outside of their specific historical contexts. We must learn how to be sensitive to this important difference.

For Reflection and Discussion

1. Give examples of how time-bound statements can be obstacles to interreligious dialogue.
2. How can the information about new religious movements help us in interreligious dialogue?
3. What is the meaning of the term "polemics"?
4. What is the meaning of "contextual meaning" as opposed to "universal meaning" in relation to scriptural verses?

CHAPTER SIX

What Christians and Muslims Need to Know

Hebrews, Israelites, and Jews

We should begin by clarifying some terms. All the people who practice Judaism today are Jews, but other names were applied to Jews or their forebears, or were taken on by them in earlier periods of history. In the earliest period, according to the Bible, the progenitors of Judaism such as Abraham, Sarah, and the other patriarchs and matriarchs of biblical history were *Hebrews.* This term may actually reflect a socio-economic position of tribal pastoral nomads that occasionally took on other temporary jobs in the areas in which they wandered in the ancient Near-Eastern world. Whatever the original meaning, the Bible usually refers to Hebrews as the ancestors of the Israelites who lived before the revelation of the Torah. Jews rarely refer to themselves these days as Hebrews.

The Hebrew Bible[1] regularly refers to the "Children of Israel" (*beney yisra'el*), which is often translated simply (and correctly) as Israelites. Genesis 32 narrates the story of when Jacob wrestled with a mysterious being on the bank of the Jabok River. When that creature was not able to prevail over Jacob, it gave him the name *Yisra'el* (Israel), which is translated there as the one "who struggles with God and with humanity and prevails" (Gen 32:29). Jacob, along with his wives and consorts, Rachel, Leah, Bilhah, and Zilpah fathered twelve sons who represent the twelve "Tribes of Israel."

Many generations later, according to the Hebrew Bible, those tribes stood at Mount Sinai and there received the Torah, the core of Jewish revelation and scripture. The tribes standing at Sinai represent the children of Jacob, thus the "Children of Israel." To use common Jewish parlance, they are simply "Israel,"

Distinguishing terms...

Hebrews: early nomadic tribes of the Middle East

Israel: members of the family of Jacob, whose name was changed to Israel

Jews: the tribe of Judah, one of Jacob's sons; later applied to all descendants of Israel

which became thereafter the common name for the monotheistic tribes that inhabited the Bible lands and lived according to the laws and cultural and social norms established by the authority of the Torah. They are the ancestors of today's Jews.

Under Kings David and Solomon, through most of the tenth century BCE,[2] all the tribes of Israel were united under one monarchy. But they then split into two separate and often competing kingdoms. The northern kingdom was the largest and comprised ten of the twelve tribes, so it was naturally referred to as Israel. The southern kingdom was dominated by the powerful tribe of Judah, so the name Judah eventually became the common name referring to all the people living there.

The northern kingdom of Israel was destroyed by the Assyrian Empire in the eighth century, BCE, and the southern kingdom by the Babylonians in the sixth century BCE. The ten tribes of the north lost their individual tribal identities after their defeat and assimilated into other cultures—thus the so-called "lost ten tribes." But much of Judah was exiled intact to Babylon and clung to its particular identity. When those Judeans were allowed to return to the Bible lands some seventy years later under the auspices of the Persian emperor who conquered Babylonia, the returnees went to their old home in the south (which included Jerusalem), known as Judah. Those who reconstituted that community, though a mix of survivors from most of the tribes, identified themselves primarily as Judeans, and they all were eventually called Judeans—or Jews.

Among those Jews were a few people who retained their tribal identity as Levites because the tribe of Levy was the tribe that was assigned to carry out all the required duties of the Temple in Jerusalem. Within that tribe were some clans who were identified as *cohanim* or priests. Some of the men in these tribes carried out the very specific duties of sacrifice in the most sacred and restricted sections of the Temple. Even today, some families can be identified as descendents of the tribe of Levy and the clans of the priests. Thus we can find common Jewish family names of Levy, Levine, Levin, Lowey, etc., and Cohen, Kahn, Kogan, and Kane.

Today Jews tend to call themselves just that: Jews. But Jews have always tended to refer to themselves as Israel in their writings, and Israel became a more formal and often more intimate self-designation. The Bible lands are sometimes referred to in the Bible as the "Land of Israel," referring to the area that the Hebrew Bible understood God to have assigned to the Jewish people. So the people of Israel feels a very special relationship with the Land of Israel. The modern nation-state that we know today as Israel is not the official name of that place. Its formal name is *medinat yisra'el*: the "State of Israel," but this has been shortened in informal discourse simply to "Israel." This shortened name is sometimes confusing since Israel is a very common term that in traditional Jewish texts always refers to a people and *not* to a nation-state.

For Reflection and Discussion

1. Jews see themselves as carrying on the faith tradition of Abraham, as do Muslims and Christians; Jews, Christians, and Muslims are "family." What implications does this have for dialogue among members of the three religions? (For example, sometimes family members have more difficulty bringing fresh perspectives on one another because of long-standing patterns of relating.)
2. Do you understand the theological difference between "Old Testament" and "Hebrew Bible"?
3. How would you describe in your own words the origin of the name "Jew"?

Tribes and Religions

Religion in the ancient Near East was intimately associated with ethnicity. Nations in the ancient world were not nation-states as today, but were rather fluid collections of related clans and tribes. Ancient Israel had its twelve related tribes, each of which lived in adjacent tribal areas and formed a coalition when they joined together as the Israelite people. The Canaanites made up a different coalition of tribal groupings, as did the Babylonians, the Persians, and other tribal confederations in the ancient world. Each tribe or tribal coalition had its own Gods that it believed protected it and provided sustenance by granting fertility for its crops and herds. These Gods were not considered by anyone to be universal Gods. They were, rather, powers that affected only the tribal people with whom they were associated. One was born into a tribal religion and remained within it until one died. Personal identity as a tribal member included membership in that particular tribal religion.

In those days, there was no possibility of religious conversion because one could not simply go off and change one's ethnic, tribal identity. The Bible allows Edomites and Egyptians, for example, to become part of the people of Israel only after they had lived among the Israelites for three generations (Deut 23:7–8). This is because it took that length of time for them to lose their old ethnic-tribal identity and assimilate into Israelite culture and religion. This assimilation included the acceptance of the God of Israel. In fact, the name "God of Israel" that occurs hundreds of times in the Hebrew Bible, points to the belief among the Israelites that only they understood the meaning of monotheism. The God of Israel was the God of the universe, but because only the Israelites recognized that, it was *their* notion—"their" God. Of course the Israelites knew that the God of Israel was also the God of all peoples, as is so beautifully articulated in such biblical passages as Isaiah 2 and Micah 4, among others.

> In the days to come, the Mount of the Lord's House shall stand firm above the mountains and tower above the hills; and all the nations shall gaze on it with joy. And the many peoples shall go and say, "Come let us go up to the Mount of the Lord, to the House of the God of Jacob; that He may instruct us in His ways and that we may walk in His paths." For instruction shall come forth from Zion, the word of the Lord from Jerusalem. Thus He will judge among the nations and arbitrate for the many peoples. And they shall beat their swords into plowshares and their spears into pruning hooks; nation shall not take up sword against nation. They shall never again know war. (Isaiah 2:2–4)

Most of the history of Israel that the Hebrew Bible represents, however, is a period of tribal religions. People worshiped the Gods that were associated with their tribe, and since tribal identity was unchangeable because it was understood as a kinship identity, so was one's relationship with one's God or Gods. Our concept of religion as a faith or belief system simply would not make sense in the context of the ancient Near East. One could not change one's God in exactly the same way that one could not change one's family or kin.

The concept of conversion appears to have arisen with the Greeks, who developed different philosophical schools. The elite among the Greeks could study the various philosophies and choose the school that made most sense to them. That notion of choosing a philosophical system was naturally applied later also to religion. One could choose a religious system that seemed most reliable or true.

This change in the notion of religion from a purely tribal association and custom to a belief system and practice that could be studied and then joined, was a change that occurred only at the very end of the time period represented by the Hebrew Bible. The Judaism of today represents a combination of both notions. According to traditional Judaism, a newborn child is automatically Jewish simply because he (or she) is born of a Jewish mother. This is the "tribal" aspect of Jewish identity. It is familial, based purely on kinship association. But anyone can become Jewish by studying Judaism for a significant period of time and then, after learning about its practice and organizing beliefs and assumptions, decide that it is the religious system that makes most spiritual and personal sense, a religious system in which he or she truly believes. That person then goes through a religious ritual that affirms the acceptance of Judaism.

The "tribal" aspect of Jewish identity is something that has often puzzled Christians. It seems strange to observe some Jews that seem to "belong to" rather than "believe in" Judaism. This may not be the ideal from the perspective of Judaism either, but such Jews are most certainly considered to be a part of Israel in any case. This tribal notion is not foreign at all to Muslims, for like the Jews they also have a certain tribalism in the notion of the *umma* or "super-tribe" of Muslims all over the world.

For Reflection and Discussion

1. People can "belong to" Judaism (tribal identity) or "believe in" Judaism (accept Jewish beliefs). Is this true in any way for Christians and Muslims as well?
2. Is tribalism in your opinion a stumbling block to interreligious dialogue? In what ways?
3. Why was conversion, and therefore missionizing, not a conceptual possibility in the ancient Near East? When and why did the possibility of conversion arise?

Not a Biblical Religion

In the early thirteenth century CE, a movement emerged under the aegis of the Catholic Church that collected Jewish books such as the Talmud and collections of Midrash (these literatures will be discussed shortly) and burned them in the city square of Paris. The reasons behind this travesty are complex, but the major reason from the standpoint of the Church was that these books must be destroyed because they prove that Judaism had continued to evolve and progress beyond the practices and theologies that were supposedly condemned by certain arguments in the New Testament. Judaism was condemned by the traditional Christian misunderstanding[3] of Paul for being moribund, and Jews were condemned for refusing to get with the times and follow the newly emerging ideas that were being put forward by Jesus and his followers. Centuries later there was a certain fear among some in the upper echelons of the medieval Church hierarchy that acknowledgment of an evolving Judaism would cancel out some of the arguments of the New Testament and early Church Fathers against Judaism.

In fact, however, Judaism had been evolving for many centuries before, during, and after the period during which Jesus preached to the Jews and Gentiles of Galilee. And in fact, Jesus himself, a rabbinic Jew with many close ties to Pharisaic Judaism, belonged to an age during which a number of movements within Judaism had already emerged, and new ones continued to emerge after his death. These Jewish religious movements were grappling with historical changes in local and international politics and culture, science, and technology. They attempted to come to terms with how these changes influenced contemporary ideas in philosophy and theology, and they brought about new developments in culture and cultural styles and expectations, local worship practices, and language. All of these tested and even threatened the establishment expressions of human spirituality and religious tradition that were currently in place among the Jews of Judea. But before we can make sense of some of these important and complex issues, we need to go back to the origins of Judaism.

From Idolatry to Monotheism

Most contemporary scholars of ancient Israel do not believe that the earliest layers of the Hebrew Bible contain a theology that could be called genuine monotheism. There is no disagreement, however, that by the period of the classical prophets in the sixth century, BCE, the religion of ancient Israel had become a form of true monotheism. That evolution took time and effort—a lot of effort. The Hebrew Bible depicts a long and difficult struggle within ancient Israel to arrive at and then remain faithful to a true unity of God that was not sidetracked by the distractions of the popular and enticing practices of multitheistic peoples around whom and with whom they lived.

Israel remained basically true to monotheism, even though it seems to have been quite unpopular among Israel's neighbors. The Israelites and later, Jews, were only a small minority among the peoples of the ancient Near East, and only they had consistent faith in the One God. The Assyrian and Babylonian emperors who destroyed the Israelite polity claimed that their deities defeated the God of Israel. Despite their humiliation, the Jews clung to God, even in defeat, within a larger polytheistic world where only they worshiped a singular God.

The Hebrew Bible finds consolation in the God of mercy who will someday redeem Israel and return to them in love. In this biblical discourse, God chose Israel to be God's holy or royal people, even if that choosing included chastisement. *Nachamu, nachamu `ami* quotes the prophet, Isaiah. "Comfort, Oh comfort My people, says your God. Speak tenderly to Jerusalem, and declare to her that her term of service is over, that her iniquity is expiated, for she has received at the hand of the Lord double for all her sins" (Isaiah 40:1–2). "Hear this word, O people of Israel, that the Lord has spoken concerning you, concerning the whole family that I brought up from the land of Egypt. You alone have I singled out of all the families of earth—that is what I will call you to account for all your iniquities" (Amos 3:1–2). Given the religious situation of that period, when the only people who considered monotheism were the Jews, it should not be surprising that the concept of the "chosen people" would have emerged.

For Reflection and Discussion

1. What do you understand monotheism to mean? Why was it significant that the Jews were monotheistic?
2. What does it mean to you that Jesus was a rabbinic Jew?
3. Judaism has always been an evolving religion. Has this been true for Christianity and Islam as well? If so, what implications does this hold for interreligious dialogue?

A "Chosen People"

What *is* meant by chosen-ness? Do Jews consider themselves the "chosen people" to the exclusion of all others? Does it mean that only the Jews are "saved?" That the Jews consider themselves the only children of God while all others are condemned to damnation? Does it mean that God loves only Israel and has no love for others? No. None of these fearful understandings reflect the meaning of chosen-ness in Judaism.

The concept of chosen-ness—of being chosen from among the other peoples of the world—came out of a specific historical context in the ancient Near East. As noted above, for many centuries, Israel was the only monotheistic community in a vast and varied sea of multi-theistic peoples. Israel was often on the defensive in this world, and the temptations of idolatry were powerful. The Hebrew Bible portrays God's relationship to Israel in parental terms: "I had resolved to adopt you as My child, and I gave you a desirable land—the fairest heritage of the nations; and I thought you would surely call Me 'Father,' and never cease to be loyal to Me" (Jeremiah 3:19). God is depicted as punishing Israel for its transgressions like a father his child, and as rewarding and encouraging Israel for its ability to cling to God in the face of temptation and adversity.

Statements of chosen-ness in the Bible, therefore, are really encouragement or consolation for the difficulties that befall a believing monotheistic community under constant pressure from surrounding polytheistic peoples. The Hebrew Bible does not teach salvation for Jews and damnation for others. Salvation and damnation are simply not part of the worldview expressed anywhere in the Hebrew Bible.

This contextual meaning of chosen-ness does not seem to have been understood by some Jews, from ancient days to the present. As we have noted above, certain historically contextual scriptural teachings are taken out of context and applied as a universal truth. The result is that some Jews have, on occasion, mistakenly claimed that they are the chosen of God, all other peoples and individuals excluded. This position has tended to have been taken when Jews were under great stress such as during periods of oppression. Maimonides, on the other hand, the great medieval Jewish rabbi and philosopher, understood the chosen-ness of the Jews to be their unique position of introducing monotheism to humanity. The Jewish role was to arrive at the concept first, but the role of Christians and Muslims was to spread it throughout the world.[4]

Chosen-ness and the "Other"

All religions include both inspiration and influence. Inspiration in the religious context is the divine voice that inspires the uniqueness of religion through God's revelation in prophecy, text, or the living word of God incarnate. Influence is the shaping of that inspiration by human hands and minds, making sense of it and placing it into paradigms of human thinking so that it can be understood by regular people. The *idea* of a monotheist Israel, chosen by God among a huge surrounding sea of multi-theistic peoples, became closely associated with the phenomenon that we agree is monotheism. The idea of chosen-ness became so intimately associated with monotheism that the latter seemed impossible if it were not considered the only *chosen* expression of the divine will. The divine inspiration of monotheism to humanity thereafter was often formulated in the language of chosen-ness, not only among those Jews who misunderstood the limited historical context of the biblical expressions, but also by some Christians and Muslims.

The Letter to the Romans, for example (9:7), argues that the Jews are no longer the chosen Israel. It is now the *children of the promise* who are God's beloved, meaning only those promised eternal salvation through Christ, to the exclusion of others.[5] And Islam often tends to consider Muslims the new chosen, for only those who profess the particularity of Islam represent the true understanding of the divine will.[6]

The question of Paul that asks whether only Jews are the children of God, is a condemnation of the elitist interpretation of chosen-ness. It is also an argument between Jews, because what eventually became the new religion of Christianity was originally a sect of Judaism. The New Testament records many cases of argument between Jewish groups that many years later were understood as arguments between adherents of two separate religions: Christianity and Judaism.

In the first century during the emergence of the religious movement that eventually became known as Christianity, there was no single Jewish representation of monotheism. The Jesus movement, Pharisaism, Sadduceeism, Essenism, and other expressions of monotheism competed with one another

The Jesus movement began as a Jewish movement. In the first century, Rabbinic Judaism became the dominant expression of Judaism and survives to this day. During the same century Christianity came to be viewed as distinct from other expressions of Judaism and from Judaism itself.

within the larger polytheistic environment of the Roman Empire. Each considered itself a better representation of the divine will than the others, but for a while, despite their arguments, they managed to live with one another. Eventually, however, all could agree with one another only that, sadly, just one expression of monotheism was the "right" expression.

What we call Rabbinic Judaism became the manifestation of those Jewish movements that became dominant and survived the vicissitudes of history, while the others declined and eventually disappeared. This process was occurring at the same time the movement that eventually became Christianity was surviving the same historical forces. Consequently, Rabbinic Judaism was becoming the "establishment" as Christianity was emerging as the major religious competitor. Judaism's role was thus reversed, changing from innovator that threatened the established religions of its origins, to the established religion that was threatened by the innovator! The same kind of turnaround occurred when Christianity met emerging Islam, and when Islam was confronted with new religious movements that emerged from it.

Each subsequent expression of monotheism accepted the idea that only one could be "right." Only one could have access to the divine "truth." The old idea of chosen-ness that developed out of a particular historical context when the Israelite religion was the only expression of monotheism among multi-theistic religions became a paradigm of monotheism in general. This expectation, unfortunately, hardly allowed religion to give space for other honest spiritual formulations of the divine will.

In every case, newly emergent religions and establishment religions were at odds with one another. Each threatened and each was threatened. But the believers of each system never considered *themselves* threatening, nor did they consider that there may be more than one path to the Almighty. They considered only the opposition threatening, and thus blame was always laid on the *other*. This is the state of religious interaction that we have inherited. With few minor exceptions, this religious view of the other has been dominant until our own generation. As will be explained in the following chapters, each religious system has developed its own sense of chosen-ness, and it is this problem, among others, that needs to be addressed when engaging in interreligious dialogue.

For Reflection and Discussion

1. What might be a reason for the emergence of the idea of chosen-ness in ancient Israel?
2. How and why was the idea of chosen-ness so closely tied to the concept of monotheism?
3. "Being chosen" offers both comfort and challenge. Do you think this is true for Jews, Christians, and Muslims? Does the understanding of chosen-ness offer the same comfort and challenge to members of each religion?

The Torah and the Talmud

The term *torah* means learning or instruction. Capitalized, it refers to the most sacred instruction to the Jews: the first five books of the Hebrew Bible. The Hebrew Bible is divided into twenty-four books. The first five—Genesis, Exodus, Leviticus, Numbers, and Deuteronomy—make up the Torah, sometimes also called *chumash*, meaning roughly "The Five." The second category is the section called Prophets, and the third is called "Writings." All are sacred to Judaism, but the 613 commandments or *mitzvot* by which many traditional Jews comport themselves, are found in the first five books, the Torah.

The Torah contains hundreds of commandments, and it does not number them. Judaism refers to what Christians call the "Ten Commandments" as the "Ten Statements," since the first and arguably central statement of the list is actually a theological declaration rather than a commandment. And Judaism does not limit the expectations of Jewish behavior to these Ten. The number 613 is provided by the Talmud,[7] an encyclopedic collection of tradition, commentary, theology, folklore, and even medical advice that was redacted in Mesopotamia (today's Iraq) around the end of the sixth century, CE. The Talmud is made up largely of dialectic discussion among the greatest Jewish minds of Late Antiquity, who engaged virtually all known aspects of science, law, scriptural interpretation, and belief in their protracted and complex discussions.

The Talmud is actually a discrete piece of literature, but sometimes "the Talmud" is used as a general reference to Rabbinic Literature in general, which

Distinguishing terms...

Torah: the "written law" expressed in the first five books of the Bible; sometimes applied to the entire Bible

Talmud: the "oral law" of leading rabbis of Late Antiquity collected together around the end of the sixth century of the Christian Era

includes other categories such as early exegesis of the Bible called *midrash* and religious poetry called *piyyutim*. It was this continuing production and evolution of sacred Jewish texts that was so problematic to some of the leaders of medieval Christianity.

There are no Pharisees today. The Judaism of the Pharisees, Sadducees, and other ancient Jewish groups depicted in the New Testament did not survive the destruction of the Jerusalem Temple in 70 CE. And just as the Christianities of today reflect but do not duplicate the religion of the Jesus Movement in the first century, so too do today's expressions of Judaism reflect but not duplicate the Judaism practiced during the period when the Jerusalem Temple functioned.

The Destructions of Jerusalem and the Meaning of Exile

The great Temple in Jerusalem, the symbol of God's indwelling or *shekhinah* among the people of Israel, was twice destroyed. It was destroyed first by the Babylonians in 586 BCE. The prophets wrote that it was God's decision to bring the Babylonian armies to Jerusalem to destroy the Temple, and the rabbis attributed the destruction to the ultimate sins of idolatry and bloodshed. It is hard to imagine the horror of the end of God's presence among the people. Christians can probably imagine the shock and trauma, because it must parallel the feelings expressed by the apostles at the death of their rabbi Jesus, who represented and even epitomized God's indwelling within him.

In great compassion and mercy, however, God brought the Judeans back to Jerusalem and Judea three generations later, and allowed them to rebuild the Temple. That Temple held firm, often in the face of great adversity, for more than 500 years until it was destroyed a second time in 70 CE, this time by the Romans. The rabbis attributed this destruction to groundless hatred between Jews, which invalidated the very purpose of religion and spirit. The Jewish group that eventually became the great religious community of Christianity interpreted the destruction as a statement that the "old" system represented by

Judaism was no longer meaningful. The destruction was proof of a new divine dispensation established for Christians.

The Jewish group or groups that eventually became the world of Rabbinic Judaism interpreted the destruction differently. To them it was a statement that the system represented by the Temple sacrifices was no longer meaningful because it was not accompanied by true devotion of the spirit. The result of the Jewish sins of causeless hatred and shallow devotion was exile from the beloved Land of Israel. The very essence of exile is punishment. The lesson drawn was to try ever harder to engage in the business of good religion, even under the debased conditions of exile, where Jews would no longer be in charge of their own political destiny. God remains compassionate and merciful, however, and will again bring back the people of Israel in love. But no one knows when that will occur. Until the modern period, most Jews believed that it would occur in conjunction with the coming of the Messiah, who will redeem not only the Jews but the entire world.

Jews Under Christianity and Islam

The remainder of the historical story of the Jews until the twentieth century is a story of exile. For the next two millennia, in almost every corner of the world, from eastern China to South Africa, Australia, and the Americas as well as Europe, Jews have built their own communities and have governed themselves internally while living under the political and military governments of foreigners. This has been the case not only in far-flung regions of the world, but also in the biblical lands themselves, first under the Romans, then under the Byzantine Christian Roman Empire, and then under various Muslim empires and governments aside from a brief interim period under the Crusader kingdoms.

From the internal Jewish perspective, all non-Jewish rulers treated the Jews badly. The Jews were treated cruelly and their religion abused. Over a period of literally thousands of years, Jews in most parts of the world internalized a sense of persecution by outsiders that is deeply ingrained into a most basic Jewish worldview. Massacres and persecutions were meticulously recorded by Jewish chroniclers. Poems were written in great detail about the mass murders of the Jews by the crusaders in the German cities along the Rhine (Mainz, Wurms, etc.). Jewish travelers wrote about the ill-treatment they witnessed or learned had been meted out to their brethren in foreign lands. And the retelling of horrible torture and cruelty is recited regularly in Jewish liturgies, especially on *Yom Kippur*, the holiest day on the Jewish calendar, and *Tisha Be'Av*, the day commemorating the destructions of the Jerusalem Temples and other Jewish catastrophes. Given the great length of time during which Jews lived everywhere as minorities, given the largely insular and second-class existence of Jews throughout the world, and given the Jewish penchant for writing about it, such an internalization of persecution and abuse should not be surprising.

There is no question that Jews have been persecuted. Legal systems established in Christian Byzantium as early as the fifth century legalized discrimination against Jews, and Islamic law immediately established parallel degradation in the areas under its control. From the perspective of the academic historian whose job it is to examine history objectively, the abuse of Jews and Judaism must be examined alongside the abuse of minorities in general.

Before the modern period, nonconformity was rarely tolerated. It was simply assumed that groups not considered "normal" in the eyes of the majority would not be protected in the same way as others. In all the lands where Jews were persecuted, other minorities were persecuted as well. These often also included racial and ethnic minorities, women, gays, and lesbians, those born with birth defects or later crippled, and others. They also included, of course, even co-religionists whose theologies or practices did not conform with the practice of the establishment's religious orthodoxy, whether in Christian lands or in Muslim lands. Heretics were often sought out and killed in both Christendom and in the Islamic world.

This is not the place to chronicle and compare the relative intensity of persecutions. Christians and Muslims, however, if interested in engaging in productive dialogue with Jews, must be sensitive to the general Jewish view of themselves as believers who have "always" been unjustly persecuted for no reason other than their tenacity in belief. Non-Jews who observe Jewish communities in the United States are sometimes surprised at this outlook because they observe American Jews sometimes insisting vigorously on experiencing themselves as victims, despite their great social and material success.

Jews who are interested in engaging in productive dialogue with Christians and Muslims must take note of this observation as well. It will help to take into consideration the fact that the abuse of Jews has not been unique. All minorities tend to suffer abuse. Whenever abuse was acute in relation to Jews, it was invariably so also in relation to other minorities. Unfortunately, prejudice seems to be a part of culture (if not human nature in general), and all cultures and political systems contain multiple minorities against whom prejudice is expressed. Christians and Muslims who wish to engage in dialogue with Jews must be sensitive to the deep-seated Jewish cultural view that they have been unjustly persecuted throughout history, merely because they are who they are.

For Reflection and Discussion

1. The Talmud provides a window through which to view and understand the Torah. Do Christianity and Islam have similar instruments that guide them in interpreting Scripture?
2. True or false: All of us can point to victimization among our ancestors, but some groups in the past were more victimized than others. What has been your experience of this?
3. What guidelines would you offer for being sensitive to past victimizations during interreligious dialogue?
4. How would you incorporate giving and receiving forgiveness into a dialogue process?

CHAPTER SEVEN

Jews and Modernity

Throughout most of the Middle Ages, the Jewish population of the world tended to congregate in Islamic lands. But by the late 1700s, the majority of the world's Jewish population lived in Christian Europe. This was a period that had been very powerfully affected by the ideas of the Renaissance and the Christian Reformation. Both contributed greatly to the modern concept of Enlightenment and the resulting emancipation of Christian minorities. Two Enlightenment ideas had very important results for the Jews of Europe. The first insisted that every man (women were not generally considered equal in this regard) should be judged according to his own individual merits and not, as was previously the case, according to his family, class, or religious status. This allowed the possibility for Jews to integrate more fully into European society. The second idea insisted that every individual is capable of applying reason and personal judgment to decision-making and need not rely blindly on tradition. This allowed Jews, like their Christian neighbors, to reevaluate the meaning of their religious tradition for the modern age.

The Jews were not integrated into European society evenly. In many places Jews were not granted equal status until the twentieth century. In some, they were never accepted as equals; and in others, their emancipation was entirely reversed and worse when millions were murdered during the Holocaust. Despite this unevenness, however, the Emancipation forever altered the status of Jews in the West because it established the principle that all peoples who engaged positively on behalf of the nation-state should be entitled to the same rights and responsibilities of citizenship.

Without the creation of the modern nation-state, the Jews of Europe might never have been freed from their long history as second-class inhabitants. Modern national identity helped to blur the distinction of religion that had nearly crippled Europe for centuries with bloody military wars and debilitating political and economic battles. The modern, secular nation-state that emerged toward the end of the eighteenth century was far less concerned with the religious beliefs or practices of its various groups of citizens than with the success of the state as whole. The state depended on the willingness of its citizens to contribute to the national cause through military and civic service, paying taxes, and generally contributing to the good of the whole.

Jewish Emancipation and integration into the new national identities of European society had a major effect on Jewish religious practice as well. Jews inevitably applied the ideas of modern Europe to Jewish law, ritual, philosophy, ethics, and daily practice. The result was both a reduction in the power of religion to influence the behavior of Jews and an increase in factionalism and divisions among the Jews as they responded to the challenges of modernity.

Jewish Responses to Modernity in the West

Jewish Emancipation occurred first in Western Europe and the United States. For the first time in thousands of years, Jews found themselves free from restrictive laws. They could live outside a ghetto, send their children to public schools, learn any craft or trade, employ Christians, were free to dress as other Europeans, were not restricted to their homes on Sunday mornings and Christian holidays, allowed to go to public parks and places of amusement, etc. For many Jews, this was an invitation to abandon their Jewish identity entirely and assimilate into the secular nation-state or even to convert to Christianity.

The Judaism that had been the basis of their culture for centuries had developed in a different time and place. To many, it seemed at odds with the modern aesthetics, sensibilities, and ethics of Europe. One response was to modernize or reform Judaism to make it more compatible with the modern age. This was undertaken by a wide and varied group of rabbis and laity who are sometimes referred to as the early "reformers."

Reform Judaism

Some of these reformers were instrumental in developing what is called today Reform or Progressive Judaism. The earliest reformers began by reforming the prayer service to bring it into line with Western sensibilities. They also subjected the study of Judaism to the same rigorous scientific methods being employed by other sciences. They reexamined the philosophical underpinnings of Judaism, the meaning of God and Torah, reward and punishment in the afterlife, the meaning of the end of time, and the role and responsibility of the Jews in an integrated world. The result of their exploration was the emergence of a form of Judaism that they hoped would be far more relevant to the modern world.

One of the major innovations of Reform was to reexamine the place and meaning of the divine commandments. The Reform Movement in Judaism distinguished between ritual commandments and moral-ethical commandments. They considered the ritual commandments of Judaism such as the particular (kosher) food laws, use of Hebrew prayer and other forms of Jewish ritual practice to have been developed by the ancient rabbis in order to separate Jews from a world populated entirely by idolaters or people who would harm Jews. Since the Western world had become entirely monotheistic as Christianity and Islam became universal religions along with Judaism, and because Jews were afforded equal protection by the law, they felt that there was little need to keep the particular rituals that set Jews apart from other civilized peoples. This strongly reduced the cultural differences between Jews and others, while Reformers retained the major theological distinctions.

One result of this change was to rid the distinction of nationhood from their view of Judaism. They considered themselves nationally equal to their non-Jewish neighbors, while at the same time remaining religiously distinct. The Jews of France, for example, could therefore consider themselves entirely French from the national perspective, while retaining their religious distinction in the same way that French Catholics and Protestants retained a religious differentiation while remaining national brethren.

Reform Judaism was a force of some importance in Europe but remained always a minority among Jews. In the United States, however, Reform became the largest and most powerful Jewish expression. One of its American hallmarks was the emphasis that every individual Jew, rather than merely obeying the dictates of his rabbi, had the right and the obligation to learn Bible and Tradition and then to make a personal decision about Jewish practice and observance based on personal knowledge. The result of this "democratization" of Judaism was to encourage a great variety of religious practice. Many Reform Jews choose to pray in English rather than in Hebrew and to observe only a very few commandments.

Orthodox Judaism

The reformers of the early nineteenth century were a small minority of Europe's Jews. Many other Jews left their Jewish heritage entirely as they were allowed to assimilate into the modern European nation-states and assume a national identity to replace their Jewish identity. Both groups, the reformers and the assimilationists or secularists, were viewed with great alarm by some Jews who believed that the modernists failed God by refusing to observe the Torah commandments in all their details. As a reaction to the modernizing trends, groups of Jews began to close themselves off from the dangers of modernity by forming tightly-knit communities in which they could avoid its temptations.

Some urged their fellow Jews to remain true to the letter of the law, while integrating the trappings of modern European dress and aesthetic. Others insisted on the complete social and cultural segregation of Jews from modern society. All together, these groups formed what is today called Orthodox Judaism. Some communities of Orthodox Jews established greater restrictions to social and cultural interaction with non-Jews than had even the traditional Judaism of the ancient and medieval periods. The slightest tampering with tradition was condemned and new restrictions enacted in order to protect Jews from the temptations of modernity. This moved the radical expressions of Orthodox Judaism in the opposite direction of secularization or Reform Judaism.

Conservative Judaism

Conservative Judaism has taken a "middle path" between those of Reform and Orthodox Judaism. The leaders of Conservative Judaism agreed with the reformers that the entire history of Judaism was one of change and development, and that Jews and Judaism always responded creatively to the challenges of history. However, they disagreed with the more radical reformers about how far it was possible to go in allowing the modernization of Judaism. Three areas stand out as sacred in the Conservative position of Jewish observance: their devotion to the Hebrew language in prayer services and other Jewish ritual activities; the observance of Jewish dietary laws (*kashrut*); and traditional Sabbath observance. Conservative Judaism, like Orthodox Judaism and contrary to Reform, insists on strict observance of the ritual Commandments of Judaism, but it is more lenient in its interpretation of how to do this. Thus, certain foods are permitted to be eaten by Conservative Jews that are forbidden by Orthodox Jews, while Sabbath observance for Conservative Judaism is far more observant than that of Reform.

The overwhelming majority of practicing Jews living in the United States is almost equally divided between Reform and Conservative practice, although Reform is somewhat larger. Orthodox Judaism in the USA represents a strong and influential but small minority. In the state of Israel, however, the overwhelming majority of practicing Jews are Orthodox, with Conservative and Reform Jews very small but growing minorities. About half the population of Jews in the United States are unaffiliated with any religious movement. These are often called "secular" Jews—Jews who retain a feeling of Jewish identity but engage in little or no religious practice such as prayer or holiday observance. In Israel, more than half of the Jews are secular. Although the majority of religiously practicing Jews in Israel are Orthodox, they make up only about twenty percent of the total Jewish population of the country.

Reconstructionist Judaism and Jewish Renewal

The three major Jewish expressions mentioned above emerged in Europe in response to the Enlightenment in Europe and the Emancipation of the Jews. Two newer Jewish movements have been born in the American context during the twentieth century. Both emerged out of Conservative Judaism, either directly or indirectly, and both are more engaged in one way or another in recapturing the communal nature of traditional Judaism that has been overtaken by the great American emphasis on individuality. A hallmark of

Modern Expressions of Judaism

- **Reform:** Jews who adapt most to modern ways; began in the early nineteenth century
- **Orthodox:** Jews who hold most strictly to traditional expressions of Judaism
- **Conservative:** Jews who seek a middle ground between Reform and Orthodox
- **Secular:** Jews who identify with being Jewish but engage in little or no religious practice
- **Reconstructionist:** Jews who emphasize communal decision-making
- **Jewish Renewal Movement:** Jews who emphasize neo-mystical elements of Judaism

Reconstructionist Judaism in the current generation is the emphasis on communal decision-making, as opposed to reliance upon Jewish tradition or rabbinic leadership only. The Jewish Renewal Movement has emphasized a neo-mysticism that places emphasis on the individual spiritual quest as enabled by the community. Both movements are still quite small, though they have exerted an influence on the American Jewish community out of proportion to their actual numbers.

For Reflection and Discussion

1. Why, with Emancipation, do you think some Jews choose to abandon their Jewish identity altogether?
2. How was Reform Judaism a response to modernity?
3. How did Jewish Orthodoxy respond to the destabilizing threats of modernity and Emancipation?
4. Are there Christians and Muslims who emphasize religious expressions similar to the various groupings that exist in the Jewish community? (For example, are there "secular" Muslims and Christians who hold strictly to traditional beliefs and practices?)

Judaism and Modernity in Eastern Europe

Until the modern period, Jewish identity could be defined as a kind of religious nationhood. This sense of nationhood was not that of modern nationalism defined by the modern nation-state, but rather a feeling of identity and camaraderie with all Jews anywhere in the world. Whether living in Baghdad, Jerusalem, Paris, or Cracow, Jews both considered themselves and were considered by their non-Jewish neighbors to be different from the majority of people living in their cities and countries. What bound Jews together wherever they lived, in China, Yemen, Morocco, or Poland was a common religious belief and practice and a common way of conducting their daily lives, whatever languages they spoke and whatever regional variances they expressed in their local cultures.

This sense of religious nationhood is closer to the Islamic *umma* (Arabic, people) than the current Christian fellowship because the religious precepts of Judaism include behavior as well as faith, going far beyond that of acceptable religious belief. The position of Jews as second-class citizens wherever they lived helped to form a powerful particularist identity over the centuries and millennia. Jewish identity remains a powerful force, even among Jews who define themselves as agnostic or atheist. Even atheism does not invalidate a person's Jewish identity according to Jewish law, for even a Jew who sins is still a Jew.[1]

Emerging Eastern European Nationalisms

Prior to the modern period, a person's identity was based primarily on class, family, religion, gender, and region. With the development of the modern nation-state, religion became, theoretically, only a private matter. The modern nation-state became one's primary focus of identity. Although the Jews of Western Europe were largely included in the transition from pre-modern to modern determinations of identity, in Eastern Europe where the overwhelming majority of the Jews lived in the nineteenth century, Jews were not emancipated. Particularly in the Russian Empire, the Jews suffered as much or more than other national and ethnic peoples under the yoke of the Czar. Toward the end of the nineteenth century, many of the ethnic peoples living in the Russian Empire attempted to free themselves from Czarist rule and form modern nation-states. In contrast with the situation in Western Europe, however, the Jews of Eastern Europe were not accepted as participating members of the newly emerging nationalisms. Whether in Poland, Ukraine, Romania, or Russia, and even where they spoke and dressed like the local people, they were excluded from the national liberation movements. Not only did they suffer pogroms—massacres—under the Czar, the Jews suffered the same treatment by activists in the national liberation movements.

Eastern European Jews responded to their miserable life in the nineteenth and early twentieth centuries in a number of ways. Many tried to escape by immigrating to Western Europe and the Americas, and well over a million came to the United States between 1880 and 1920. Others hoped to find solace and even redemption by delving ever more deeply into religious Judaism. An important portion of Eastern European Jews became active in universalist political movements that hoped to end prejudice and inequality by creating a world of economic and social equality through socialism or communism. Another population of Jews responded to their misery, including their rejection by the national liberation movements, by agreeing with those who rejected them that the peculiar nature of Jewish nationhood prevented their integration into the modern European nation-state.

Wherever they were, these Jewish nationalists concluded, they were rejected as Jews. Even secular Jews who had completely abandoned their religious practice were excluded from the nationalist liberation movements on the basis of their Jewish identity. What exactly was it about their identity that made them unfit for the nationalist movements? Certainly not religion, for many of the Jewish nationalist leaders were also secularists or anti-religious. One group of Jews came to the logical conclusion that their rejection was based, not on their *religious* identity as Jews, but on their *national* identity as Jews. They personally witnessed the fact that even overcoming religious prejudice did not allow the Jews to be accepted fully as people. Moses Hess, one of the earliest Jewish nationalists, came to the following conclusion: "We shall always remain strangers among the nations....Religious fanaticism may cease to cause hatred of the Jews in the more culturally advanced countries; but despite Enlightenment and Emancipation, the Jew in exile who denies his nationality will never earn the respect of the nations among whom he dwells."[2]

The Modern Jewish Nationalism of Zionism

There was little hope for the Jews to join the nationalist movements of Eastern Europe, and the Jews were suffering heavily from the violence of robbery, rape, and even massacres at the hands of their peasant neighbors, and even from the regional and national governments that should have protected them. Jewish nationalists therefore called for the creation of a Jewish nation where, under their own government and police force, they would no longer be victims of the hatred and prejudice of other religions and nationalities. Long before the Holocaust, these Jewish nationalists came to the conclusion, logical given their own historical experience, that living at the mercy of peoples who hated them was no longer tenable. In the modern period, many national peoples were ridding themselves of the yoke of foreign control by forming their own nation-states where they could decide their own destiny. This is possible also for the Jews, they declared, because Jews also make up a national people.

European theorists of nationalism at the time determined that national peoples were defined by a common history, common language, common land, and common vision. Jewish nationalists claimed that the Jews had all these criteria of nationhood. Their common history was well-known and obvious, and their common language was the ancient tongue of Hebrew that Jews learned

Distinguishing terms...

Zionism: Movement advocating existence of Israel as a nation-state for Jews

throughout the world. But not all Jews had the same vision. Many were piously awaiting the coming of the Messiah, others sought to modernize Judaism, while still others wished to secularize and assimilate. The nationalists aspired for a Jewish state.

An additional problem was the one of a common land, for Jews had been living throughout most of the world for many centuries and had not controlled their own political destiny for nearly two millennia. Some Jewish nationalists were content to build a Jewish nation-state on any land in the world that might become the exclusive possession of Jews. Most nationalists, however, insisted that there was only one land that truly qualified as a Jewish national territory, and this was the land that had been settled, farmed, governed, and defended by Jews for over a thousand years: the Land of Israel. The Jewish nationalist movement became the Zionist movement when it insisted that only Zion—one of the biblical names for the ancient Jewish capital of Jerusalem and therefore representative of all the Land of Israel—must be the location for the rebirth of the Jewish people in the form of a modern nation-state.

Zionists remained a minority movement among the Jewish people until the Holocaust, when the Jewish people observed most of Europe standing by if not assisting in the nearly successful genocide of the Jews. The fact of world complicity if not activity in the destruction of Jews convinced the Jewish people, with only a very few exceptions, to support the building up of the Land of Israel as a modern Jewish state where Jews would finally govern themselves and therefore cease being at the mercy of peoples who did not care about their welfare.

For Reflection and Discussion

1. What were some of the motivations for Jews to develop a sense of modern Jewish nationhood?
2. How was modern Jewish nationhood different from traditional (pre-modern) Jewish nationhood?
3. Why did this development occur in Eastern Europe rather than Western Europe?

4. If you were a Jew living in Europe during the eighteenth century when nationalism was emerging, would you have:
   - piously awaited the coming of the Messiah without getting involved in politics?
   - worked for a nation-state for Jews?
   - attempted to assimilate into the dominant culture in which you lived?

The Holocaust

The Holocaust has left an indelible mark on the soul of the Jewish People. Although attempts at genocide have been made to other peoples before and after World War II, never have such careful planning, huge expenditures of resources, and monumental human efforts been devoted to the destruction of another group of humans in the history of humankind. As may be expected, Jews have responded to the Holocaust in a variety of ways. Some have abandoned their religious commitment in the belief that God had abandoned them. Conversely, others have become more pious and committed to religious practice as a result of the horrors of the Holocaust.

Jews have responded differently to the Holocaust also in terms of their relations with the non-Jewish world. One response has been to become determined to work diligently in order to prevent such hatred and violence from being directed toward any human group on earth. According to this response, because Jews were victims of the most horrendous crime in human history, Jews have the awesome responsibility (having collectively experienced this unprecedented crime), to help ensure that such an act never occurs again.

Another response to the Holocaust has been to turn away from the world and concentrate only on Jewish survival. According to this response, as innocent victims of the most horrendous crime in human history, and as sufferers of indescribable horrors inflicted upon them by many nations of the world while the remainder of the world stood by without interfering, the Jews owe the world nothing. Even leaders of disinterested parties such as the Arabs of Palestine in the 1930s and '40s are not considered innocent by many Jews. The great Arab nationalist leader Hajj Amin al-Husseini, for example, mufti and longtime leader of Arab nationalism in Palestine, collaborated with Nazi Germany as one of its chief propagandists to the Arabs and as a recruiter and organizer of Muslim volunteers, supporting and aiding the Nazi program for the extermination of the Jewish people. Therefore, according to this position, no people, including Palestinians and Muslims, can claim that they have nothing to do with the Holocaust.

The Holocaust has cast a certain shadow over the relations between Jews and Arabs because Jews tend to lump Arabs along with other peoples that stood by and allowed the destruction of European Jewry. Conversely, Arabs tend to consider themselves innocent of the Holocaust, which they claim was purely a European phenomenon. Arabs and Muslims who are concerned for the rights of Palestinians living within Israel and Palestine, and those who have been exiled from the region, feel that they have been made to bear the punishment for the crimes against the Jews perpetrated by Europeans and Christians. The pain of victimization, accusation, and blame is deep and not easily forgotten. It may be transcended in part through honest dialogue and discussion, but people can and must learn to live together even when there cannot be a full understanding between them.

The State of Israel

The State of Israel was established in 1948, only three short years after the end of the Holocaust, and it was established through war and bloodshed. As mentioned previously, most Jews today completely support the right of Jews to have their own nation-state. The religious teachings of the Bible and the Talmud, however, have been interpreted both in favor and against the establishment of a modern Jewish state. The argumentation of both positions is complex and sometimes obscure, but from the religious perspective, the issues revolve around the idea of the messiah in Judaism.

After the destruction of the Second Temple and the Dispersion of Jews by the Romans in the aftermath of that destruction, the rabbis came to the conclusion that the Jewish people were destined by God to remain in exile until the coming of the Messiah. According to these rabbis, it was no longer possible or even desirable for Jews to control their political destiny until the Messiah would come and redeem not only the Jews, but the entire world.

The Zionist movement for the establishment of a modern Jewish state, on the other hand, was begun and peopled almost entirely by Jews who did not adhere to the strict theological and religious principles of traditional Judaism.

They neither agreed with the interpretations of their rabbis nor followed their guidance. On the contrary, they called for the establishment of a modern, secular state for Jews in order to end Jewish persecution and to provide them with freedom from oppression and the constant fear of violence. The Zionists were therefore opposed by most Jewish religious leaders from the outset.

Religious opposition to Zionism was partially a response to previous attempts by Jews in ancient days and in medieval times to gain political independence. These attempts had all ended in failure and the subsequent destruction of large Jewish populations. The lesson that Jewish religious leaders took from these disasters was that Jews must wait until God decides the time is right for redemption. According to their understanding, only God can decide this. The attempt to "force the hand of God" by working through political channels to create a Jewish state would only bring the wrath of God and another horrible destruction to the Jews. The Zionists therefore remained almost exclusively secularists.

By the 1930s, however, a new religious interpretation of Zionism began to evolve with the thinking of Rabbi Abraham Isaac Kook, an influential rabbi of the Jewish community of Palestine.[3] He suggested that the secular Zionists were not really "forcing the hand of God," but were rather, and inadvertently, actually carrying out God's divine plan by creating a Jewish state, thereby beginning the process of Redemption. According to Kook, God's will is inscrutable, but the signs suggest that the final Redemption is near at hand. Religious Jews are therefore obligated to assist the Zionists, or at least not condemn them, for their work in building up the Land of Israel.

The horror of the Holocaust was interpreted by some anti-Zionist Orthodox Jews as that horrible punishment that would befall the Jews for attempting to force the hand of God. For most other Jews, however, whether Orthodox, Conservative, Reform, or secular, the Holocaust confirmed that only a Jewish state would succeed in protecting the Jews from some future disaster.

The success of Israel's War of Independence in 1948, and even more so, the victory of the 1967 war, was interpreted by many Orthodox Jews as divine signs that the Redemption is at hand. Orthodox Judaism has therefore became more and more Zionist during the second half of the twentieth century, for it tends to place Israel fully within the process of reaching a final and imminent Redemption. Zionism itself, however, has undergone many changes and developments. While some Zionists continue to call for Jewish political control over all of the biblical Land of Israel, the overwhelming majority are moving increasingly toward accepting a smaller state that can be in close and cooperative relationship with its Arab and Muslim neighbors.

For Reflection and Discussion

1. What are some of the different ways that Jews have responded to the Holocaust?
2. Why did some Orthodox Jewish communities oppose Zionism?
3. What watershed event in Jewish history overturned most Jewish opposition to Zionism, and why?
4. The relationship between Israel and its Arab neighbors is a political matter, not a religious one. Is it necessary to address this political situation as part of interreligious dialogue? If so, what guidelines would you suggest for including this topic in a dialogue process?

Post-Modern Judaisms

Our current age is increasingly being referred to as "post-modern." The connotations are numerous, but for Judaism and Jewish practice and ideas, it has meant that Jewish living and thought has begun to transcend the boundaries of modernist thinking. There are "post-denominational" forms of Judaism that feel comfortable with incorporating varied aspects of Jewish life deriving from strict orthodoxy to liberal reform, and even movements to join aspects of Judaism with Buddhism or native American religious traditions. There are also Jewish "post-Zionists" who support the State of Israel but call for far more Arabized or even partially Islamized forms of national culture that will bring Israel culturally into greater harmony with its Middle Eastern surroundings. What is most important to remember is that although Jews feel very closely connected to other members of their religious-national civilization and culture, there are a wide variety of expressions of Judaism and Jewish culture. Some are religious and some secular, but all relate to the peoplehood or nation of Jews as a unity.

Judaism and Dialogue

Since the Christianization of the Roman Empire in the fourth century until only very recently, Jews have experienced religious "dialogue" almost exclusively as attempts to prove Judaism wrong and convert the Jews to other faiths. In actual fact, however, Jews, like Christians, engaged in proselytizing before the fourth century. But when Christianity became the official religion of the Roman Empire, it became a capital crime for Jews to proselytize. That ended any such inclination rather quickly. The Islamic world enacted similar laws. As a result of these imposed restrictions, Jews imposed their own protective ban against any behavior that might be construed as missionizing. This internal ban against proselytizing became so much a part of Jewish culture that Jews lost even the memory of reaching out to non-Jews.

Unlike Christian missionizing, however, Jewish proselytizing did not teach that salvation required Jewish beliefs or practices. In fact, Judaism has regularly expected that righteous Gentiles will attain the "world to come" just like righteous Jews.[4] Although dialogue is the opposite of proselytization, Jews are very sensitive to the possibility that so-called "dialogue" may mask missionizing. For successful dialogue, it is important that all the participants listen to one another and not enter the process with any goal other than the desire to learn from the others.

CHAPTER EIGHT

What Jews Need to Know about Judaism in Dialogue

Judaism is not incompatible with dialogue. In fact, Judaism is a "dialogic" religion. Traditional Jewish learning takes place through *machaloqet* or taking opposing positions on principle and working through them, and is thus dialogical at its core.

The important phenomenon of *machaloqet* developed in Judaism as a response to the observation that the Bible, like all Scripture, often does not take a monolithic or uniform position on issues (though on certain issues it is unswerving, such as the falseness of idolatry and the idea that there is a single God who is responsible for the universe). But on many other issues, Scripture often refrains from providing a single unambiguous message. The lack of absolute consistency in scripture is troublesome to some, but it seems to be just a part of the reality of Scripture in general. Jewish sages throughout history took this reality to mean that humans need to analyze and discuss what may appear inconsistent in scripture, to struggle and theorize the possible meanings of the divine word in order to act on our understandings of God's expectations of us.

From the earliest period we know of Jewish learning, competing schools argued and debated one another. This is exemplified by the generations of *zugot* or scholar-pairs, that eventually became schools of interpretation and legal discourse. Famous early scholar-pairs include: Yose ben Yo`ezer and Yose ben Yochanan; Yehoshua ben Perachya and Nitai the Arbelite; Yehudah ben Tabbai and Shimon ben Shetach; Shemaya and Avtalyon, culminating in the two schools of Hillel and Shammai. Both schools were of equal academic stature, but God favored the school of Hillel for a very important reason that is explained in the Talmud (Eruvin 13b).

> Rabbi Abba said in the name of Shmuel: For three years there was a dispute between the school of Shammai (Beit Shammai) and the school of Hillel (Beit Hillel), the former asserting, "The proper legislation (*halakhah*) is in agreement with our views." Then a heavenly voice issued, announcing "Both are the words of the living God, but the *halakhah* is in agreement with the rulings of Beit Hillel." Since, however, "both are the words of the living God," what was it that entitled Beit Hillel to have the *halakhah* fixed in agreement with their rulings? Because they were kindly and modest, they studied their own rulings and those of Beit Shammai, and they even mentioned the conclusions of Beit Shammai before their own.

The tradition of parallel schools continued for over a thousand years in the Land of Israel and in the great academies in Babylonia (today's Iraq) under the Persian and Muslim empires. The existence of the famous Babylonian Jewish academies at Sura and Pumbedita exemplified the dialogic approach, even as they competed with one another like the competition of great colleges and universities in our own age. To this day, study in traditional religious academies known as *yeshivot* takes place as a series of dialogues or arguments (*machaloqot*) that a pair or more students engage in with one another over the meanings of sacred text. The purpose of this dialogic methodology is not to win arguments, but rather to deepen understanding by trying to see how far one can carry out a particular position. It is not unlike forensics today, where debate competition is not intended to prove an absolute truth, but rather to deepen one's grasp of complex issues.

Judaism in Dialogue with Other Religions

But these deeply Jewish expressions of dialogue all occurred *within* the larger Jewish community and rarely between Jews and non-Jews. The reason for this is not intrinsic to Judaism, which stresses dialogue in general between different views. The reason for the rarity of dialogue with other religions is, in fact, more a result of history. When religion became state-sponsored and state-enforced beginning with the Christian Byzantine Empire and continuing with the Islamic Caliphates and Sultanates, it became dangerous for Jews to engage in dialogic religious discussion with non-Jews.

There were notable exceptions to this rule. The most famous is during the height of the Islamic achievement in the Middle Ages under the Abbasid

Caliphate that was ruled from Baghdad, and the revival of the Umayyad Caliphate in Spain. The climate was not always ripe for dialogue, even under enlightened rulers, and Jews were always aware that these exchanges of ideas were taking place under the military rulership of a foreign empire. One cannot compare such dialogues favorably with what is possible in the West today.

The other major exception was the rare occasion when Jewish and Christian scholars engaged in real dialogic discussion with one another in Christian Europe. This was more unusual than in the Islamic world, and in both cases dialogue could become a means for ruling powers to obtain information to support polemical argument against their Jewish subjects. Even this tradition of negative polemics constitutes a form of dialogue, however, though not the kind that is of use to us in the modern world. Polemics literature sometimes claims to record actual discussions between peoples of different faiths, though it always constructs the discussions in a way that "proves" the truth of the religion of the writer over the religion of the other. Reading the polemics literatures in Judaism, Christianity, and Islam can nevertheless help us to understand what issues were of concern, threatening, or problematic to our religious leaders and intellectuals in earlier days. Very often they articulate some of the very issues that divide us today.

Thus far we have considered three kinds of "dialogue" in Jewish history: that of *machaloqet* or argumentation within the Jewish community; that of actual verbal discussion and argument between Jews and Muslims or Christians; and that of formal religious polemic that is carefully written in order to prove the "truth" of one religious system or theology over the other(s). None of these are particularly good models for the kind of dialogue we need to engage in today.

Positive Dialogue Today

Today, dialogue is not making points or winning arguments. The purpose of dialogue is not to make believers *of* the dialogic partners, but rather to foster and gain better understanding *with* the dialogic partners. Dialogue today is listening and learning. It is a way to reach out to other religious people by learning how they feel and what they believe. And it is a way to learn about the self by learning about the other. It should not be threatening to either party because it should not be an argument or an attempt to prove the rightness of one system of belief or practice. Dialogue today requires no relinquishing of personal beliefs.

> **Two effective forms of dialogue:**
>
> - working together in social action, social justice projects
> - examining Scriptures together in small groups

A rapidly shrinking world requires greater understanding across religious as well as cultural boundaries. Too many misunderstandings lie behind the willingness of people to engage in violence against the other. With interreligious dialogue and respect, even without deep understanding, we can learn to live better and with greater dignity, both with ourselves and with the religious other. The compassion and appreciation that is learned and achieved from interreligious dialogue extends to all spheres of human interaction, thus making this world just that much more humane and livable.

Types of Dialogue

Jewish-Christian dialogue is often structured around theology, and Jewish-Muslim dialogue is often structured around "issues" such as war and peace. But dialogue need not be centered on sitting around tables and discussing theology or issues. The word, "dialogue" is derived from two Greek words that mean "speaking across." It is any kind of discourse that involves exchange. Some of the best dialogue emerges when two different religious groups or communities engage together in social action or social justice projects. Through these activities, adults or youth or entire families can get to know one another and get to know one another's beliefs and attitudes toward living.

In my experience, some of the most effective dialogue for stimulating thinking about our own faith and that of the religious "other" happens in the reading of one another's sacred texts. When two Scriptures are learned together in intimate study groups of two to four, the participants begin to learn not only the texts themselves, but also a wide range of related issues. These include the participants' interpretations that they bring into the discussion. Some of these interpretations are formal, traditional positions. Others are absorbed informally, simply by growing up in a particular religious civilization. When studying a text with co-religionists, we often fail to notice the special ways that we read our sacred texts intuitively from our natural religious contexts. But when we study together with people of other faiths who do not share our intuitive readings and hence come at them from a different angle, they help us learn how we read our own texts and therefore expand the depth of our own readings.

For Reflection and Discussion

1. In what way is Judaism inherently a "dialogic religion"?
2. Why did Jews view dialogue with other religions with suspicion until only recently?
3. What are some of the main differences between pre-modern "dialogue" and dialogue today?
4. Besides the two specific types of dialogue mentioned here, what other forms of interaction between religions would be mutually beneficial?

CHAPTER NINE

Jewish "Red Buttons"

All religious communities have suffered in one way or another from misunderstandings or religious slander and defamation. All religious communities have suffered persecution at some time in their history at the hands of outsiders. All religious communities have certain "red buttons" that when pressed by outsiders, can end the dialogue. This is not to say that any subject is necessarily taboo. It is only that certain subjects are sensitive and must be handled with care. Not all members of the same community have the same "red buttons," nor when they do are they felt by all with the same intensity. It is a good idea nevertheless to tread gently (if at all) on known "red buttons" of the other when engaging in dialogue.

One such subject for Jews is the Holocaust. Another can be the state of Israel. Others can include traditional defamations of Jews such as the claim of the forged so-called "Protocols of the Elders of Zion" that the Jews control the world, or that they control the world economy, the media or Hollywood, or even old medieval libels that occasionally surface even today.

The Holocaust is probably the most sensitive "red button" for Jews today. With nearly every Jew having lost relatives or relatives of friends in the attempted Nazi genocide of European Jewry, one cannot in any way make light of the experience. To Jews, no genocide in human history can even compare with the experience. An attempt to do so would be considered disrespectful of the living and of the dead. Any suggestion that the Palestinians, despite their suffering, have experienced something of the caliber of the Holocaust might end any dispassionate discussion on the spot. On the other hand, such a suggestion is not dialogue, but rather competition and argument, which is not a means for promoting understanding.

This is not to label the Holocaust as a taboo subject. On the contrary, it is of great interest to Jews, who wish that non-Jews understand the importance and horror of the event for Jews. Some non-Jews who have engaged in dialogue with Jews might have had enough of hearing how unequaled the Holocaust is in terms of human suffering. But sometimes one simply must endure it, as the Holocaust has become a sacred event for the Jewish group consciousness.

The other major "red button" for Jews is Israel. For some, Israel can do no wrong, and any critique of the country or of its government is a slander against the Jews as a whole. For most Jews, Israel is a sacred part of Jewish life, but it is not without reproach. Many Jews feel great frustration over Israel's military and political acts against Palestinians but feel that Israel has been forced by outsiders to engage in such acts in order to defend itself against annihilation. Even when clearly justified, criticism leveled against Israel can end meaningful dialogue if it is not couched in supportive language or after a deep level of trust has developed among the dialogue partners.

Conspiracy accusations are always frustrating because they can never, by definition, be disproved. There can be no hard proof of any conspiracy theory because if there were, it would be proven and therefore no longer a theory. Any group accused of being involved can never be cleared by anybody within or outside the group because either the persons offering the disclaimer are part of the conspiracy (so they would never admit their involvement), or they are being victimized and used by those involved in the conspiracy and would therefore never be a recipient of insider information about it. Accusations of Jewish conspiracy control of anything can therefore be extremely frustrating and upsetting to some Jews, though it may be only annoying to others.

Jewish religious and secular culture contains an oft-repeated theme of persecution. This has been a part of the Jewish worldview for millennia and may have come from the ancient past when the ancient Israelites were the only community in the world to believe in monotheism. The Holocaust has clearly intensified this feeling of persecution, and repeated Arab, Muslim, and Palestinian calls to destroy or dismantle the State of Israel have also strengthened this sentiment. In America today the Jews are one of the most successful communities in terms of educational, economic, and social achievement. This success has not dampened the existential anxiety of persecution for most Jews, however, so even inadvertently making light of this anxiety is likely to diminish the willingness of Jews to engage in dialogue.

Self-criticism is a central part of Jewish life, and this includes humorous self-criticism. Jewish humor is often self-deprecatory, and "Jewish jokes" are often funny because they tend to be vignettes of Jews making fun of themselves. Such Jewish humor originated as internal discourse, however, and was not intended for outsiders. But as Jews became emancipated and integrated into the larger society, they have felt more comfortable sharing their humorous self-criticisms with non-Jews. We can all laugh at such humor, but it is sometimes easy to go one step beyond the acceptable when an outsider tells a "Jewish joke." At that moment the joke is no longer self-deprecatory but racist. Jews may appear good-humored about the joke, but there will often develop a subsequent tension that is unnecessary and can be harmful to trustful dialogue. It is better for non-Jews to leave the Jewish jokes to the Jews.

At the bottom of all the "red button" issues for Jews is an anxiety about antisemitism. Anti-Semitism is a serious issue for Jews, even in the United States where anti-Semitism is strictly taboo and where racism against people of color, Latinos, Asians, and anti-Islamism (or "Islamophobia") seems to be much more prevalent. All minorities have their anxieties, and anxiety is usually based on real experience. It is best to be sensitive to the anxieties that one is aware of, and to be ready to offer apologies when accidentally treading on sensitive issues. It is also quite acceptable to expect Jewish partners in dialogue to take the same care with the "red button" issues of the other.

For Reflection and Discussion

1. What are some of the most important "red button" issues that should be kept in mind when engaging in dialogue with Jews? Have you ever encountered these personally?
2. What does it mean to say that for Jews the Holocaust has become a sacred event? Have there been similar sacred events for Christians and Muslims?
3. In your opinion, is anti-Semitism still a problem in the United States today? in the world?
4. How would you describe some of your own "red button" issues when it comes to dialogue?

PART THREE

Preparing for Dialogue: Christianity

LEONARD SWIDLER

CHAPTER TEN

What Jews and Muslims Need to Know

The first thing to be aware of about Christianity is that there have been, and are, many understandings and lived versions of Christianity. There are, to begin with, the three major branches of Christianity: Catholicism, Orthodoxy, and Protestantism. Further, some versions of Christianity have been optimistic, some pessimistic, some absolutistic, some tolerant, some other-world-directed, some this-world-directed, and so on. However, in the latter half of the twentieth century, most of Christianity took a dramatic turn in the direction of what might be called Modernity. What I aim to do now is to present a general picture of modern Christianity (without forgetting the more traditional versions, which also continue to exist), and then point out some of the common ground that all three of the Abrahamic traditions—Judaism, Christianity, and Islam—stand on together, as well as their true differences. But before I can turn to modern Christianity, I need to trace the founding and subsequent trajectory of Christianity leading up to it, albeit in a compact manner.

At the heart of all of the versions of Christianity stands Jesus of Nazareth, *Yeshua ha Notzri*, as he was called in his native Semitic tongue. (I will be using that original form, Yeshua, mainly because it helps to keep in the consciousness of readers the most oft-forgotten—especially by Christians—fact of the Jewishness of Jesus. Hence, to understand something of Christianity we must first understand something of Yeshua, and that in turn entails understanding something of the Hebrew and Jewish traditions.

Hebrew Religion

The ancient Hebrews thought and spoke in the theistic mode, that is, thinking and speaking of ultimate reality as person—someone who could know and could freely decide and could love. They eventually came to a monotheistic understanding, which became characteristic not only of their religion but also of the three major religions which sprang from their roots: Judaism, Christianity, and Islam. The story of the development of the Hebrew religion is set down in "The Book" (*Biblos* in Greek). In its beginning it tells of one God who is the source of all reality through creation (not *ex nihilo* [out of nothing]; that is a later Christian doctrine).

Yeshua ha Notzri means "Jesus of Nazareth" in Hebrew. Jesus would have been known by some form of this name to his family and acquaintances.

The crowning point of creation was humankind, made in God's image. Human beings were persons who could know, freely decide, and could love. Modern critics of religion would say that rather than humanity, *homo*, being an Image of God (an *Imago Dei* in St. Jerome's influential Latin) God, *Deus*, is actually an image of humanity, *imago hominis*. Modern theistic adherents of religion would respond that both are doubtless true in different but analogous ways.

In this tradition everything that exists is good simply because it has being, and this being springs from God, who is all good. Then whence evil? For to the Hebrews, as to everyone else, it was obvious that there was evil in the world, indeed in every human being. Their answer was that human beings themselves are the source of evil, for by their free will they can refuse to choose the good, and their choice then is called evil. This understanding is embedded in the story of the "fall" at the beginning of the book of Genesis: Because humanity did not follow the right order of its nature, the "self," as created by God, in God's image, it became "dis-ordered" in its relationship to its own self and its creator, and in turn to all the rest of creation. Here was the first "domino theory."

The way to live an authentic human life is to live according to one's authentic "self," one's Image of God—one's *Imago Dei*. Perceiving that *Imago Dei* became difficult, however, after the "fall" and so, according to the Hebrews, God arranged for special help to be made available, at least to a Chosen People, the Hebrews, who in turn were to be "a light unto the nations." This special help was God's instructions, God's *Torah*, on how to live a true human life, one in accordance with one's true self, the *Imago Dei*.

Thus, the Hebrew religion was basically optimistic, for the source of all reality was the one God, who was goodness itself. God's creation was as it says in Genesis "good," *tov*, and in the end even "very good," *mod tov*. But it also took account of the presence of evil in humans and prescribed its elimination by the human returning to its original authentic self, the *Imago Dei*, the clear path to which was indicated by God's *Torah*. And the heart of the *Torah* was justice and love, or even simply love, for, as Pope Paul VI much later said, "justice is love's minimum."[1]

The summary of the *Torah* was the twofold commandment of love of God and love of neighbor, and the former could be carried out really through the fulfillment of the latter, the love of neighbor. Who, then, is the neighbor who is to be loved? The Hebrew prophets appeared in the history of the Hebrew people to make it abundantly clear that what God desired was not "burnt offerings" but rather a just life. This meant not only treating everybody fairly, but preeminently loving the oppressed, the powerless, of society, and they specifically spoke of the poor, the widow, and the orphan, the most powerless of society.

Judaism

In the first millennium before the Christian Era the Hebrew people became a united kingdom, suffered division into two parts, one of which, Israel, was largely destroyed in the eighth century BCE and the second of which, Judah, was carried off into Babylonian exile in the sixth century, only to return to rebuild Jerusalem. By this time the Hebrews had rather firmly committed themselves to monotheism and more and more focused on carrying out God's *Torah* as the essence of an authentic human life. It is from this post-exilic period onwards that one speaks of Judaism.

Later, around 167 BCE, the Pharisees, who have had such unwarranted bad press in the Christian tradition, appeared on the scene. Among other things, they were responsible for prayers referring to God as a loving "Father" and such teachings as the Resurrection of the body. Most of all they showed the "way" (*halakhah* in Hebrew) to lead a just human life by laboring to make concrete the more general obligations found in the "written *Torah*," the Bible. Eventually their commentary came to be understood as the "oral *Torah*," written down first in the *Mishnah* (200 CE) and the *Talmuds* (Palestinian 400 CE, Babylonian 500 CE). In all these reflections, it should be noted that for the Pharisees as for Jews in general, the big question was not, "What must I *think*?" as it was for the Greeks and later also too for Christians, but rather "What must I *do*?"

The Pharisees, of course, were not the only Jews at the beginning of the Christian Era who laid claim to have the right teaching about an authentic human (Jewish) life. There were others: Saducees, Essenes, Zealots, and Hellenists, among others. One of those "others" was the Galilean Jew Yeshua of Nazareth, who in many ways was close to the Pharisees but also critical of at least some of them.

Yeshua of Nazareth

As noted, Yeshua was a Jew, religiously as well as ethnically. He was born of a Jewish mother, studied the Jewish Scriptures (the Hebrew Bible, of course, not the New Testament), was addressed as "rabbi," and carefully kept the *Torah* or Law. Indeed he declared that he "had not come to abolish the Law but to carry it out" (Matthew 5:17). Like the Pharisees, Yeshua also specified the general great twofold commandment of love of God and neighbor. All his teaching and all his stories were aimed at making God's instructions, God's *Torah*, concrete. And like the other prophets—his followers also called him a prophet—he epitomized the love of neighbor in reaching out to the powerless. When asked who is leading an authentic human life, who will "enter into the kingdom of heaven," he answered: "Those who give drink to the thirsty, food to the hungry, clothing to the naked, visit the sick, visit those in prison" (Matthew 25:31–46). For Yeshua, because he was a good Jew, the real question was not "What must I *think*?" but "What must I *do*?"

This then, in brief, was the Good News, the "God-spel," Yeshua taught, that the Reign of God was near, indeed, "within you" (*entos hymon*), and that letting "God reign" in their lives would lead them to joy now, and "in the world to come." Thus the first followers of Yeshua, who of course were all Jews, found in him a special "way" (*halakhah*) to "salvation." Remember: "Salvation" comes from the Latin *salus*, meaning primarily a full, healthful, whole, and therefore holy, life. A secondary meaning of the term is to be "saved" by something or someone from the outside—which became the dominant usage by Christians only from the third century onward.

For Yeshua's first Jewish followers, this salvation, this (w)holy life, was attained by following what Yeshua "thought, taught, and wrought." They sensed in him an inner wisdom and authenticity (what he thought), which issued in his extraordinarily insightful and inspiring teachings (what he taught), which in turn were reflected in his self-emptying life and death for others (what he wrought).

Yeshua made it clear that although he understood himself called to address in his lifetime the "children of the House of Israel," his notion of one's neighbor was the widest possible: It included not only one's geographical neighbors, one's relatives, one's ethnic companions, it even included one's enemies, as the story of the good Samaritan graphically illustrates. Yeshua even broke through that most ancient pattern of oppression, sexism, for, as the gospels make clear, "Jesus Was a Feminist,"[2] even to the point that some ancient writers claimed that his feminism was one of the reasons for his condemnation!

The first followers of Yeshua obviously grasped the heart of what he "thought, taught, and wrought," though unfortunately his feminist example faded from Christian view until the twentieth century. Despite the apocalypticism of the time, their understanding of the following of the "way" of Yeshua (*hodos* in New Testament Greek, just like *halakhah* in Rabbinic Hebrew, and later *shar'ia* in Islamic Arabic) was not the preaching of pie in the sky bye and bye; rather, the fulfillment of the commandment to love God could be accomplished only through the fulfillment of the commandment to love one's neighbor. "If any one says, 'I love God,' and hates his brother, he is a liar; for he who does not love his brother whom he has seen, cannot love God whom he has not seen" (1 John 4: 20).

For Reflection and Discussion

1. Is reaffirming and examining closely the Jewishness of Jesus and his early community a necessary step toward interreligious dialogue between Jews and Christians? How might this be?
2. What is your understanding of "salvation"? How is the concept similar and different in the three Abrahamic traditions?
3. What does the name Yeshua imply for you? Does using it enhance the dialogue process? Why or why not?

Christology

Yeshua clearly was an extraordinary charismatic healer, teacher, and prophet. But at least some of his first followers saw something else very special, very Jewish, in him; they saw him as the *Meshiach*, Messiah (*Christos* in Greek), the Anointed One, who, as promised in the Scriptures, would among other things free Judea from Roman occupation. But he did not. Instead the Romans crucified him. At first Yeshua's followers were crushed. Two of them were reported to have said, "But we had hoped that he would be the one to set Israel free" (Luke 24:21). But the power of Yeshua was too great for it all to run out in the cracks of the rock of Golgotha. His followers believed that Yeshua rose from the dead and further empowered them to go forth to preach his Good News.

But what about the messianic claims of Yeshua's followers for him? He did not become the new political king of Israel. They, or at least some of them, did not drop the messianic claims. They simply transformed and spiritualized the understanding of Messiah. However, as the "Way" of Yeshua moved from the Jewish to the Greek world, the Greek term "Christ" grew in usage and importance, and in a way that it became fused with another Jewish title given to Yeshua, namely, "son of God." The latter, which was a term used by the Jews to refer to kings and holy men, was obviously meant in a metaphorical way. In the Greek "field of force," however, the metaphorical title "son of God" moved in a few centuries to the ontological title "God the Son," as reflected in the Trinitarian formula of the Council of Nicaea (325 CE).

Many modern critical-thinking Christians, being aware of what occurred in the paradigm shift from the Jewish metaphorical thought world to the Greek substance-ontological thought world, ask themselves what the intended meaning was at the beginning of the process. One way some have of putting it is that the followers of Yeshua saw in him a transparency of the divine. He appeared to them to be so radically open to all being, including the Root of being, God, that he was completely filled with Being. Thus, he was a meeting point of the human and the divine, an enfleshment, an incarnation of the divine, as all humans ought to be and in principle can be. Yeshua himself urged: "Be you perfect as my heavenly Father!" Thus, some modern Christians see this original Jewish perception of Yeshua as more "orthodox," "right-teaching," than some of the later Greek ontological-substance formulas.[3]

In this way Yeshua becomes for Christians a model of how to live an authentic human life. In him they meet ultimate reality, the divine, so that in a preeminent way he is for them *the* door to the divine—to be sure, not the only possible point of entrance, but for them the one that informs all others, just as they see that Gautama does for the Buddhists, Muhammad for the Muslims, etc.

At the same time it is also clear from the New Testament, especially from the Pauline writings and the Gospel of John, that there was a tendency early in the history of the followers of Yeshua to become "Christocentric" rather than "theocentric," that is, a tendency to "foreshorten" the follower's gaze from where or whom the mediator was pointing to, God (*Theos*), to the mediator himself (*Christos*). This did not mean that Paul and John forgot about God and concentrated solely on Christ. It does mean, however, that in their writings there is a great emphasis on getting to God through Christ, whereas in the Synoptic Gospels (Matthew, Mark, and Luke), which mainly portray Yeshua's teaching and actions (complicated, to be sure, by being seen through the lenses of the early faith communities) the strong stress is on God rather than on Christ.

Moreover, it is important to note that Paul overwhelmingly talks about, not Yeshua, not Jesus, but about Christ, Jesus Christ, Christ Jesus. Most often Christ for Paul was not a concrete human person, but much more a spiritual "force" or "life," so that he could write things like, "I live now not I, but Christ lives in me." This notion of a "spiritual life" entering into one's own interior life fit quite well with the Semitic way of understanding and speaking of the world, but it was all too liable to be "ontologized," understood as a "substance," in the Greek thinking world of the Roman Empire. This unfortunately did happen much too extensively with many later followers of Yeshua. And when the "mind of Christ" was thus ontologized, the notion of salvation also tended to be understood as something coming from the outside, as if one were "saved" by Christ as by a sort of cosmic lifeguard, rather than be understood in its original meaning of being healthy, whole, holy. Salvation came solely by "Other Power," (*tariki* in Japanese Buddhism) and not at all by "Self Power" (*jiriki*).

A question then arises: Must one make a choice between Yeshua and Christ? I and many contemporary Christian thinkers believe the answer is, yes and no. The yes part of the answer is that one must choose Yeshua if one wants to be a Christian, because for such a follower the Jew Yeshua of Nazareth is the key to the meaning of life and how to live it.

However, how this Yeshua comes to inhere in one's life is a complex process. It is obvious that he must in a variety of ways be "spiritualized" so he can be "interiorized" in another person's interior life, and consequent external behavior. Early in the history of the followers of Yeshua a major way that "interiorizing" was named was with the term Christ. Hence, the answer is, no, one need not choose between Yeshua and Christ. A Christian can build his or her Christian life on the foundation of Yeshua, on what he "thought, taught and wrought," as a model, and, having thus been energized, strive to live accordingly—and at the same time understand and refer to that interiorized "energy" as Christ, as Paul did, for example.

It is a matter of appropriate balance, but, of course, what constitutes a proper balance in one individual and one culture and at one time and in one place, may not be precisely the same in others. Our human reality is plural; hence, our means of *salus* must correspondingly match it in it plurality.

At the same time it must be recalled that in the Greek thinking world of the fourth and fifth centuries, the articulation by Christians (by then almost entirely non-Jews) of their understanding of Jesus the Christ (Yeshua the Jew was largely lost from Christian consciousness by then), was worded in the prevalent Greek "substance" philosophical concepts and language. Jesus was declared to be "truly God and truly man, *vere Deus et vere homo.* How this apparent contradiction was to be correctly understood has been a challenge to all subsequent Christian theologians. Meeting that challenge has resulted in a long trail of solutions being declared heterodox by various Christian authorities.[4]

For Reflection and Discussion

1. Is it likely that Jews and Muslims who openly engage in interreligious dialogue would "accept Jesus Christ"? Would engaging in interreligious dialogue likely lead Christians to reject Jesus as sole and unique savior of the world? Why or why not?
2. What is your understanding of Yeshua/Christ? Do you think that your understanding is shared by most Christians? By Jews or Muslims?
3. What is the likely Jewish response to the traditional doctrine on the nature of Jesus Christ? To the alternative view?
4. What is the likely Muslim response to the traditional doctrine on the nature of Jesus Christ? To the alternative view?

The Christian Religion and Its Development

By the fourth century and even before, the religion *of* Yeshua had largely, though of course not entirely, become the religion *about* Christ. It was no longer simply Yeshua's "way"; it had become Christianity, the state religion of the mighty Roman Empire. In the ensuing centuries, the Christian Church spread throughout the Roman Empire and then eventually beyond it.

Some form of Christianity also moved eastward from Israel into adjacent lands and by the fourth century reached India, but it had relatively little impact there. One version of Christianity, Nestorianism, moved into China in the sixth century, but again had relatively little influence. In the fourteenth century Catholic Christianity came into the north of China, brought by Franciscans and supported by the Mongolian emperor, but in less than a century it largely disappeared along with the Mongolian dynasty.

Then in the sixteenth century, the great Catholic missionary movement, paralleling European discovery voyages and colonization, brought a Catholic version of Christianity to India and from there to Japan and Korea, and only later to China. Under the initial leadership of the Jesuit Francis Xavier, Christianity made great strides in Japan, with many hundreds of thousands becoming Christian by the first third of the seventeenth century. But then its own success contributed to its downfall as the new rulers, the Tokugawa shoguns, decided to close Japan off from outside influence, and Christianity was perceived as an outside religion. Bloody persecution brought about many deaths and drove what few Christians remained underground without clergy or normal ways to sustain themselves.

In China, developments were somewhat similar in that after a very difficult but brilliant beginning by the Jesuit Matteo Ricci, several hundreds of thousands of Chinese had become Christian by the end of the seventeenth century. But then out of theological myopia, and probably also a good deal of jealousy on the part of the Franciscans and Dominicans against the Jesuits, the papacy took a number of restrictive and intolerant steps, the so-called "Chinese Rites Dispute," which put Christianity in such an unfavorable position that the number of Christians instead of continuing to grow, shrank in the eighteenth century to a small remnant.

Matteo Ricci (1552-1610) was an Italian Jesuit missionary. He learned and lived Chinese culture, presenting himself as a Confucian sage while he introduced the Chinese intelligentsia to Christianity and engaged them in dialogue using their own categories of thought and expression. He gave us the Latinized name "Confucius" by which we know the great Chinese sage Kung fu-tzu.

Only in the nineteenth century did Protestant Christianity launch its missionary movement—largely paralleling, though with a certain time lag—the spread of the British Empire, coming into India, China, Korea, and Japan, the latter two only in the last third of the nineteenth century, when those two countries were forcibly opened up to the West.

All this was initially done to "save the souls" of the "heathens" who if not baptized would go to hell. Despite huge efforts, Christianity has had relatively little success in the Far East, except in the Spanish colonized Philippines, and in most recent times in southern Korea, where perhaps as much as forty percent of the population has become Christian in the past few decades. Likewise, Christianity had little success in converting Muslims in dominantly Muslim countries, though great efforts were expended. Conversion among Muslims, again, tended to fail because Christianity was perceived as the religion of the outside colonizers.

North and South America became largely Christian as a result of the efforts of both Catholic missionary work and European colonizations. Much of sub-Saharan Africa likewise became Christian, either Catholic or Protestant, while much of what had been Christian in northern Africa and the Near and Middle East gradually became Muslim after the conquest by Arab Muslim armies.

After Christianity became the established religion in the Roman Empire in the fourth century, it took on many of the trappings of Greco-Roman culture, including a very strong stress on "what to think," generating a plethora of lengthy creeds. These creeds were the source not only of unity but also of divisions. Each time a new creed was devised, a new division was enacted, and many of the resulting "non-orthodox" churches still exist today. A much larger division was solidified in 1054 with the split between Eastern and Western Christianity, usually known as Orthodox and Catholic Christianity respectively. This was followed by another major division of Western Christianity in the sixteenth century, known as the Protestant Reformation. Each of these three major branches of Christianity took a rather absolutist view and insisted that they were true and correct, and those who differed from them were consequently wrong. Of course, for almost all Christians, non-Christians were even more wrong!

For Reflection and Discussion

1. How would you describe the transformation to Christianity that took place during the fourth century?
2. Why did Christianity have so little success in converting people in the Far East during the period of European expansion?

3. Are missionary programs (seeking converts) and interreligious dialogue conflicting activities?
4. Is there a way to engage in missionary activity that is compatible with the spirit of interreligious dialogue? What might this be?

Eastern (Orthodox) Christianity

Christianity was formed along with Rabbinic Judaism out of the womb of a Proto-Judaism which evolved from pre-exilic (sixth century BCE) Israelite religion. As noted earlier, it all started with the Jew, Rabbi Yeshua ha Notzri, whose teaching quickly spread among the Jews and "fellow-travelers" (*Phoboumenoi ton theon*, "God-fearers" in New Testament Greek) in the Roman Empire, especially in the eastern half. The major centers of Judaism, and hence subsequently of Christianity, were Jerusalem, Antioch, Alexandria, and Rome. These Christian communities eventually were named "patriarchal" communities or sees (Latin *sedis*, seat). With the triumph of Constantine (and Christianity with him) as sole emperor, and his building of a new city on top of the Greek city Byzantium, modestly naming it Constantinople (the "Second Rome" as the capital of one of the usually two concurrent emperors), that city became a fifth ancient patriarchal see in the fifth century.

All the early formative theological debates were resolved in universal, "ecumenical" councils held in the Greek East. Of the seven widely recognized ecumenical councils (from 325 to 787 CE), three were held in Constantinople itself and three in "suburbs," Nicaea (I and II) and Chalcedon; only the Council of Ephesus (431 CE) was held a couple of hundred miles distant. A representative of the Church of Rome was always present and given respect, but only as the *primus inter pares*, "first among equals." The decisions of these councils were called "orthodox," "right teaching," and of course also produced defeated communities. A number of these ancient so-called "non-orthodox" Christian Churches, such as the Coptic Church of Egypt, the Armenian Church, the Nestorian Church, still exist today.

The fall of the Roman Empire in the West (last emperor in Rome died in 476 CE) began a division between Eastern and Western Christianity, both understanding themselves to be adherents of orthodox Christianity. This division took place gradually in the latter centuries of the first millennium and was "fixed" in the year 1054 with the mutual excommunications of the leaders of both Eastern and Western Christianity. Already in the ninth century the Patriarch of Constantinople began to be called the Ecumenical Patriarch, meaning the titular head of the Eastern Orthodox Churches, rejecting the universal authority of the pope, the bishop of Rome.

> **Distinguishing terms...**
> Orthodox Christians: refers to those Christian communities formally separated from the pope of Rome after the East-West Schism of 1054.

The Orthodox Churches tend to be related to nations, e.g., the Greek Orthodox Church, the Russian Orthodox Church, and the Serbian Orthodox Church. This is both a strength and a weakness. The Church usually uses the language of the people in their liturgy, bringing them closer, but too often the Church can become a surrogate for a narrow nationalism. In its history, the Orthodox Church often suffered from "caesaropapism" without a pope, that is, it was dominated by the civil authority. For example, all of the seven ecumenical councils were called by the emperors (and once by the empress), and were not valid until promulgated by the emperor!

The emphasis of the Orthodox Church has been on the importance of the liturgy and spirituality, particularly the mystical dimension. For example, *Hesychasm* (Greek *hesychia*, quietness), a piety that focuses on the "Jesus Prayer," was denounced by some theologians as superstition, but it has become an accepted part of the Orthodox tradition. Also, although there was a huge, long-lasting "Iconoclast Controversy" (725-842 CE), the Icon (Greek *Eikon*, painted wooden images of Jesus and saints; now making up the *Iconostasis* in front of the altar in Orthodox churches) has become the expression and source of a deep, mystical spirituality.

The Orthodox clergy usually are married—distinct from Catholic clergy, who since the twelfth century are to be celibate, though the practice has often been honored in the breach—although since the sixth century Orthodox bishops are always chosen from celibate monks. Monasticism developed vigorously in Eastern Christianity, but was different from that in the West where a plethora of different religious orders were founded over the centuries, such as Benedictines, Dominicans, Franciscans, Premonstratentions, and Mercedarians. In the East, monasticism focused on individuals and on individual monasteries, without the organizational structure of specific religious orders. Western Christianity's development of Scholastic Philosophy and

Theology in the Middle Ages (largely fostered by the religious orders) and subsequently was not matched by the Orthodox Church. Rather, its emphasis remained on interior spirituality, personal piety, and the liturgy.

Orthodox Christianity has had a long and very bloody history of contact with Islam. The western half of the former Roman Empire was already in the hands of various Germanic barbarian tribal leaders when in the seventh century the Muslim armies swept across Christian North Africa and into Spain and France. They settled and largely "Islamicised" North Africa and much of Spain, though they were gradually over centuries driven from the Iberian peninsula, the final blow coming in 1492. However, the military struggle of Islam with the Eastern Roman Empire continued incessantly until the final collapse of the Roman Empire in 1453 at the hands of the Muslim Turkish armies.

At the same time there was an amazing positive interaction between the new Islam and the ancient Greek culture such that Islamic civilization reached a cultural level comparable to that of the Eastern Roman Empire. It is to this symbiosis, which during the high Middle Ages attained a Golden Age of creative interaction among Jews, Christians, and Muslims in the Iberian peninsula, that we should look to as an exemplar of interreligious dialogue and cooperation to match and surpass in the Third Millennium.

For Reflection and Discussion

1. What do Orthodox Christians understand to be the position of the pope, and why?
2. What is the role of the liturgy, icons, and mysticism in Orthodox Christianity? Have you ever had experienced an Orthodox liturgy?
3. What are the similarities and differences between monasticism and the clergy in Eastern and Western Christianity?
4. What in your opinion is the best way to approach historical conflicts among religions when engaging in interreligious dialogue?

Western (Catholic) Christianity

Although there is nothing in the New Testament about Peter being in Rome, an early Christian tradition places him there during the persecution of the Emperor Nero and asserts that he was crucified (upside down!) and buried under the site of St. Peter's Basilica on Vatican Hill, Rome. Tradition also places the execution of Paul in Rome. Nevertheless, as the center of the Roman Empire, Rome and its head of the Christian community could lay claim to a primacy of the universal Christian community once Christianity became the established religion of the empire in the fourth century. It should be remembered, however, that all of the almost universally recognized first six Ecumenical Councils (from 325 to 680 CE) took place in the "Second Rome," Constantinople, or its environs (except Ephesus in 431), and were all both called and validly promulgated by the emperor or empress, not the pope or any ecclesiastic.

Hard times befell the Western Roman Empire, which gradually succumbed to the invading Germanic barbarian tribes so that, as noted, the last Roman Emperor died in 476 CE. Slowly thereafter the former western part of the Roman Empire sank into the so-called Dark Ages, suffering further from the centuries long onslaught by Nordic warriors.

The light of learning and civilization dimmed, being held aloft almost single-handedly by the Christian Church. Two of the most important of the vast number of contributions of the Christian Church to what became Western Civilization were the founding of monasteries, both male and female, starting in the sixth century. These multiplied geometrically during the High Middle Ages—which became stabilizing, educating, humanizing, and spiritualizing forces in an otherwise grim world—and the founding, starting in the twelfth century, of universities. Beyond that, the Church was the soul patron of the arts and a generally civilizing force.

Since during the Middle Ages (500-1500, the period between the fall of the Roman Empire in the West and the beginning of the modern world with the discovery of the New World (1492) and the Protestant Reformation (1517), the Church was one of the very few institutions that wielded power in western Europe. Gradually the Church, usually through bishoprics, monasteries, and convents, acquired more and more land, and the power that went with it in a feudal society. After centuries of acquiring land, bishops or abbots or abbesses became *de facto* political princes as well as spiritual leaders, which of course led to abuse.

The Bishop of Rome, who was likewise the Patriarch of the West and also claimed to be the Pope of the Universal Church (hence the symbolic three-tiered papal tiara), also began to acquire political power, particularly after the gift of the

"Papal States" in the center of Italy by the Frankish king Pepin in the eighth century, which was later affirmed by his son, Charlemagne. The papacy dipped in prestige later in that and the next century, becoming the object of machinations, murder, and mayhem, but reestablished itself as a primary political as well as spiritual force in the eleventh century under the leadership of the Benedictine monk Hildebrand who became Pope Gregory VII. The papacy reached its acme in the thirteenth century, and then began to decline in influence with the imprisoning of Pope Boniface VIII at the beginning of the fourteenth century. This was followed by the Western Schism (when there were two and briefly three men who claimed to be pope!), further followed by fifteenth-century Conciliarism, which declared the Ecumenical Council superior to the pope, and then the *piece d'resistence*, the sixteenth-century Protestant Reformation (more of that below).

The Catholic Church recovered in the sixteenth and seventeenth century Counter-Reformation, which moved to reform the Catholic Church from within and to gain for itself as much as possible the newly European colonized world of the Americas, Asia, and Africa. Huge energies were invested not only in the vast mission projects, but also especially in education and the arts. This Counter-Reformation character with its sense of triumphalism largely marked the Catholic Church until the Second Vatican Council (1962-65).

The leadership of the Catholic Church reacted largely negatively to the French Revolution (1789-1815) with its emphasis on freedom, especially during the long pontificates of Gregory XVI (1830-46) who crushed the flourishing *Aufklärung Katholizismus* with his 1832 encyclical *Mirari vos*, declaring religious liberty *deliramentum*, and Pius IX (1846-78), two of the most reactionary popes of history. It was during the latter's pontificate that the doctrine of papal infallibility (which had been specifically condemned by Pope John XXII in the fourteenth century) was declared (Vatican Council I, 1869-70). Under the leadership of Pope Leo XIII (1878-1903), the Catholic Church moved away from reaction to support the working classes and democracy, giving rise to *Reformkatholizismus*, Modernism, *Rinnovamento*, and Americanism—all to be swept away by his successor Pope Pius X (1903-1914) in his Anti-Modernism Heresy Hunt.[5]

In the first half of the twentieth century the Catholic Church slowly crept out of the intellectual ghetto its leadership had enforced, and exploded into full Modernity with the Second Vatican Council (1962-65), whose full potential has only begun to be applied (more below).

For Reflection and Discussion

1. What positive roles did the Catholic Church play in western Europe during the Middle Ages?
2. What were the various nineteenth-century Catholic responses to the Enlightenment and liberalism?
3. Why do you think Christianity eventually flourished in the Roman Empire and Judaism did not?
4. Were "Christianity" and "European civilization" synonymous from the fourth century into the modern era? Would you answer differently in regard to Europe today?

Protestant Christianity

The Protestant Reformation began in Western Christianity in 1517, the year Augustinian Friar Martin Luther allegedly nailed ninety-five theses to the door of the church in Wittenberg, Germany—a customary way to launch a debate, one of the primary entertainments of the time. This debate, however, was more than just entertainment; it challenged many of the accepted positions of the papacy. As the very name indicates, it was an attempt to reform the Catholic Church, not to break away, though in the end that is precisely what happened. Attempts all along the way were made to bridge the gap between where Luther and his supporters stood on the one hand and the papacy and its supporters on the other hand—alas, finally to no avail as the Catholic Reform Council at Trent was launched in 1545, at the last minute without Lutheran participants.

The gist of the Reformation was expressed in several slogans with the term "only," *sola*, at its heart. They answered several questions, each of which were answered by "*sola* x," whereas the Catholic answer was "*et* x *et* y," "*both* x *and* y." The key two questions with the Protestant and Catholic answers were as follows:

How am I saved?	*Sola fide* By faith alone	*Et fide et bonis actionibus* By faith and good works
How do I know what what to believe?	*Sola Scriptura* By Scripture alone	*Et Scriptura et traditione* By Scripture and Tradition

There were, of course, many more doctrinal issues involved, and underneath much economics and politics, so that whole political bodies were swept into what became the Lutheran Church, and during the Counter-Reformation back into the Catholic Church. At one point the serfs took the opportunity to attempt to break away from the power of the nobility, but Luther urged the princes to kill and slaughter them! Not all authority was to be challenged.

Families of Reformation Churches

Once Luther and his supporters made the break, others followed suit, going in various directions. In the end, there were four major "families" of Reformation Churches that developed. Besides the national 1) Lutheran Churches (as still exist, e.g., in Germany, Sweden, Denmark, and Norway), there grew up the so-called 2) Reformed Churches, mainly under the inspiration of the French lawyer John Calvin operating out of Geneva. The various national Reformed Churches (e.g., the Hungarian Reformed Church, the Dutch Reformed Church), the Presbyterian Churches, and other related churches form this family of churches.

Then there was the so-called Left Wing of the Reformation, also called the 3) Radical Reformation. These churches took the Lutheran principle of individual interpretation of the Bible even further and broke away from a relationship with the prince, the state. Hence, they advocated religious freedom and separation of church and state. They likewise were pacifist, being sometimes known as the peace churches. They sprang up in the German-speaking area and were initially called *Wiedertäufer* (baptize again—Anabaptists), because they were convinced that one had to be an adult to have faith and baptism in order to be saved—hence, their original infant baptism could not qualify. There are several such churches still in existence, such as the Amish (the famous Pennsylvania Dutch), Mennonites, and Church of the Brethren. The Society of Friends or Quakers follow in this spirit.

The fourth family of churches stemming from the Protestant Reformation is that of the 4) English Churches. At the beginning of the Reformation, King Henry VIII of England was a vigorous opponent, even being given the title "Defender of the Faith" by the pope for a small anti-Lutheran book he wrote (to this day English monarchs ironically are formally dubbed such during their coronation).

Henry's father, King Henry VII had come to the English throne after a decades-long bloody civil war, the "War of the Roses," which was fought because Henry VI had had no son, and hence the succession was disputed. Henry VIII was married to Catherine of Aragon who bore three daughters, but no sons. Since no one then knew that it is the male sperm that determines the gender of offspring, Henry determined to avoid future civil war by gaining an annulment of his marriage with Catherine and marrying someone who would give him a son. That would mean that Catherine had been living in fornication and their daughters were bastards, a condition Catherine's brother King Philip II of Spain found unacceptable, and so informed the pope. It should be recalled that the Kingdom of Naples on the southern border of the Papal States also belonged to Spain. Eventually Henry despaired of receiving an annulment and declared himself the head of the Church of England, confiscated the vast lands of the monasteries and convents and distributed them to lesser nobility to insure their perpetual support. Thus was born the Church of England, or Anglican Church, and eventually its "offspring" throughout the British Empire and descendants, for example, the American Episcopal Church and, in the eighteenth century, the Methodist Church.

Other Christian churches sprang up later in the nineteenth and twentieth centuries from these Protestant roots, such as the Seventh-day Adventists, the Pentecostal Churches, and the Holiness Churches. Multiplicity was cherished, with the result that there are approximately 350 Protestant denominations in the United States, and in South Korea there are dozens of different Presbyterian denominations alone!

Development of Protestantism

The first period of Protestantism was that of the Reformers: Luther, Calvin, Zwingli, Bucer…, which was followed by that of the Confessional Writings, starting with the 1530 Augsburg Confession and ending for the Lutherans with the writing of the Concordance Formula in 1588 and for Reformed Protestantism in the 1619 Synod of Dordrect. Although the Reformers tended to reject scholastic philosophical language in favor of the Scriptural Word, the third phase of Protestantism was that of Protestant Orthodoxy wherein the correct philosophical formulation was insisted on, precipitating still further bloody religious wars, and culminating in the Thirty Years War (1618-48) which embroiled all of Europe, decimating the land of the Reformation, Germany. It finally ended with the Treaty of Westphalia, which fixed upon the then "liberal" principle: *Cujus regio, ejus religio*, "Whose reign, his religion." This was an advance because now conquered people were not forced to choose between conversion or the sword, but could also elect emigration.

Distinguishing terms...

Cujus regio, ejus religio: the principle that people are required to take the religion of their local ruler (specifically Catholic or Lutheran)

The fourth phase was that of Pietism. Many Protestants were horrified by the bloodshed resulting from insistence on doctrinal purity and argued that love of God and of neighbor was the essence of Christianity and that devout feeling was more important than the correct creedal words. As the seventeenth century turned into the eighteenth, the Age of Reason stole upon Europe, and also had a profound impact on Protestantism as well, leading to the fifth phase of Protestantism. The role of reason grew ever more influential, as exemplified by the beginning of modern critical Scripture scholarship in J. S. Semler (1725-91), "the father of German rationalism."[6]

(It should also be noted that the Enlightenment had a huge effect on Catholicism of the time as well, producing a kind of "Vatican II Catholicism" a hundred and fifty years before that Council in 1962-65, known as *Aufklärung Katholizismus*, which was eventually crushed by Popes Gregory XVI and Pius IX.[7])

The Enlightenment in Europe was followed by Romanticism with its stress on the affective and a sensitivity to the historical, the dynamic dimensions. In philosophy, Fichte, Schelling, and Hegel led the way (later supported by physical sciences as exemplified in Darwin's 1859 *On the Origin of Species*), and in Protestant thought Frederich Schleiermacher (1768-1834) gave expression to the *Zeitgeist* with his "Liberal Theology," the sixth phase. He argued that dogmas such as the Trinity were not really descriptions of how God is in himself, for we finite humans are not capable of truly grasping and expressing the infinite. Rather they are finite human expressions reflecting the human experience of the divine in particular times and situations. According to Schleiermacher, the work of the theologian is not to investigate the truth or falsity of these expressions, for neither can be proved, but rather to study their origin in the history of the Church. It is this emphasis on the subjective and historical as well as his distrust of the speculative powers of humans that made Schleiermacher the father of "liberal theology."

Schleiermacher set the tone for the rest of the nineteenth century, which not only embraced the sense of history but also the idea of progress. In addition, the social sciences, sociology, anthropology, psychology, the historical-critical method, all appeared on the scene and were applied by Protestant scholars to the understanding of Christianity and religion in general by scholars like Albrecht Ritschl, Ernst Troeltsch, and above all Adolf Harnack.[8]

All this optimism seemed to come to a crashing conclusion with the absolutely devastating World War I (1914-18). It had been thought that humanity had progressed beyond the irrationality of war, but this war was the most irrational of all. All the reasons for starting it were amazingly stupid, beyond the usual greed and ambition. Its conduct was overwhelming in its senseless butchery of millions in trench warfare, which year after year meaninglessly pushed back and forth over the same blood-soaked acres, led by an incredible series of inept, incompetent, amazingly stupid generals on all sides. Instead of arriving at the dream of rationality, humanity arrived at the nightmare of irrationality.

This disaster led to the next, the seventh, phase in Protestantism, "Dialectical Theology," launched by Karl Barth with his 1919 *Letter to the Romans.* Barth rejected liberal theology and returned to the Bible as the word of God breaking in from outside of human history. It must be seen as "other" from us humans and therefore not subject to study like other texts.

He maintained that theology needed to speak not the language of the history of religions or psychology, but rather the language of revelation, of the Bible. Here too, he insisted, was its proper subject matter: the revealed acts of God, not the philosophy of religion and the historical evolution of the human spirit. There was need for a new "dogmatics," which would be exclusively a theology of the Word of God in its content, method, and vocabulary. For when the attempt is made to synthesize revelation with "reason," theology suffers both from malformation—casting revelation in a particular intellectual form—and from constant change, since human knowledge is always being remolded to new shapes or even cast aside completely. Barth, of course, was not alone in leading this Dialectical Theology, but was joined by a number of outstanding theologians, such as Emil and Peter Brunner, Frederich Gogarten, and Eduard Thurneyson.

Existentialist philosophy played a major role for the very influential German theologian Paul Tillich, who used the then current existentialist thought to make the gospel *au courant*, and the equally influential German biblical scholar Rudolf Bultmann, who argued for the demythologization of the New Testament so as to understand it as proclamation, *kerygma*, to which every human must existentially respond.

The turn toward dialogue, first with Catholics in the wake of Vatican II, and then increasingly with non-Christian religions, and again with Modernity, led Protestantism into its eighth phase, which might be called 8) "Theology of Dialogue." In some ways the tasks of Liberal Theology have again been taken up, but with a greater concern to bring the church structures into the dialogue. Here Protestantism is greatly influenced by developments in post-Vatican II Catholicism.

For Reflection and Discussion

1. What are the major families of Protestant Churches? Are you familiar with any of these in particular?
2. What are the major phases of Protestant thought over the centuries? Which of these is of most interest to you?
3. What are the contemporary Protestant attitudes toward other Christians, other religions? How might you discover this?
4. Given the many branches of Christianity, do you think it is possible for a member of one Christian community to speak for other Christians during interreligious dialogue? Is there greater internal diversity among Christians than among Jews and Muslims?

The Christian West, Modernity, and Global Civilization

Modernity is characterized by a focus on this world, on freedom, by a critical turn of mind and eventually a historical sensibility. This began to happen in Western Christendom with the Renaissance and accelerated with a series of revolutions as Christendom mutated into Western Civilization, and is now emerging into Global Civilization: The sixteenth-century World Discovery Revolution, the seventeenth-century Scientific Revolution, the eighteenth-century Industrial Revolution, the eighteen/nineteenth-century Political Revolutions, the twentieth-century Information Revolution, and the third millennium Dawn of the Age of Global Dialogue.

The twentieth century in effect began in 1914 with the beginning of World War I. It reached its nadir in 1939-45 with World War II, and ended in 1990 with the Fall of the Berlin Wall and the end of the Cold War. About two-thirds of the way through, momentous changes began to surface, starting in a number of instances in America, but not limited to there. In fact, the 1960s was a momentous turning-point decade for the entire world: 1) American Catholics broke out of their political ghetto in the election of President Kennedy; 2) the American civil rights movement began a transformation of the Western psyche; 3) the anti-war, environmentalist, anti-Establishment and related movements in the West brought the transformation to a fever pitch; 4) through Vatican Council II (1962-65) the Catholic Church took a dramatic turn and leapt into what might be called Modernity, and edged even beyond.

The Fivefold Copernican Turn

As seen earlier, the Catholic Church weathered the storm of the sixteenth-century Protestant Reformation, launched its own Counter-Reformation, largely embraced the Enlightenment, the *Aufklärung*, only to be thrown back to pre-Enlightenment in mid-nineteenth century, then to move forward again around the turn of the century, only once again to be retrenched the first five decades of the twentieth century. But then a kind of historical miracle occurred when Pope John XXIII in 1959 called the Second Vatican Council to lead the Catholic Church in an *aggiornamento*, "updating," to "throw open the windows of the Vatican." The curial forces of reaction, which had been in possession for half a century, were stunned, fought back viciously, but nevertheless were soundly defeated.

Some refer to this dramatic turn in the Catholic Church as a "Copernican Turn." As the medieval 180-degree turn in astronomy led by Copernicus went from geocentrism to heliocentrism, much of Christianity through Catholicism made a fivefold Copernican Turn in the last four decades. That fivefold turn included: 1) the turn toward a historical sense, 2) the turn toward freedom, 3) the turn toward this world, 4) the turn toward inner reform, and 5) the turn toward dialogue.

The Turn toward a Historical Sense

For centuries the thinking of official Catholicism was dominated by a static understanding of reality; it resisted not only the democratic and human rights movements of the nineteenth and twentieth centuries, but also the growing historical, dynamic way of understanding the world, including religious thought. This changed dramatically with Vatican II where the historical, dynamic view of reality and doctrine was officially fully embraced (unfortunately John Paul II largely resisted that radical turn in inner-church matters; the future under his successor, Joseph Ratzinger, Benedict XVI, remains to be seen).[9]

The Turn toward Freedom

The image Catholicism projected at the end of the 1950s was of a giant monolith, a community of hundreds of millions who held obedience in both action and thought as the highest virtue. If the pope said, "have babies," Catholics had babies; if he said, "don't associate with Protestants and Jews," Catholics avoided them like the plague; if he said, "believe in papal infallibility and Marian dogmas," they believed. For a hundred years (but really not much more than that!) Catholics were treated like children in the Church, acted like children, and thought of themselves as children. With the Second Vatican Council, however, this very unfree image and reality was utterly transformed. Suddenly it seemed humanity, including Catholics, became aware of their "coming of age," their freedom and responsibility. This was clearly expressed in many places, but perhaps nowhere clearer than in the "Declaration on Religious Liberty,"[10] which was drafted by the American Jesuit John Courtney Murray, who had been silenced by Cardinal Ottaviani, the head of the Holy Office in the 1950s—precisely for writing that religious liberty was compatible with Catholicism.

The Turn toward This World

As noted, until very recently the term "salvation" was understood exclusively to mean going to heaven after death, its root meaning from *salus* of a "full, healthy life" being largely lost in Christianity after the third century.[11] Thus often Marxism was not far from the mark when it claimed that Christianity (and religion in general) was mainly concerned about "pie in the sky bye and bye." But that focus shifted radically with Vatican II, especially as reflected in the document, "The Church in the Modern World," which in effect, though without the later name, launched Liberation Theology, a commitment to shaping a just world in this life.

The Turn toward Self-Reform

Since the sixteenth century, inside the Catholic Church even the word "reform" was forbidden, to say nothing of the reality (there were periods of notable exception,[12] but they were largely obliterated—even from Catholic church history textbooks!). At the beginning of the twentieth century, Pope

Pius X, leapfrogging back to his prior predecessor Pius IX, launched the heresy-hunting Inquisition of Anti-Modernism, crushing all creative thought in Catholicism for decades. In the middle of the twentieth century, leading theologians were again censured and silenced (e.g., Jean Danielou, Henri de Lubac, Pierre Teilhard de Chardin, John Courtney Murray, and Karl Rahner).

But Pope John XXIII burst those binding chains and called the Second Vatican Council. As noted, he spoke about "throwing open the windows of the Vatican" to let in fresh thought and bring the Church "up to date." Indeed, the Vatican II documents even used that neuralgic word "reformation." "Christ summons the Church, as she goes her pilgrim way, to that continual reformation of which she always has need." "All [Catholics] are led to...wherever necessary undertake with vigor the task of renewal and reform," and insisted that all Catholics' "primary duty is to make an honest and careful appraisal of whatever needs to be renewed and achieved in the Catholic household itself" (*Decree on Ecumenism*).

The Turn toward Dialogue

For centuries, especially since the sixteenth century, the Catholic Church has been largely trapped in a kind of solipsism, talking only to itself and shaking its finger at the rest of the world. When, for example, a committee of Protestant churchmen shortly after World War I visited Pope Benedict XV to invite the Catholic Church to join in launching the Ecumenical Movement to work for Church reunion, he told them that he was happy they were finally concerned about Church unity, but that he already had the solution to the problem of Christian division: "Come home to Holy Mother the Church!" The forbidding of Catholic participation in dialogue was subsequently constantly repeated (e.g., 1928: *Mortalium animos*, 1948: *Monitum*, 1949: *Instructio*, 1954: barring of Catholics at the Evanston, Illinois World Council of Churches World Assembly).[13]

John XXIII and Vatican II changed all this inward-gazing attitude radically. Ecumenism was now not only not forbidden, but "pertains to the whole Church, faithful and clergy alike. It extends to everyone" (*Decree on Ecumenism*). Pope Paul VI issued his first encyclical (*Ecclesiam suam*, 1964), specifically on dialogue:

> Dialogue is *demanded* nowadays....It is *demanded* by the dynamic course of action which is changing the face of modern society. It is

> *demanded* by the pluralism of society and by the maturity man has reached in this day and age. Be he religious or not, his secular education has enabled him to think and speak and conduct a dialogue with dignity.

At Vatican II Catholics were taught—especially in the "Constitution on the Church," the "Declaration on Religious Liberty," the "Decree on Ecumenism," and the "Declaration on the Relationship of the Church with Non-Christian Religions"—that to be authentically Christian we must cease being enslaved by our tribal forms of Christianity; we must stop our fratricidal hate; we need to recall our Jewish roots and the fact that the Jewish people today are still God's Chosen People, for God's promises are never revoked; we need to turn from our imperialistic convert-making among Muslims, Hindus, and other religious peoples and turn toward bearing witness to Jesus Christ by our lives and words, toward helping the Muslims be better Muslims and the Hindus be better Hindus. This will help us love our own liberating traditions not less, but more. (See Appendix 2 for the text of the "Declaration on the Relationship of the Church with Non-Christian Religions.")

For Reflection and Discussion

1. What is Modernity and what were some of the factors that brought it about? How do you think it has affected dialogue?
2. What consequences did Catholic self-reform have for non-Catholics? How has that affected dialogue?
3. What bearing did the Vatican II *Declaration on the Relationship of the Church with Non-Christian Religions* have on Catholic relations with Jews, with Muslims? How might you discover this?
4. How dominant is each of the five characteristics of a modern worldview in Judaism, Christianity, and Islam today?
5. Do you associate these five characteristics with contemporary Catholicism? Contemporary Protestantism or the Eastern Orthodox churches? Why or why not?

CHAPTER ELEVEN

Connections or Corrosives?

Liturgy and Ritual

Like all religions, Christianity has an abundance of worship practices, and they vary widely depending on the variety of the denomination in question. The ends of the spectrum have been designated as, first, High Church, which in addition to the cognitive dimension, places a great emphasis on the importance of symbols and ceremonies: in short, on the full uses of all the senses—colorful vestments, highly developed music, reading/preaching, sacred food, incense, gestures—in the worship of God and the spiritual nourishing of the individual and community. The opposite end of the spectrum is known as Low Church, where the employment of the senses is very largely eschewed, which are often seen as leading the believer away from the inner, spiritual reality of the Transcendent God. Its stress is on the Word, namely, God's revelation as found in the Bible, and then as expounded at considerable length in the sermon, and reflected further in the singing of manifold verses of hymns.

The vast majority of Christians belong to the High Church tradition, including the largest tradition by far, Catholicism, and the second-largest tradition, Eastern Christianity, Orthodoxy. Much of the Anglican tradition, as well as significant portions of the Lutheran also tend toward High Church, whereas those coming from the Reformed and Radical Reformation traditions tend toward the Low Church style.

Central to the High Church tradition are what are known as sacraments. These are key ceremonies which play central roles in the lives of individual believers and in the community. There are customarily thought to be seven, depending on the church in question. Five of the seven, whether or not they are formally called sacraments, have to do with different stages/states of human life. The first is baptism, the rite of initiation, and the last—usually administered at death's door—is anointing of the sick, formerly called extreme unction by the

Distinguishing terms...

Liturgy: public, communal religious ceremonies

High Church: style of worship with emphasis on external symbols and rituals

Low Church: style of worship with minimal ceremony, emphasis on the Word in scripture, sermons, and the singing of hymns

Catholic Church. In between is confirmation, a rite of passage into adulthood. Then there are the two "states of life," matrimony and holy orders. The sixth sacrament is penance (or reconciliation), that is, a confessing of sins committed and a granting of God's forgiveness. The seventh is the central act of worship, the Eucharist (also variously named Mass, Holy Communion, the Lord's Supper, the Holy Liturgy).

The Eucharist (from the Greek, *eucharistia*, thanksgiving) stems from the earliest years of Christianity when the first Jewish followers of Yeshua gathered for the ceremonies ending the Sabbath (Saturday sundown) and remained in vigil until the following sunrise when it was initially expected that the Second Coming of Yeshua would occur (Sunday, the "third" day after Yeshua's Crucifixion, the Resurrection). When the *parousia* (Greek: arrival, as it was called), did not happen, the followers of Yeshua in customary Jewish fashion blessed and broke bread and drank wine "in memory of him" (1 Corinthians 11: 25), which was then followed by an *agape*, a "love feast."

Beyond the sacraments or their equivalents in the High Church tradition, there also developed a plethora of prayers, ceremonies, and rituals, spilling over into pious practices and devotions covering every dimension of life.

As noted, in the Low Church tradition most of the above is seen as distraction from the spiritual, which is to be nourished by the Word of God as found primarily in the Bible. Sunday worship in this tradition consists mainly of the reading of biblical passages and lengthy preaching on them, plus the singing of hymns. The senses outside of hearing were to be quieted so as to allow the Word of God to sink into the soul. The custom of reading, quoting, and reflecting on the Word, the Bible, outside of church has also spread widely in much of Protestantism.

The Mystical Life

Mysticism refers primarily to the knowledge of ultimate reality, God, in a direct way often called contemplation, and hence is similar to intuition, which is *im*-mediate knowledge, as opposed to discursive reason, which leads to mediate knowledge, as in a syllogism. Human knowledge of God normally is mediate, that is, humans know God indirectly, through faith (i.e., trust in an authority), the wonders of creation, etc. However, some humans in all religions claim to have a more direct knowledge of God. In its purest form it is a kind of contemplation wherein the devotee simply rests in the presence of God. However, the term mysticism is also used to cover any kind of claimed knowledge of God or the "beyond-human" by means other than rational, immediate knowledge, ranging from "orthodox" religious believers through "Gnostics" (Greek *gnosis*, knowledge—those who sought or claimed to have special knowledge of the beyond-human) to the superstitious (those who imagine the real existence of the unreasonable).

Christianity along with Judaism (particularly through the Kabbalah) and Islam (particularly through Sufism) and other religions as well has a strong mystical tradition which runs the gamut from orthodox through gnostic to the superstitious. At its beginning, the Yeshua of the Gospel of John is among other things clearly a person who has immediate experience of God: "Father...as you and I are one....Who sees me sees the Father" (John 17). This tradition courses strongly throughout subsequent Christian history, creating a huge delta in the Middle Ages and thereafter with many male and female mystics of great renown: Hildegard of Bingen, Angela of Foligno, Catherine of Siena, Francis of Assisi, Thomas à Kempis, John Tauler, Meister Eckhart, John of the Cross, Teresa of Avila, and Thérèse of Lisieux, to name but a few.

This mystical tradition is likewise strong in both Judaism and Islam. In Judaism, as mentioned, there is the still tradition of the Kabbalah, although it has at times moved somewhat in the direction of gnosticism. The eighteenth century Eastern European movement of Hasidism (Hebrew *hasid*, pious), led by the Baal Shem Tov (Master of a Good Name) fostered the Jewish mystical tradition. Perhaps even stronger is the mystical tradition of Islam, named after its initiators of the eighth century, the Sufis (Arabic *suf*, wool, after the plain wool cloak these mystics wore). Sufism produced a number of well-known male and female mystics, including as Ghazali, Rumi, Ibn al-Aribi, Omar Khayyam and Rabi'a of Basra. Of the last it is said that one day she was seen running through the streets of Basra, (present-day Iraq) with a torch in one hand and a bucket of water in the other. When asked what she was doing, she replied that she was going to put out the fires of hell and burn down paradise so that people would no longer love God out of the fear of the one and the hope of the other, but purely for God's self.[1]

Among the true mystics, there seems to be very little division, whether they are Jewish, Christian, Muslim, Hindu, or Sikh. All seem to be aiming at the love of God, and God's most beloved creatures, humans.

For Reflection and Discussion

1. What do you see as the appeal of High Church forms of worship?
2. What do you see as the appeal of Low Church forms of worship?
3. Is mystical experience the same whether the mystic is Jewish, Christian, or Muslim?
4. Do you think members of one religious community should participate in the rituals of another? What general guidelines would you propose regarding, for example, Jews who attend a Catholic Mass, Christians who attend Friday services at a mosque, or Muslims who go to synagogue services?

The Meaning of Revelation

As noted earlier, all three of the Abrahamic religions are religions of God's revelation, which has been distilled in writing in Sacred Scriptures. For the Jews the Book (*Biblos*) is the *Torah* (Hebrew, teaching), including the Pentateuch, the Prophets, and the Writings (all of which the Christians called the Old Testament, but now more frequently the Hebrew Bible). For Christians it is the Hebrew Bible and the New Testament, whereas for Muslims it is the Al-Qur'an (Arabic, recitation), which corrects and supplements the earlier revelation of the *Torah* and *Injil* (Arabic, gospel-derived from the Greek *euanggelion*—but meaning the whole New Testament).

The art and science of understanding the various meanings of the words of revelation have been highly developed over the centuries in all three traditions. Manifold efforts have been expended to obtain the precise text in each case and then to probe its several layers of meaning. Supposedly the devotional use of the scriptures is to be based on the best "scientific" understanding, or at least not be contrary to it. The increasing application of critical-thinking tools to the understanding of the several Scriptures, especially since the eighteenth century Enlightenment, has led to a great deal of controversy within each tradition.

The extreme reaction to the critical study of the Scriptures is usually labeled "fundamentalism," coming from an early twentieth century conservative American Protestant movement which proclaimed certain "fundamentals" that Christianity must adhere to. One of these fundamentals was the so-called literal interpretation of scripture. I say "so-called" literal interpretation because it is in fact *their* interpretation, not necessarily that of the original writer—which is borne out by the further fact that there are hundreds of different understandings of the Bible text, which have given rise to more than 350 Protestant denominations in America alone.

The Catholic position, and in large part the Orthodox Christian position as well, is not that of biblical fundamentalism. This is also true for large parts of Protestantism, but there are nevertheless tens of millions of Protestants who either embrace fundamentalism and its literalist interpretation of the Scriptures, or tend in its direction. In Judaism, a spectrum of attitudes is also found, but outside of ultra-Orthodoxy, literalism is not strong. There is also a full spread of opinions in Islam concerning how to understand revelation. The differences in all cases really are not so much along the lines of the three religions, but how best to understand ancient religious texts, the gap ranging from the critical understanding to the uncritical traditional understanding. Because Christianity and Judaism both for the most part have had to run the gauntlet of the challenge of critical thought starting over two hundred years ago, and Islam largely only for several decades, the demarcation appears to be between Judaism and Christianity as over against Islam. However, the real point of division is not the religion but critical thought.

Jihad, Colonialism

Since September 11, 2001, fingers are pointed and shouts of colonialism and *jihad* are heard. These mutual accusatory attitudes constitute barriers to dialogue between Christians and Muslims. Let's first take a brief look at colonialism. It is true that from the eighteenth through the first part of the twentieth century Europe colonized much of the Muslim world, and Muslims are surely justified in resenting it. Almost all the countries where Muslims were in the majority came under European control in the course of the eighteenth to twentieth centuries.

At the same time, however, it should also be remembered that the Islamic world did not become Islamic by peaceful means either. Islam, despite its name, also colonized by military might the whole now Islamic world outside of Arabia, and this expansive military colonization continued at least up to the latter part of the seventeenth century, when in 1683 the Ottoman Empire besieged Vienna. Indeed, it was only during the first part of the twentieth century that Southeastern Europe broke free from centuries-long Ottoman conquest and occupation (though to this day, a small portion of the European continent stills remains under Turkish colonization).

Jihad is an Arabic word meaning "struggle," and from the earliest time of Islam it had two meanings, the inner or greater and the outer or lesser *jihad*. The inner *jihad* is the struggle to submit oneself inwardly to the will of God, living according to God's precepts. The outer *jihad* is to struggle to protect religion. It is the latter that has come to predominate in the public image, and, indeed, as already mentioned, too frequently has been misused as an excuse to launch violence against others that in no way is a protection of religion, but frequently is the opposite.

Of course modern Western colonialism was at times carried on under the arrogant banner of *mission civilisatrice* or *White Man's Burden*. This was especially galling for those longtime Muslim countries which in previous centuries had been culturally superior to Western Christendom. This form of domination quickly evaporated after World War II, but the countries of Muslim majority are still struggling to develop. The effort on the part of critical-thinking Muslims is made extremely difficult by the prevalence of political authoritarianism in the Muslim world and the strong attack of Islamists, that is, those political ideologues who manipulate the religion Islam as a means to gain political power.[2]

For Reflection and Discussion

1. What is fundamentalism? Is it present in all three Abrahamic religions? Have you experienced it?
2. How do you understand the relationship between colonialism, crusades, and *jihad*?
3. Should Scripture be subject to scientific investigation and critical analysis? Why or why not?
4. How should the legacy of colonialism and *jihad* be addressed in relationships between Christians and Muslims?

CHAPTER TWELVE

Modernity: Bond or Barrier?

There are a number of issues which are the source of major divisions between Judaism and Christianity on the one hand and Islam on the other. They all stem from developments that have occurred in the past two hundred years, since the eighteenth century Enlightenment, first in the West, and now increasingly everywhere. The source of these serious tensions can be cast as a single word: Modernity.

Religious Liberty

Since at least the time of Israel's incorporation into the Roman Empire the century before the Christian Era, Judaism has favored religious liberty. But what of the other two Abrahamic religions? What about their attitude toward religious liberty?

In the early centuries of Christianity in the Greco-Roman world, Christian writers were strongly in favor of religious liberty. For example, in the third century the North African Christian Tertullian wrote: "It is a fundamental human right, a privilege of nature, that all human beings should worship according to their own convictions; one human person's religion neither harms nor helps another. It is not proper to force religion. It must be undertaken freely, not under pressure."[1]

In a way, a high point of religious liberty, and thus much of the basis of human rights, was reached publicly with the universal declaration for the whole Roman Empire in the Edict of Milan (313 CE) by Emperor Constantine: "We should therefore give both to Christianity and to *all others* free facility to follow the religion which they may desire."[2] This moment of freedom was short-lived, for in 380 CE, the Edict of Thessalonica was issued by Emperor Theodosius, stating, "It is our will that all the peoples who are ruled by the administration of Our Clemency shall practice that religion which the divine Peter the Apostle transmitted to the Romans."[3]

After the Constantinian embrace of the Christian religion in the fourth century, Christian leaders quickly switched to the position that the state had the responsibility of seeing that the truth was protected and favored—and of course Christianity had the truth. In theory, of course, no one was to be forced to accept Christianity, but frequently the theory was not translated into practice. With the development of medieval Christendom in the western half of the former Roman Empire, almost everyone became Christian, with the exception of the Jews, who for the most part were allowed to continue a separate existence, often in ghettos—as long as they did not teach any non-Jews about Judaism.

Even Thomas Aquinas, that great saint and scholar, followed the repressive thought of the time: Their crime is even greater than that of counterfeiters, for "it is much more grievous to corrupt the faith...than to falsify money." Therefore, heretics "may not only be excommunicated, but may justly be killed." The Church should properly tolerate their existence for a while, so long as there is some reasonable hope of conversion, but when that is gone, then heretics "must be cut out like rotten flesh," as Jerome says. They should be handed over "to the secular judge to be exterminated from the world through death."[4]

The insistence on the true religion, Christianity, continued to and past the Reformation until the U.S. Constitution's 1789 Bill of Rights: "Congress shall make no law concerning the establishment of religion or the free exercise thereof." There was widespread resistance to the eighteenth century Enlightenment's efforts to spread religious liberty, led by the two reactionary mid-nineteenth century popes, Gregory XVI (1830-46) and Pius IX (1846-78). As noted earlier, they said of religious liberty and freedom of conscience: "From this poisonous spring of indifferentism flows the false and absurd, or rather the mad principle (*deliramentum*) that we must secure and guarantee to each one liberty of conscience; this is one of the most contagious of errors."

Fortunately in the middle of the twentieth century the Catholic Church caught up with the great majority of Protestant Churches, which by that time had endorsed religious liberty. At the Second Vatican Council the Catholic Church issued an authoritative document insisting on religious liberty for all:

> The human person has a right to religious freedom. This freedom means that all human beings are to be immune from coercion on the

> part of individuals, social groups and every human power.... Nobody is forced to act against his convictions in religious matters in private or in public....Truth can impose itself on the mind of humans only in virtue of its own truth (*Declaration on Religious Liberty*, nos. 1, 2).

The history of Islam was not very different. In theory no individual or community was to be forced to embrace Islam. It states in the Al-Qur'an, "concerning religion, there shall be no coercion" (Qur'an 2:256) In addition, "If it had been thy Lord's will, all who are on the earth would have believed, all of them. Wilt thou then compel mankind, against their will, to believe!" (Qur'an, 10, 99). A. Yusuf Ali, in his translation of the Al-Qur'an, comments on that verse in this way:

> Men of faith must not be impatient or angry if they have to contend against Unfaith, and most important of all, they must guard against the temptation of forcing Faith, i.e., imposing it on others by physical compulsion, or any other forms of compulsion such as social pressure, or inducements held out by wealth or position, or other adventitious advantages. Forced Faith is no faith.[5]

But in practice the *jihad*, in the sense of a Holy War against non-Muslim states, not infrequently was in fact launched aggressively. Although the *millet* system (Non-Muslim religious minorities were permitted to apply their own law concerning family matters) allowed non-Muslims within a Muslim-conquered state to practice their religion, the non-Muslims were clearly second-class citizens—which doubtless encouraged conversion to Islam, and surely not the contrary. The Tunisian Muslim scholar Mohammed Talbi notes:

> But it is a fact that at certain times and places they (*dhimmis*—non-Muslims in Muslim dominated countries) suffered from discrimination. Roughly speaking, things began seriously to worsen for them from the reign of al-Mutawakkii (847-861 CE). The discrimination, especially in matters of dress, took an openly humiliating shape. The oppression culminated in Egypt during the reign of al-Hakim (996-1021 CE)....In the medieval context of wars, hostilities, and treacheries, this policy of discrimination or open oppression was always prompted, or strongly backed, by the theologians.[6]

At various times during the intertwined history of Christianity and Islam, one side or the other pointed, usually with justification, an accusing finger at the other as a brutal aggressor. In fact, neither Christianity nor Islam can claim to have been predominantly the victim and the other the aggressor; the acid of history dissolves any such claim from either side. *Jihad* and the Crusades easily match each other in gratuitous aggressiveness.

Hence, the record of both Christianity and Islam concerning religious liberty is fraught with negatives. It is only with the secular 1789 U.S. Constitution that religious liberty was assured by a state, and it began to spread across the world. Secularism properly understood does not mean hostility toward religion, but a non-preferential treatment of each and all religions.

Religion-State Relations

In the past, it has often been claimed by Jewish dialogue partners that Judaism is different from Christianity because, unlike Christianity, Judaism is a holistic religion which includes politics as well as all other aspects of life (many, perhaps, had Israel in mind). Exactly the same kind of argument has been put forward by Islam.

In this, unfortunately, they are both forgetting that Christendom was exactly the same for well over a millennium—the Constantinian Era. It is only when Christendom, the West, began to break out of that mischievous marriage of religion and state (only allegedly virtuously "holistic") that it embarked on the path of human freedom with its limitless possibilities of creativity.

Separation of religion and state? This was and is an unthinkable position not only for present-day Israel and for traditional Muslims, and especially current Islamists, but also by the vast majority of Christians over the centuries until just a few decades ago. This is made dramatically clear by the words of Pope Gregory XVI in his 1832 encyclical *Mirari vos*:

> We cannot foresee any happier results for religion and the civil power from the desires of those who so warmly advocate the separation of Church and State and the rupture of the agreement between clergy and Empire. For it is a well-known fact that all the most ardent lovers of liberty fear more than anything else this concord that has always been as salutary and as fortunate for the Church as it has been for the State.[7]

Gregory's successor, Pius IX, issued in 1864 his Papal Bull *Quanta cura*, whose bombastic language not only echoed the most authoritarian condemnations of his medieval predecessors, but also preempted that of the Islamists a hundred years later:

> Wherefore those our predecessors have with apostolic fortitude continually resisted the nefarious attempts of unjust men, of those who, like raging waves of the sea, foaming forth their own confusion and promising liberty while they are the slaves of corruption, endeavored by their false opinions and most pernicious writings to overthrow the foundations of the Catholic religion and of civil society, to abolish all virtue and justice, to deprave the souls and minds of all men, and especially to pervert inexperienced youth from uprightness of morals, to corrupt them miserably, to lead them into snares of error, and finally to tear them from the bosom of the Catholic Church.[8]

He then referred to the chief errors of the time which he had enumerated to some extent in earlier writings. The first error he specifically mentioned was that of a separation of Church and State. Then he castigated freedom of conscience.

> These false and perverse opinions are so much the more detestable by how much they have chiefly for their object to hinder and banish that salutary influence which the Catholic Church, by the institution and command of her divine Author, ought freely to exercise, even to the consummation of the world—not only over individual men, but over nations and sovereigns—and to abolish that mutual cooperation and agreement of counsels between the priesthood and governments which has always been propitious and conducive to the welfare both of Church and State (Gregory XVI, Encyclical, August 13, 1832, [*Mirari vos*])....Contrary to the teaching of the holy Scriptures, of the Church, and of the holy Fathers, these persons do not hesitate to assert, that "the best condition of human society is that wherein no duty is recognized by the Government of correcting by enacted penalties the violators of the Catholic religion, except when the maintenance of the public peace requires it."
>
> From this totally false notion of social government they fear not to uphold that erroneous opinion most pernicious to the Catholic Church, and to the salvation of souls, which was called by our predecessor Gregory XVI (lately quoted) the *insanity* [*deliramentum*] Encycl. August 13, 1832), namely, that "liberty of conscience and of worship is the right of every man; and that this right ought, in every well governed State, to be proclaimed and asserted by the law."[9]

Again, fortunately, all this was reversed in the Catholic Church by Vatican II in its 1965 *Declaration on Religious Liberty* wherein it insisted on a separation of religion and the state as the necessary guarantee of complete religious liberty. Hence, it is abundantly clear that the separation of religion from the power of the state, along with religious liberty, is something that appeared in human history only since the eighteenth-century Enlightenment and has been resisted by all traditional religion: Judaism, Christianity, Islam, Hinduism.... The union of religion and state is not something peculiar to Judaism or Islam, but to all religions—until most recent times, when the separation of religion from the power of the state emerged, along with other such human advances as democracy and human rights.

For Reflection and Discussion

1. What was the attitude and practice of Christianity toward religious liberty before and after Constantine?
2. What has been the attitude of Judaism, of Islam, toward religious liberty? What has been their attitude toward the separation of religion and state?
3. If people believe that their religion represents the truth, shouldn't they work to have the values and beliefs of their religion become "the law of the land"? Why or why not?
4. Give examples of specific issues around which this question is being debated in our society (e.g., the Ten Commandments displayed in courthouses, no alcohol in Muslim-dominated countries).

Human Rights

The notion of human rights is not something that was initially championed by religion, any religion. Seeds of human rights can be found in the roots of various religions, but one would have had to have the developed idea already in order to discern it there in its early stages. Human rights can be seen in embryonic form in the creation story of Genesis, for instance, in Athenian democracy (just for the top layer of society), in the *jus gentium* of Roman law, but it is only with the eighteenth century Enlightenment that the idea and the beginning of the reality emerged—and was vigorously resisted by most religions. Now almost every human on earth demands them! And many religions advocate them.

It may seem to many that contemporary Islam opposes human rights. However, in fact, except for Saudi Arabia, all Muslim states that were independent at the time supported the Universal Declaration of Human Rights in

1948.[10] All Muslim states that have become independent since then have endorsed the Declaration. Muslim states have also endorsed other relevant resolutions of the General Assembly of the United Nations, such as the "Declaration on the Elimination of All Forms of Intolerance and of Discrimination Based on religion or Belief."[11] Many Muslim states are signatories to specialized human-rights instruments, including the "International Covenant on Civil and Political Rights" and the "International Covenant on Economic, Social, and Cultural Rights."[12]

Nevertheless, as the Sudanese Muslim scholar Abdullahi An-Na'im writes:

> A fundamental problem facing both Muslims and non-Muslims who wish to engage one another in serious interreligious dialogue has been the traditional Muslim position that all non-Muslims perforce will be second-class citizens in any state where the Muslims obtain political power. A similar domineering attitude prevailed until just a few decades ago in Roman Catholicism, making it almost impossible for Catholics to enter into dialogue with non-Catholics until Vatican II (1962-65).[13]...Clearly, an essential question for dialogue with Islam, then, is whether full equality between Muslims and non-Muslims can be reconciled with the major sources of Islam, the Al-Qur'an and *sunna*. If so, how?[14]

Those Muslims convinced of the validity of the idea of human rights, which by definition are due to every human being equally, have a severe challenge. Their tradition as lived until recently does not allow for the equality of non-Muslims with Muslims. To move to truly implementing human rights for all citizens, drastic reform of the traditional Muslim law, the *shar'ia*, will have to be undertaken, or a move to secular law—which is the conclusion of An-Na'im and other Muslim scholars.

This, however, is the situation not only for Islam, but for all traditional religions. They were all formed in a time of relative isolation from or hostility toward other religions. Recall, for instance, the huge resistance in the leadership of the Catholic Church from the time of the French Revolution until after the middle of the twentieth century. Even where the issue appeared to be resolved, as in India with its secular government after independence in 1948, the forces of traditional Hinduism are reasserting themselves—pushing 150 million Muslims more vigorously in the direction of a secular government guaranteeing all citizens their human and civic rights.

Only by dialogue and cooperation, locally, regionally, and globally, can Jews, Christians, Muslims, and others build a peaceful world without oppression.

Status of Women

A major sore area between Judaism and Christianity on the one hand and Islam on the other is the status of women. It appears to many that Judaism and Christianity are arguing for the equality of women with men and Islam is arguing for the protection of women by men—making for a great tension between the two groupings.

Again, it is largely a matter of the difference in time. Before the nineteenth century, even the sons of the eighteenth century Enlightenment thought women were inferior to men and needed to be protected. The nineteenth and twentieth centuries rang with the struggle of women for emancipation from dominance by men and equality with them, that is, a right to make their own choices. From the beginnings of both Judaism and Christianity, women were second class. The first century Jew Josephus summed it up for then burgeoning Judaism: "The woman, says the Law, is in all things inferior to the man,"[15] and his contemporary, Paul of Tarsus, echoed the same idea: "Let a woman learn in silence with all submissiveness. I permit no woman to teach or to have authority over men; she is to keep silent."[16] Of course, it is rightly claimed that the Jew Yeshua "was a feminist," but nobody, Jew nor Christian, followed him in this radical position for almost two thousand years![17]

Since the beginning of the first European women's feminist movement in the first half of the nineteenth century, the status of women in Western civilization has advanced greatly, and continues to do so. The lot of women in both the majority of Christian Churches and Judaism has improved dramatically. In most of the Protestant Churches women can fill all positions of authority. The same is also true of three of the four branches of Judaism: Reform, Conservative, and Reconstructionist. Unfortunately that is not yet true in either Catholic or Orthodox Christianity or Orthodox Judaism, though considerable progress has been made. The struggle continues unabated.

All scholars grant that Muhammad improved the lot of women in Arabia during his time. Some extreme apologists even argue that the introduction of Islam into an area always improved the status of women. Critical Muslim scholars, however, will usually agree with Khalid Duran: "Admit that the advent of Islam did not bring about an all-comprehensive revolution in favor of women as some apologists would have us believe."[18] In fact, in his very recent book attempting to explain Islam to a contemporary audience, Duran devotes one of five sections of his book to "Women: The Most Vexing Question." He deals with all the vexing issues, including veiling of women, female genital mutilation, and "honor killing"[19] The struggle in Islam for the equality of women is clearly joined, and will doubtless go on for decades. A recent indication of that appeared on the front page of the July 31, 2003 *New York Times* where it was reported that the appointment of a female judge in Iraq was protested "because it contradicts Islamic law." A woman cannot be a judge because "women are always ruled by their emotions."

In whatever religion women do not have equal rights with men, there is today a strong or at least emerging movement for equal rights for women. As in secular society, these movements will have their ups and downs, their extremes and mainstreams, but it is clear from secular history that they will persist, and doubtless will ultimately prevail. And why not? At the very beginning of the Bible it states "God created humanity in the image of himself, in the image of God he created it, male and female he created them." (Gen 1:26–27) Man and woman were created simultaneously as the very images of God. How could they be unequal?

Only by dialogue and cooperation, locally, regionally, and globally, can Jews, Christians, Muslims, and others address the issue of the status of women and build a world without oppression.

For Reflection and Discussion

1. What is the present attitude of Judaism, Christianity, and Islam toward human rights?
2. Does concern for human rights, and specifically women's rights, reflect the beliefs and teachings of the three religions, or must religious beliefs be set aside to achieve human rights?
3. Are people who have no religious affiliation in a better position to advocate for women's rights since they do not carry the cultural and historical baggage of discrimination found in the Abrahamic religions? Why or why not?

PART FOUR

Preparing for Dialogue: Islam

KHALID DURAN

CHAPTER THIRTEEN

What Is Interreligious Dialogue and What for?

"People of the Book! Come to a *word* common *between* us: that we worship none but God" (Al-Qur'an 3 64).[1]

Here Islam's Sacred Scripture proposes to Jews and Christians a get together for dialogue, for that is what the term means in Greek: "a word between," *logos dia*, in Arabic *kalima baina.*

What can we achieve through dialogue? What purpose does it serve? In its most basic sense dialogue aims at good neighborly relations. This may sound like a platitude, yet it implies so much. Good neighborly relations may be the outcome of esoteric intercourse among philosophers. They may just as well be the outcome of students playing the devotional music of different faiths, or members of different communities playing religious music together. Good neighborly relations may also be the outcome of Muslims inviting Christian neighbors to festivities, or joining Jews in a fast on Yom Kippur. If dialogue were to achieve nothing more than good neighborly relations, that alone would be worthwhile. *Al-jar qabla d-dar*: "first we care for the neighbor, then for ourselves."

Neighborly relations are rarely as good as they seem because beneath the surface prejudices and misconceptions keep on smoldering. Sarajevo, for example, taught us a bitter lesson. Antagonisms accumulated over centuries may surface with a vengeance, at any moment. In Bosnia, good neighborly relations were taken for granted, and then in the 1990s paradise burst into flames. There was little conscious effort at buttressing them by means of purposeful dialogue. The most solid basis for respect is knowledge, respect for one another's convictions based on mutual knowledge. And the surest means to such mutual knowledge is dialogue—a process of probing one's own tradition and that of the partner. This facilitates acceptance of the other as he or she is. It helps Jews and

Christians see us as we see ourselves, rather than have them look at a picture of us that may be distorted, or at least may not depict us faithfully.

Muslims have a rich legacy of approaching religious life in other traditions positively. Moroccan Muslims join in the annual *hilula*, the pilgrimage to the shrine of a Jewish saint near the city of Fes.[2] There are many such examples from various parts of the world. Most of that belongs in the realm of spiritual dialogue; it is not built upon any conscious effort at enlarging our own understanding of religious life in other traditions. But there also exist precedents when this went hand in hand with an academic dialogue seeking to challenge and correct the way many of us used to approach other religions. Those precedents of enriching our understanding call for a resumption of the dialogue from earlier times.

The temptation to regard one's own community as the best is surely universal. Christians' affirmation of dialogue has created an awareness of this and consequently Christians have come to adopt a critical attitude toward self-righteousness. Many reject the absolute authority they used to attribute to their own religious identity. Do we not find similar attitudes among Muslims? Surely, but equally strong is the temptation to isolate from others, especially among Muslim diaspora communities in the West.

Who Are We? A Basic Point of Self-Understanding

For Muslims there are a number of reasons to advocate dialogue as "cooperation for humanity." First and foremost is the fact that *islam* in itself was originally intended as something like a global ethics. Prophet Muhammad (p)[3] did not set out on his mission bent on founding a new religion. He was driven by the desire to bring people back to the original faith of Abraham (p). He understood that the various types of Christianity and sects of Judaism all sprang from the same source. Since they had come to differ among themselves, he saw his task in reestablishing the original Abrahamic religion, *islam*.

The primordial purport of the revelation to Muhammad (p) was not to create yet another community in addition to the already existing Christian Churches and sects of Judaism. The original mission was to bring all of them together on a common platform: the reconstituted Abrahamic origin of them all. This, however, did not materialize, and Islam turned into a new religion, number three after Judaism and Christianity.

Muhammad (p) made it his mission to bring people back to *islam* in that original sense. He did not intend to convert people to a religion of his own; he wanted to make them convert—or reconvert—to the religion of Abraham (p). To this end the prototype of Abrahamic religion had to be reconstructed, and that became the religion of Islam, at least in its ideal sense as enshrined in the revelation of Al-Qur'an.

This may sound odd to someone who associates the word *islam* with the religion of Islam as we know it today, with the world community of Islam as a political and social phenomenon with a long history. Let us forget about Islam in this sense for a moment and bear in mind that the word *islam* has a meaning in Arabic. It signifies "submission to the will of God" and "peace." In that sense *islam* is the same as *salam*, which is the same as the Hebrew *shalom*, meaning peace, with the underlying connotation of soundness and wholesomeness.

It is in this sense that we have to understand such verses of Al-Qur'an that speak of *islam* as a precondition for salvation: "Whoso desires another religion than *islam*, it shall not be accepted of him" (3:79). "The true religion with God is *islam*" (3:17). The reference here is to *islam* in its theological meaning, not to Islam in the sociological sense as the communal base for the Caliphal empire.

There are mystics and *islamic* reformers who stress the literal meaning of the word *islam* over against the communal meaning of Islam, that is to say that the present-day community of followers of Islam is one thing, and the ideal notion underlying the term *islam* is another. No Jew or Christian could possibly have any objection to *islam* in the sense of peacefulness and submission to God. In this ideal sense of the word, *islam* remains a goal for all of us alike: Jews, Christians, Muslims. Today's followers of Islam are often as remote from the ideal meaning of *islam* as are Jews and Christians, while many Jews and Christians are in fact very close to *islam*.

Most of us consider Imam AbuHamid Al-Ghazali (d. 1111) to have been an authentic spokesperson for *islam*. In his book *Faisalu t-tafriga* this orthodox theologian expressly stated that non-Muslims can be saved, provided they live a life of honesty and sincerity.[4] A towering scholar of our age, Egypt's Imam Muhammad 'Abduh (d. 1905), expressed a similar opinion in his commentary[5] on the following verse of Al-Qur'an:

"Surely they that believe, and those of Jewry, and the Christians, and those Sabeans, whosoever believes in God and the Last Day, and works righteousness—their wage awaits them with their Lord, and no fear shall be on them, neither shall they sorrow" (2:59).

To keep our perspectives clear: admitting a variety of roads leading to salvation does not imply that we abdicate our faith, nor that we give up holding as true what we believe to be exact. Anyone doing so would be "among the losers in the next world" (3:85). Al-Qur'an, by a multiplicity of arguments and warnings, calls people to *islam* as the final message from God which confirms and completes all the scriptures which preceded it. The Muslim position in interfaith dialogue has been appropriately defined by the Tunisian Islamic scholar Muhammad Talibi:

> The need to adhere to our faith becomes more imperative as it becomes more lucid. Then our faith ceases to be simply membership of a sociological group and a form of subordination. It becomes a real communion and a binding commitment. And so we come back to the duty of the apostolate through witness, which is as much a question of self-respect as of respect for others.[6]

For Reflection and Discussion

1. The author distinguishes between *islam* in the theological sense and Islam in the sociological sense. How do you understand this distinction?
2. If you do not identify yourself as Muslim (sociological sense), would you be comfortable identifying yourself with *islam* in its theological meaning as the author describes it? Why or why not?
3. If you identify yourself as Muslim, are you comfortable viewing non-Muslims as "sisters and brothers" sharing *islam* in its theological meaning? Why or why not?

Reuniting the Human Family

This religion was to do justice to both major purposes with which the term religion is usually associated: an explanation of the world and ethics. In Islam, as in Judaism, the emphasis is on ethics. Given the fact that Islam, in its capacity as the reborn faith of Abraham (p), was meant to be a platform for Jews, Christians, and other monotheists, it had to be universal. It was not a message to any particular people, not a religion for Arabs exclusively. Quite the contrary. The basic assumption underlying Muhammad's message, one that is clearly and frequently stated in Al-Qur'an, is that God sent messengers to all peoples. Every people had its messenger. Jesus (p) was understood as a messenger to the Jews primarily. Finally there was to be a messenger for all humanity, Muhammad (p).

Islam aims at unifying humankind. Accordingly, the ethics of this prototype of Abrahamic religion had to be universal. The express purpose was to do away with particularisms of an unnecessarily conflictive nature, such as divisions by caste and class, racial superiority, and religious supremacy. As for the *per se* differences between races and religions, Al-Qur'an recognizes them as originating out of divine wisdom. Humanity is to know itself through difference from other men and women. Human variety serves the purpose of understanding about humanity. The differences help to shape identity. Humans need not be all the same, as that would be highly impracticable. "We created you as nations and tribes so that you may know one another" (Sura 49, verse 13). Within the general framework of human relations, humans are given multiple choices of self-realization.

This is a contentious issue within Muslim communities and the *umma* (world community) in general. Despite Al-Qur'an's clear-cut statements regarding the wisdom of variety, there are always sections of the community desirous of greater uniformity, which mostly means "Middle Easternization." Not without reason have some anthropologists accused Muslims of cultural leveling and creating a *homo islamicus* (the *mard-e musulman* or "Muslim Man" with the poet-philosopher Muhammad Iqbal). Islam, it is said, enforces a high degree of uniformity on otherwise very diverse parts of our world. The *homo islamicus* is a kind of monolithic human being, more conditioned by the Middle Eastern background of the nascent *umma* than any other tradition or particularism.

Al-Qur'an calls for unity of humankind, stipulating the measure of human oneness required for peace and harmony. At the same time it points out the divine wisdom in creating diversity. The decisive factor then is the general framework of the human community. The Muslim community is to provide the model for the ultimate unification of humankind. Unification, we conclude from Al-Qur'an, means closeness despite diversity, not uniformity.

For Reflection and Discussion

1. The author claims that Islam calls for unity, not uniformity. Nonetheless, aren't there core beliefs and principles (that is, some uniformity) required of any *umma* (world community)? If so, what would they be?

2. Is there a common source for such beliefs and principles? If so, what would it be?
3. Is there ever a time when people should call for uniformity? How might people discern when they should push for sameness and when they should accept and advocate diversity?
4. According to the author, human diversity is a manifestation of divine wisdom. Give some examples to support this belief.

If the Muslim community is to serve as a model for such unification, how can this be made meaningful to "People of the Book"? (People of the Book are Jews, Christians, and other monotheists who believe in a revealed Scripture.) Those are saved even if they do not become "members." In what other way can they join the enterprise? How do we interlink our model community with other communities, or with the human community at large? We are not the only ones aspiring to provide a model for the ultimate unification of humankind. In what way can those efforts be coordinated? Are there novel ways of speeding up the process by "going it together"? Here dialogue has a major role to play.

Both Jews and Christians claim universality. We have a tendency to assign a particularism to them that they refuse to recognize as theirs. Some Muslims tell Christians that they are mistaken in being Christians because Jesus was sent to the Children of Israel.

This may be an interesting point of debate for historians of religion, but we have to recognize that there is a Christian belief system that has its own history and validity. According to this belief system Jesus' mission was to all humankind, not different from what our belief system tells us about Muhammad's mission. Several Western scholars of Islam have argued that Muhammad (p), at least initially, thought of himself as a prophet to his own people, and expanded this self-view into a universalist claim only later on.

To us this sounds plainly absurd, if not insulting. Christians feel no different when we try to convince them that Jesus came only to guide the Jews and not to save humanity as a whole.

Jews are less unanimous in defining this issue, however, in the course of more than 3,000 years they have absorbed into their community groups of Arabs, Berbers, Egyptians, Ethiopians, Khazars, and quite a few others. We ought to recognize that their belief system knows a larger universalist scope than we are wont to think.

CHAPTER FOURTEEN

Jewish-Christian-Muslim Dialogue Today

In view of anti-Western hostilities in parts of the Muslim world, one might feel inclined to ask whether there is any prospect at all for Jewish-Christian-Muslim cooperation. In actual fact there is just as much encouraging news, if not more, than all those well-publicized negative facts.

On the negative side we witness excesses such as the firing on Christian congregations and the burning of churches and monasteries in Egypt. It started with a "war of the stickers." Copts and Muslims had developed a habit of displaying their religious creed on their cars. Some automobiles seemed to serve more as sectarian campaign trailers than as private vehicles, until the Egyptian government passed a law prohibiting this "war of the stickers" in 1985. This propaganda war was an unfortunate development indeed, because there was a time, back in 1919, when all Egyptians—Copts and Muslims alike—fought for the liberation of their country from foreign domination. In those days they used to demonstrate with flags bearing Crescent and Cross. In retrospect one might deplore that this did not become Egypt's national flag. (Farag Foda, an Islamic scholar who used that symbol on his party flag was gunned down in 1992.)

Today, in Spain, white flags bearing a red Crescent and Cross are a common sight, as if Islam and Christianity had at last merged, after centuries of futile enmity. This is not meant as a syncretism but as a fusion of godly efforts, born of a simple necessity. Every year more than a million Muslims, most of them working in France, Belgium, the Netherlands, and Germany, pass through Spain on their way to North Africa to spend their vacations at home. Once they have converged from the various countries where they toil, the trek becomes one huge caravan traversing Spain from North to South. Spaniards call this *la ruta de los marrogies*, and all along this "Route of the Moroccans" the Spanish Red Cross and the Moroccan Red Crescent join hands and set up mixed first aid centers. This resulted in the birth of a new symbol, Crescent and Cross together on one flag, illustrating an exemplary unity of purpose shared by both communities.

Any emphasis on the challenges posed by natural calamities, especially the devastating drought that ravaged most of Africa in the 80s, may sound platitudinous. All the same, it may be time to ponder the far-reaching effects of this challenge to both religious communities. Ethiopia, for a while the country worst affected, has a population that is roughly half Christian and half Muslim. Regrettably some of the Western aid was motivated by a distinct commitment to Christians qua Christians, while oil-rich Arab states sometimes give the impression as if their primary—if not sole—concern is to keep starving Muslims alive, and not just simply starving human beings.

As a result of backwardness, Muslims have generally lagged behind with regard to such large-scale humanitarian efforts. Of late they have made headway, and the year 1985 was a landmark in this development.[1]

At the U.N. World Summit for Social Development in Copenhagen in March 1995, three interfaith services were held. Some Christian and Muslim relief organizations formed a joint Committee on Interreligious Development Action. The committee brings together Catholic, Orthodox, Protestant, and Muslim groups, such as the International Islamic Council, based in Cairo and headed by Kamil Ash-Sharif. The committee's first initiative was to send a joint delegation to Russia to make sure that humanitarian aid reached Chechnya. The committee recognized that in Bosnia, Chechnya, and Sudan, to quote Kamil Ash-Sharif, "religion has been exploited and misused to promote hatred. It is time to present religion in its true spirit." In his view the committee took a step beyond dialogue: "We are undertaking concrete projects in development and relief. Now we are getting practical."[2]

Pride of performance and a new self-assurance may be the best guarantees for emancipation from the narrow confines of confessionalism. Gigantic salvage operations, such as those under way in Africa, will hopefully turn out to be the cornerstone of a future ecumenical *caritas* (Arabic, *khairat*). Our survival depends on such kinds of Jewish-Christian-Muslim cooperation.

Until now the most encouraging examples still take the form of local "miracles" hidden away in the bush. In Western Kenya, not far from the border with Uganda, Muslim elders pulled their resources together and founded the "Mumias Muslim Secondary School." More than half of the students and teachers are Christians. As such, this school has a model character, for it has come into existence in an area otherwise dominated by missionary schools tending to generate confessional rivalry. The Mumias Muslim Secondary School pays for its exemplary ecumenical spirit inasmuch as it does not receive financial assistance from either side, depending entirely on the sacrifices of the founding fathers and dedicated staff members. If it manages to cross those material hurdles it may become a signpost pointing toward a promising era of Christian-Muslim cooperation. A Nigerian and a Tanzanian bishop, both hailing from families that are partly Christian, partly Muslim, report of similar ecumenical initiatives in their parishes. There is no dearth of such redeeming features, despite an unmistakable rise of fanaticism on all sides in many places.

There are plenty of examples of a pioneer attitude, most remarkable perhaps in Spain, the destiny of which was shaped by centuries of war among Jews, Christians, and Muslims. Spain's ecumenical vanguard is personified by Father Emilio Galindo Aguilar who publishes a magazine on Christian-Muslim encounter, titled *Encuentro Islamo-Cristiano.* He is also running a center called *Darek-nyumba* (meaning "Your House" in Arabic and Kiswahili), catering to the needs of Christians and Muslims in their interaction: from language courses (Arabic for Spaniards and Spanish for Arabs) to counseling and religious instruction for children of mixed couples. Such activity furnishes interreligious dialogue with a solid practical base.

The ecumenical movement initiated here is called *Crislam*[3] and takes its cue from Ibn `Arabi, a thirteenth century mystic from Murcia in Spain. In many Muslim lands Ibn `Arabi is hailed as *ash-shaikhu l-akbar,* the "Greatest Saint," the most spiritual Sufi master ever. One of his poems has become Crislam's logo. He wrote that his heart had become a meadow for the deer, Torah scrolls for the rabbi, a monastery for the monk, a Kaaba for the pilgrim. "I profess the religion of love. Wherever its caravan may turn to, I shall follow."

Quite a few Jews, Christians, and Muslims, who otherwise may be fond of dialogue, might be scared away by what could look to them as an inadmissible syncretism. But syncretism is not a must, not even in *Crislam. Crislam's* objective is fairly akin to that of the "universal theology" Christian thinkers such as Leonard Swidler, Hans Küng, Raimundo Panikkar, Wilfred Cantwell Smith, John Hick, and others are heading to. Proceeding from a humanitarian commitment and the defense of human rights, they are keen on sailing forth together with Muslims.

The stress on activism is of vital importance especially for the more intellectual forms of dialogue. Experience has shown that there is a kind of dialectic relationship between dialogue as a theological discourse and dialogue as humanitarian cooperation. Whenever one of the two is neglected, the other is invariably affected negatively.

Manifestly, activism is not going to efface theoretical hurdles to a better understanding of each other's positions. As far as theological differences are concerned, the aim of dialogue is not to sweep them under the carpet. Quite the contrary: We want to gain clarity on what separates us just as much as on what unites us. The activism of Jewish-Christian-Muslim cooperation helps in this effort by instilling interfaith talks with new vitality and preventing them from falling a victim to professionalism and semantic inbreeding.

Given the present negativity, both in the Eastern Churches and in the "Islamist Movement," which has produced Al Qaida and 9/11 and its *revanche*, the Iraq war, it is gratifying indeed to witness those almost celestial circles of academics who get together every now and then in various retreats in the United States, at diverse academies in England and France, at universities in Italy and Spain, at the "Church Days" in Germany, and the Parliaments of the World's Religions. Moving in those groups of largely like-minded Jews, Christians, Muslims, and others, the participant feels elevated into spheres of paradisiacal harmony, into a world that could scarcely be better. A newcomer to such a symphony of ecumenism might find it difficult to make out who is who: a blond haired panelist turns out to be a Turk, while a Swede reveals himself as a Sufi.

This phenomenon should not be belittled as a dream world. There is, after all, some chance that such a *Crislamic* nucleus might develop into a broader movement. Otherwise there would be little hope for Western societies of which Islam has become part and parcel. Even if a hundred thousand Albanians, Turks, and other Muslim immigrants or refugees are sent back, the diaspora in North America and Western Europe is scarcely going to dwindle: four to five million in the United States, three to four in France, two to three in Germany, one to two in England—these figures will either remain constant or increase, but not decrease. The unhealthy isolation of many members of this new minority can best be overcome by a proliferation and enlargement of the *Crislamic* circles referred to above.

Such budding Jewish-Christian-Muslim cooperation is not without pitfalls. As with every other human enterprise, it is sometimes exploited for personal, professional, or political ends. These are universal symptoms of human failing that need to be guarded against. Jewish-Christian-Muslim cooperation is not immune to unsavory distortion and tendentious manipulation. Yet there are successes too. Liberation Theology, for example, is experiencing a resurgence far from the Latin American scene. Various Jewish, Catholic, and Protestant students' communities from Muslim parts of the Third World are seeking theological communication with liberation movements. This expresses, *inter alia*, a refusal to let interreligious dialogue be monopolized by career hunters. A generation concerned about the bleak prospects of nuclear war and environmental catastrophes is insisting on Jewish-Christian-Muslim cooperation as a necessity. They refuse to let the dialogue be misappropriated by what might be called "professional partners."

An increasing number of Jews, Christians, and Muslims are reaching beyond this and reason that no time should be lost with preliminaries. Recently more than 200 members of the medical profession, most of them from Western Europe, especially France, but even from Argentina, spent about a year serving with the Afghan resistance in a country ravaged by Soviet occupation forces. Afghanistan had become "a medical desert." The population, having suffered many an invasion, showed a repellent attitude toward things foreign. Many Afghans, however, were deeply impressed by the sacrificial spirit of those young Jews and Christians who risked their lives during every moment of their sojourn in the war areas, sharing the suffering of a people subjected to one of the most savage aggressions of our times. A delegation of the Afghan resistance (representing Muslim, not Islamist parties) touring Latin America did not miss the opportunity to thank bishops in Bogota and Buenos Aires for the heroic support rendered to a Muslim people by such a large number of young Christians. Hashim Zamani, "poet of the Afghan resistance," spoke of a new chapter that had been opened in Christian-Muslim relations.

A Protestant institution, affiliated with the University of Hamburg in Germany, bears the intriguing name "Mission Academy" (*Missionsakademie*). Some theologians at this academy worked untiringly for many years on behalf of the *Moros*, the oppressed Muslim minority in the Philippines. The world press occasionally mentions the *Moros* as being supported by Iran, Libya, or Saudi Arabia. Nevertheless, experts at the *Missionsakademie* in Hamburg strove hard to preserve *Moro* literature and traditions, and to make them accessible through the media, thus helping this Muslim minority to preserve its identity. It is partly due to those contributions that the *Moros* have developed a new consciousness. They have become aware that their freedom struggle is not a war between Christianity and Islam, but a popular uprising against a corrupt regime that was just as anti-Christian as it is anti-Muslim. In this way the word *Mission* acquired a new sense, denoting a Christian mission on behalf of Muslims, and vice versa.

Al-Qur'an reminds us that there exists a common platform of believers: "We believe in God, and in the revelation sent down on us, and on Abraham, Ishmael, Isaac, Jacob, and the tribes, and that given to Moses and Jesus, and that given to all prophets from their Lord. We make no difference between any of them, and to Him we surrender" (2:136).[4] In the light of this principle, it is evident that Muslims ought to enter dialogue in a spirit of reconciliation.

There are a large number of concrete issues Jews, Christians, Muslims, and other believers could best tackle together. But in a way all of these can be subsumed under the project of designing a global ethics, a moral code subscribed to by all humanity.

For Reflection and Discussion

1. Syncretism means the merging of religions, implying a watering down or dissolving of specific differences among religions as they interact and influence one another. The author advocates "a fusion of godly efforts" without syncretism. Do you think this is possible? Give examples to support your position.
2. Would you place a bumper sticker on your car that displayed combined symbols for all the world's major religions? Why or why not? What would displaying such a bumper sticker mean to you?
3. Would you display a bumper sticker of your religion alone? Why or why not? If so, what message would you want to convey with it?
4. Think about and then debate the following statement: Hatred is a violation and distortion of every religion. Mutual concern and compassion represent the true spirit of every religion.

CHAPTER FIFTEEN

Tackling Roadblocks to Dialogue

In principle, most Muslims welcome interreligious dialogue. Many, however, entertain some reservations, and sometimes these reservations are overwhelming. In general, such reservations do not belong in the realm of theory or theological qualms, rather they are the product of history and politics. These roadblocks are not anchored in the teachings of Islam. They have no place in the sources of religion. However, as a historic legacy they are perceived as tradition by many—to the extent that one might call them quasi-theological.

First, there is the problem posed by the age-old confrontation between Muslims and the followers of the earlier Abrahamic religions.

Second, there is the still fairly recent experience of European colonialism and its aftermath, the wounds of which are far from being healed. After regaining political independence, people are still chafing under a feeling of impotence in a number of Muslim countries. There is a widespread feeling of being excluded from the steering of the affairs of this world. Partly this is due to the long period of superpower rivalry when Third World nations felt like pawns in a power play of the mighty. Finally, the East-West conflict was replaced by the North-South rift, leaving much of the Muslim world with the feeling of being condemned to the role of underdogs in a world dominated by the rich industrial nations.

But there also exists a converse element of which we Muslims have to become more conscious. Many Muslims have not fully overcome their own imperial past. Centuries of glory with a proud history of political supremacy over much of the then known world, left behind in minds a "prince" complex that we have not been able to shed, no matter the painful downfall and the centuries of degrading subjugation to foreign rule.

While on the one hand clamoring for true independence and equality, some Muslims do in fact expect more. They long for a leadership role that is not easy to obtain in a world of minorities, a global village that requires partnership rather than dominance. As the anachronistic chauvinism of the twelve million strong Serb nation has shown, there are quite a few members in this world community who have great problems with the new constellation. Several nations and religious communities feel that they have yet to have their turn, that destiny has reserved a special role for them. According to some predictions, this will be the major problem of the twenty-first century: the refusal of many groups to be cut down to size, which is an unavoidable concomitant to the shrinking of our world. There are too many contenders for very few leadership positions.

At its annual convention in Prague in 1992, the "European Conference of Churches" felt greatly disturbed by the revanchist (desire to recover lost territories) currents that seem to have gripped the "Eastern Churches." Apparently the adjustment problems of Orthodox Christians match those of Muslims. Yet with more than one billion followers, Islam is a particularly large minority in our world of minorities. This Muslim minority has great difficulties in reconciling itself to a reduced role in world affairs.

This sentiment is strongest among Islamists, much stronger than among the masses of general Muslims. Islamists feel that it is not enough to be a Muslim by birth or by tradition. They visualize Islam as a political ideology and sometimes call it Islamism, referring to themselves as Islamists rather than merely as Muslims. Not a few Islamists indulge in revanchist talk, be it by inaugurating a mosque in Spain with preposterous predictions that tomorrow all of Andalusia will be Islamic once again, or be it by rejoicing over the demise of the Soviet Union and announcing that the United States will follow suit, after which Islamists will take over.[1] Since September 11, 2001, such a vision (nightmare) seems less farfetched.

Many Muslims are deeply upset by such anachronistic romanticism but face formidable obstacles combating it. Deteriorating living conditions in most of North Africa and the Middle East make people susceptible to any promise of a better world. For Islamists it is a foregone conclusion that the world will be better once they dominate it. The majority of Muslims doubt that, but feel helpless as things turn from bad to worse.

Interreligious dialogue could provide a suitable forum for a discussion of these issues. For the moment we cannot but register that these are roadblocks on the way to dialogue.

For Reflection and Discussion

1. Many Muslims, and Islamists in particular, believe that Muslims (nearly one-sixth of the world's population) should have a greater voice in world affairs than they now have. Do you agree or disagree?
2. Would you support such a development? In what ways? What forms might such involvement/empowerment take?
3. Are there more effective and more destructive ways of pursuing this goal? Explain.

Roadblocks to Dialogue with Jews

The Prophet Muhammad (p) had as his neighbors a Jewish community. That was one particular community conditioned by the age and the place they lived in. They had developed an attitude toward their non-Jewish environment that would not be shared by many other Jews. Since those Arabian Jews laid claim to the Mosaic religion, the Prophet (p) expected them to acknowledge his intent of 1) establishing a common platform for all monotheists by recreating the prototype of Abrahamic religion that could be acceptable to Jews and Christians alike, and 2) of converting idol-worshipers to Abraham's faith in The One God.

The Arabian Jews scoffed at his endeavor and ridiculed the revelations he received. They contravened a treaty they had concluded with the Prophet (p) and plotted against him by aligning themselves with his foes, the powerful rulers of Mecca who were idol-worshipers bent on crushing the nascent Muslim community in Medina.

The Prophet (p) fled his native Mecca and was requested by the inhabitants of Medina to become their chieftain. Part of Medina's population was Jewish. The Arab tribes in town partly joined Islam, partly they stayed aloof. The Prophet (p) concluded a pact with the people of Medina that was to join the different sections of the population together in a common citizenship. This pact was called *sahifa*, a term that might be translated as "holy writ." It is also referred to as *mithaq*, meaning "charter," and is often named Charta. Some call this Charta of Medina the first secular constitution because it bound people of different religions together in one common nationhood.

When talking about relations between followers of different religions, it has become customary to speak of tolerance, which is to say that we are prepared to put up with one another. The Charta of Medina was much more explicit—and more demanding. It stated: "The Jews of Bani' Auf form one nation together with the Muslims. The Jews have their religion, their followers and themselves, and so have the Muslims. He who transgresses and commits a crime does harm only to himself and to his family. The Jews shall be responsible for their financial affairs, and the Muslims for theirs. Together they shall fight those who wage war against the signatories of this pact. Their relations shall be guided by mutual sympathy, wishing each other well, and by righteous conduct, not by sinfulness."

We are supposed to wish Jews well, have understanding for them and deal with them ethically. The criterion is *birr*—and *birr* is defined in Al-Qur'an as kindness—especially kindness toward those in need of our help; hence, this is Muslims' social and moral responsibility.

The basic notion underlying the Charta of Medina is pluralism. Two communities, Jews and Muslims, agreed to form one nation under God, with the clear commitment that each one would have its religious autonomy and stick to its cultural identity. While accepting these differences, they formed one unit in face of the others, especially in face of nations hostile to either of them or to both of them together. This acceptance of difference is less surprising if we keep in mind that the Prophet (p) had a positive view of differences of opinion even within his own community. He is reported to have said: "Difference of opinion in my community is a blessing."

The Charta of Medina gave practical shape to the general principles enshrined in Al-Qur'an. The Charta says: "The Jews shall follow their religion, the Muslims theirs." This was possible on the basis of the Qur'anic verse: "I am not going to worship whom you worship and you are not going to worship whom I worship. To you your religion and to me mine" (109:4–6).

Unfortunately this first attempt at pluralism did not work out as hoped. After repelling a tribal alliance under the leadership of the Meccans, the Muslims turned on the Jews of Medina who had betrayed them. There was a tragic confrontation, resulting in the expulsion of Jews from most of the Arabian Peninsula.

In later centuries Jews and Muslims learned to turn the page and live together in many parts of the world. The experiment of Medina had failed, but elsewhere they gave it a second and a third try, and this time it worked. This living together was by no means always ideal. There was discrimination and occasional violence. In general, however, Jews fared better in the Muslim world than in Christian Europe. In some parts at least, Jews and Muslims were very close to one another. Spain is often mentioned as a shining example of a successful *convivencia* (living together), and this is by no means an exaggeration, no matter the exceptions to the rule.

Granada, the last bastion of Islam on the Iberian Peninsula, has been romanticized for many things. This was indeed an island of cultural splendor throughout the 15th century. For Muslims, Granada is Paradise lost, the lost dream of their bygone glory. Few are aware of the fact that roughly half of Granada's population was Jewish. With the shrinking of Muslim territory in Spain, many Muslims and Jews had flocked together in this last Muslim principality on Iberian soil.

After the fall of Granada in 1492, both Muslims and Jews were expelled. The majority avoided expulsion by converting to Catholicism. Later even those converts, or rather their offspring, were expelled. The last such expulsion occurred at the turn of the year 1608-1609. Significantly, Muslims and Jews mostly went together. They settled primarily in Morocco and the neighboring countries of North Africa. Others, mainly Jews, went as far as the Balkans, then part of the Ottoman Caliphate.

Such Jewish refugees introduced Spanish culture to Bosnia. There were two occasions when Turkish governors tried to create anti-Jewish pogroms in order to confiscate Jewish property. Bosnian Muslims, however, resisted those attempts and protected the Jewish citizens. At one time the Sultan had to appoint a new governor in order to avoid an uprising by the Muslims of Bosnia who were so protective.

What do these experiences demonstrate? The majority of Muslims and Jews clearly understood that the tragic events during the Prophet's life in Medina were an isolated instance that should not be generalized into an everlasting conflict between Judaism and Islam. The successful *convivencia* in Andalusia, Bosnia, and elsewhere was possible because people realized that the clash in Medina was a one-time affair, restricted to that particular community. There was always scope for a fresh start.

Muslims learned to judge the Jews in Spain, Morocco, and the Ottoman Empire on their own merit, and often they felt very close to them. So much in their religious observance is alike that to an outsider, such as a Confucianist, they look like twins.

An American professor, 'Abdullah Schleifer, converted to Islam on rediscovering the spirit of Jewish orthodoxy in a Moroccan Muslim environment strictly ruled by the *Shari'a*. He felt that the ritual differences were immaterial as compared to the oneness in essence. His impression was that such oneness is not found between any other two religions; this particular spirit is not found except with Jews and Muslims. The sameness that impressed Schleifer as positive, has impressed many others as negative. Old European prejudices against Jews are today voiced against Muslims. Turks in Germany get to hear the same insults once hurled at Jews.

Islam was the religion of the majority, and Muslims held political power. It was but natural that many Jews converted to Islam, as had happened earlier in the Middle East during the first expansion of Islam. Some two dozens of Morocco's leading families are of Spanish Jewish descent. They have been Muslims and pillars of the state for centuries; all the same, they stand by their Jewish origin, without embarrassment, no matter the poisoned atmosphere of the Arab-Israeli conflict. Similarly, many Jews from North Africa (in Israel, France, and the United States) are proud of their roots in Moorish culture. As mentioned earlier, in Morocco, Jews and Muslims together perform the *hilula*, the annual pilgrimage to the shrine of a Jewish saint. Often there are more Muslims than Jews praying at this Sufi sanctuary.

While all these positive aspects cannot be emphasized enough, it is also true that there is deep suspicion between many Muslims and Jews, reinforced by the Palestine conflict and the wars between Israel and its Arab neighbors. Initially Arabs and other Muslims took great pains to point to the racial and religious bonds between Jews and Muslims, stressing that the conflict was political, not religious, that they were opposed to Zionist ideology and the State of Israel, not to Judaism as a religion or the Jews as a people.

In the course of time such confrontations have deteriorated into an abysmal hatred with some sections on both sides. In the sixties some Islamists, notably the Egyptian Sayyid Qutb (d. 1966), took this conflict out of the realm of politics and converted it into a theological issue. Ever since, this trend has intensified, and we currently witness the production of a literature that is outright anti-Jewish, not just anti-Israeli. Some Islamists argue that this is a conflict of existence, that this world has room for only one of the two, that the Almighty prophesied the end of Jews, that Palestine will be their grave, this being the only purpose for their gathering there. It is all a struggle of existence between Al-Qur'an and the Talmud.[2]

Judaism and Islam, such Islamists aver, are incompatible and mutually exclusive. One of the top leaders of the Islamist movement, Rashid al-Ghannushi, takes the ultimate step into Nazism by declaring Jews to be the enemies not just of Islam but of all humanity, of all positive values and speaks of "a Jewish-American plan encompassing the entire region, which would cleanse it of all resistance and open it to Jewish hegemony from Marrakesh to Kazakhstan."[3]

This trend is relatively new and therefore has not yet been rebutted by many Muslim thinkers. In fact, many are not even aware of what is brewing in Islamist literature. Others are aware and are deeply shocked, paralyzed by what seems simply too outrageous to them. They consider it not only un-Islamic but profoundly anti-Islamic, and regard the evident borrowing from European antisemitic outpourings shameful and harmful to the cause of Muslims.[4]

Lately some Islamists have adopted medieval European notions of condemning Jews as the killers of Christ. By the same token, Arabs stand condemned as the people who opposed Muhammad (p) and nearly killed him. On a popular level, such an anti-Arab prejudice does in fact exist in some Muslim societies. But is that Islamic?

Al-Qur'an does not hold Jews collectively responsible for the death of Jesus (p). Some Arabian Jews seem to have taunted Christian opponents by boasting that they had killed Jesus (p). Al-Qur'an refutes that by stating emphatically "but they killed him not" (4:157). It mentions that Jews sometimes killed their prophets, as other peoples did, Arabs in particular.

Islamist literature presents an undifferentiating image of the Jews by making use of the Qur'anic verses that speak of Jewish sinners. For someone not familiar with the text as a whole, such stigmatization sounds convincing. But one could do just as well the opposite by referring only to the instances of divine grace upon Jews while omitting the instances of sin and transgression. If one were to weigh both elements in Al-Qur'an, the negative image of the Jews as transgressors amounts to only about one sixth, or less, of the references to Jews as examples of close communion between humanity and God. Al-Qur'an presents many of the biblical prophets as recipients of divine grace, as friends of God. With one or two exceptions they are all Jews—and those Jews are the heroes of the Qur'anic narration.

Al-Qur'an even exceeds Judaism by elevating David and Solomon to the rank of prophets. For Jews, David and Solomon are national heroes. They are, so to speak, the centerpiece of the Israelite pantheon. Millions of Muslims bear the names of David (Da'ud) and Solomon (Sulaiman). And what about Jesus? His name ('Isa) is more common among Muslims than among Christians. In the Hispanic world the name Jesus is not uncommon, but even that stands no comparison to the frequency of 'Isa with Muslims. Jesus was a Jew. Al-Qur'an speaks of him as a prophet to the Children of Israel, stressing his Jewishness rather than his universality.

Most important of all, Al-Qur'an explicitly speaks of the divine blessing upon Isaac, Jacob, and their offspring. The revelation also tells us how we are to understand those passages that speak of Jews negatively: "We gave her the glad tidings of Isaac, and after him, of Jacob" (11:71). "We gave him the good news of Isaac—a prophet—one of the righteous. We blessed him and Isaac. Of their progeny are some that do right and some who obviously wrong themselves" (37:112–113).

To pick out negative references to Jewish sinners as if those were God's teachings about an inherently evil people is a sin against the revelation. It is a distortion of the message enshrined in Al-Qur'an.

As for "the common man" in the Muslim world, he mostly is apprehensive of Jews because of news about attempts against the hallowed places in Palestine, especially the burning of Al-Aqsa Mosque, the massacre at the Dome of the Rock and the massacre at Abraham's shrine in Hebron. There is a widespread belief that Jews aim at creating a Greater Israel, stretching as far as to Medina in present-day Saudi Arabia. As mentioned above, in the Prophet's days part of Medina's population was Jewish, and this makes some Muslims believe that Medina is an object of Jewish vengefulness, an area Jews want to claim as their own. The irony of fate is that scarcely any Jews know the background to these fears, except for a few specialists of Islamic affairs.

These are roadblocks obstructing Jewish-Muslim dialogue. The important thing for Muslims is to spell out their fears, and for Jews to reflect upon them patiently. Those fears ought not be dismissed as fantasies of political propaganda. These issues need to be analyzed and addressed creatively, with positive assurances. Muslims need to listen to Jewish voices of reconciliation instead of imputing to Jews as a whole motives of which the vast majority are not even aware.[5]

Ethnic cleansing against the Bosnian people engendered a debate among Jews and Christians as to whether this was Holocaust or not. We Muslims do not insist in calling the destruction of Bosnia Holocaust, even though the parallels are obvious.[6] But we certainly feel consoled by the stand most Jewish organizations and many prominent individuals took in publicly denouncing those crimes against humanity as Holocaust, often in the face of opposition from those who would dispute the enormity of the crime in Bosnia or seek to minimize it, equating victim and aggressor, and averring that "all are the same and equally to blame."

Most Jews have unreservedly identified the suffering of the Muslim people of Bosnia with the suffering of the Jewish people. Jews were also in the forefront of humanitarian efforts in Bosnia. On April 6, 1995, the third anniversary of the start of fighting, when a pro-Bosnia demonstration took place on Capitol Hill, fifty percent of the participants were Jews, forty-five percent Muslims, and five percent Christians.

The Christian response has rarely been negative, but generally muted. The fact that the churches have failed to take a strong stand against the war between Orthodox Serbs and Catholics Croats, which led to the destruction of hundreds of churches, is little consolation for Muslims suffering the atrocities of both Croats and Serbs. The excuse proffered by governments for their inaction is shameful, both morally and intellectually. True, the conflict is hundreds of years old, but what political conflict does not have roots in history?

Dialogue should help us heal the wounds of the past and remain alert to the present. As Muslims we have to be more passionate in identifying with the sufferings of others and say "never again" to Holocaust. Human suffering is indivisible. The defense of human rights requires a common front of Jews, Christians, and Muslims.

An attentive reading of Al-Qur'an leaves no doubt that Muslims can under no circumstances remain indifferent to Holocaust. Our Sacred Scripture explicitly condemns the persecution of all believers and the destruction of human life. The passage that allows Muslims to resist persecution militarily is of utmost significance in this regard inasmuch as it mentions the destruction not just of mosques but of churches, monasteries, and synagogues.

"Permission to fight is given to those against whom war is made, because they are wronged. Surely God is able to help them. Those who have been expelled from their homes in defiance of right except that they say, 'Our Lord is God.' Had God not driven back one set of people by means of another there would surely have been pulled down monasteries, churches, synagogues, and mosques wherein God's name is much mentioned" (22:39).

It is an article of faith with us that not a single word in the holy text is incidental. In this particular verse churches, monasteries, and synagogues are mentioned even before mosques. Does this not tell us that we should make no distinction whether those persecuted are Jews, Christians, or Muslims?

Let us suppose at the time of the extermination of Jews at the hands of the Nazis there had been a strong Muslim power. Would it not have been the obligation of that Muslim power to intervene to save the Jews, the Gypsies, and other human masses from such slaughter? In Spain it used to be held against Jews that they were—supposedly—responsible for the Muslim conquest. From history we know that at the advent of Islam, Spain was experiencing one of the worst persecutions of Jews. According to the legend, some Jews turned for help to Muslims in Morocco. Muslims may have moved into Spain for many reasons, one of them was certainly to put an end to the persecution of Jews and Christians at the hands of the then dominant Church. It is not without reason that in its dark ages Catholic Spain treated Jews and Muslims as merely two sides of the same coin. Most Jews expelled from Spain settled in the world of Islam.

Against this background it is deplorable that the Holocaust should not have evoked a stronger response among Muslims. One would expect the film *Schindler's List* to be opposed by Neo-Nazis in Western Europe, not by leaders in the Muslim world. Such insensitivity makes one think of the widely appreciated contribution made to present-day Islamic thought by S. Muhammad Asad (Leopold Weiss), a Jewish convert to Islam. He lost his relatives in the Holocaust, and had he not happened to be in Arabia at that time, he himself would have suffered the same fate. Today many Muslims consider Asad's rendering of Al-Qur'an as the best English translation.[7] Dr. Hamid Marcus, another convert from Judaism, translated Al-Qur'an into German—only to die in a concentration camp, totally unsung in the Muslim world.[8] To the Nazis it did not matter whether he was a Christian or a Muslim, they regarded him as a Jew. Lately in Bosnia and Serbia, non-Muslims have been killed because one of their grandparents was a Muslim.

Professor Zuhdi Sharrabi (Zehdi Charrabé), a Sunni Muslim from Aleppo in Syria, managed to hide his Jewish wife and her mother in the heart of Berlin throughout the Nazi period—and refused ever to have his story told, because he felt that he had done nothing else than his most basic Islamic duty. The thriving Charrabé family he left behind in Berlin bears testimony to his Qur'anic ethics. A Bosnian Muslim woman sheltered a Jewish family in her Sarajevo home during the Nazi occupation. Fifty years later she received a special recognition for risking her life. The late Sultan Muhammad V resisted fierce pressure to have the Nazis' anti-Jewish laws enacted in Morocco.

These examples are here adduced as a kind of bridge to help Muslims on to a stronger identification with the Holocaust. From an Islamic perspective such a help should not be necessary, the teachings of Al-Qur'an being explicit on this point. The Arab-Israeli conflict over Palestine is no excuse for many Muslims' adopting a lame attitude with regard to the Holocaust.

Dialogue can help to sensitize Jews and Christians to our religious susceptibilities. It calls upon us to reciprocate by perceiving them the way they want to be perceived. There is much sense of hurt on all sides because each one sees the self-view distorted by the others. A primary function of dialogue is to alleviate this sense of hurt by accepting others as they want to be seen, not as we are used to seeing them, or as the vicissitudes of history have made us to imagine them to be.

For Reflection and Discussion

1. What is the sum total of numerous references to Jews (Children of Israel) in Al-Qur'an? Despite a conflictive start, the relations between Jews and Muslims have witnessed long periods of harmony. What reasoning makes it possible to overcome past conflicts and foster good relations?
2. Why is anti-Semitism irreconcilable with the message of Al-Qur'an?
3. The author quotes the Qur'anic passage: "To you your religion and to me mine." He says that this statement represented an affirmation of religious pluralism at the root of the earliest Muslim community in Medina. Do you believe that the foundation of your own religion affirms pluralism?
4. Would you want religious pluralism and freedom of religion to be affirmed by your nation? the community of nations? your religion? In what particular ways?

Roadblocks to Dialogue with Christians

While Christians spent the first three hundred years of their history as a persecuted minority, Muslims rose to political power almost during the lifetime of the Prophet. The abode of early Christendom were the Catacombs of Rome, that of early Islam the Caliphate of Baghdad. However, Muslims, too, started as a persecuted community in Mecca, where their fate was scarcely different from that of the early Christians in Jerusalem. Centuries later, once the seats of the Caliphate were taken, first Cordova, by the Castellans, then Baghdad by the Mongols, Muslims in many parts of the world were subjected to centuries of suffering at the hands of Christians, a long period of persecution that culminated in the seventy years of Communist rule when Islam became the prime target of a ferocious anti-religion policy.

Some of us see our entire history primarily under the aspect of that persecution. Others are unaware of the terrible fate their ancestors suffered. While Muslims should guard against a persecution complex, they need to know what Muslims have suffered just as much as they ought to know what others have suffered at the hands of Muslims. What other way is there to understand the human condition? Muslims need to be self-critical. They must desist from the widespread attitude of communalism at any price, that is to say, they must refrain from showing solidarity with those Muslims who commit crimes against humanity with the pretext of safeguarding Muslim interests. The worst such case is that of Sudan where some Islamists wage a ruthless war against African peoples on their ancestral lands—land that has never been Arab or Muslim.

Self-Righteousness or Naiveté?

There is general agreement among historians that the expansion of Muslim Empires was not accompanied by forceful conversions. The early Caliphate extended from Southern France to China in less than a hundred years, but it took centuries before a majority of inhabitants of the Middle East and North Africa adhered to the religion of Islam. Muslims take pride in the tolerance that allowed the conquered peoples to continue with their inherited faith.

European scholars have contrasted this Muslim tolerance favorably with intolerance in Christian Europe. In the tenth century there existed Muslim communities in the Hungarian Empire which comprised, *inter alia*, Bosnia. In the twelfth century, however, the Hungarian monarchy expelled Jews and Muslims, before this was done in Spain—and centuries before the first Ottoman Turk appeared in the Balkans.

Muslims have reason to be proud of the relative "modernity" of the Caliphate as a state with a semblance of pluralism. But this should not blind our eyes to the fact that Arab and Ottoman imperial rule was experienced as a foreign invasion by the conquered nations. The same applies to the rule of Muslim foreigners in India.

In several instances the Muslim invasion had aspects of a liberation of oppressed peoples—in Egypt, Persia, parts of India, and Spain. Elsewhere it was a traumatic experience for the peoples concerned. From Afghanistan, Sultan Mahmud Ghaznawi invaded India seventeen times, plundering and devastating Hindu temples.

The Ottoman conquest of Constantinople caused immense pain to Eastern Christianity. For Orthodox Christians of the surrounding countries, this was their capital. Constantinople's main cathedral, the *Hagia Sophia*, was to them what the Temple in Jerusalem was to Jews, or the Kaaba in Mecca to Muslims. This is not to be taken in a doctrinal sense, but in terms of symbolism and emotional attachment. Eastern Christianity has never overcome this loss of its capital city, just as many Muslims in North Africa and elsewhere are still bewailing the loss of the Grand Mosque of Cordova, which was turned into a cathedral after the Castilian conquest of Andalusia.

The conquest of Constantinople was neither a political necessity nor a strategic exigency. It was but lust for glory. The Ottomans could have left the old city with its churches untouched as a Greek island and built their new capital next to it—as the French did later on in Morocco.

The Ottoman conquest of Eastern Europe was not experienced as a liberation by the nations affected. Albanians, Bosnians, Bulgarians, Croats, Greeks, Hungarians, Rumanians, Serbs, almost all of them resisted the advancing Caliphal army. This fifteenth century conquest was little different from the Soviet invasion of Afghanistan in 1979.

Today the Muslims of Bosnia are paying the price of the hatred Eastern Christians developed against Islam as a result of Ottoman rule which they experienced as a foreign yoke.

It is of little use to point out to certain progressive aspects of Ottoman administration in the fifteenth and sixteenth centuries when non-Muslims could rise to key positions in a multinational state. As Muslims we must learn to view the situation of non-Muslims under Muslim rule through their eyes, not ours. There is no point in insisting, as our apologetic literature does, that non-Muslims enjoyed full freedom and had the same rights as Muslims. The Balkan peoples never wanted to be subjected to Ottoman rule in the first place, even if that brought certain advantages to some of them. Today a majority of Albanians are Muslims, but their ancestors were the ones who resisted the Ottoman invasion most fiercely.

The fact that they did not have to convert to Islam does not impress peoples of Southeastern Europe. They credit themselves with having resisted considerable pressure to do so. The Serb nobility converted to Islam and today's Serbs aver that it was the steadfastness of their Church that helped them preserve their identity after they were "abandoned" by their aristocracy. Incidentally, that Serb nobility partly merged with the Bosnians, with the result that today many Serbs regard every Bosnian Muslim as a descendant of those "traitors."

In short, Muslims must make serious efforts to understand and honor the pain of peoples who feel that they, their forebears, have suffered terribly from "us," from the ancestors of some of us. We need not accept all the anti-Muslim myths of Greeks and Serbs—many of which are spurious, but we ought to shed the self-righteousness that characterizes our reading of history all too often. The notion that conquering Muslims were greeted everywhere as liberators is a myth.

After the British crushed the national uprising in India in 1857 and consolidated their rule, thousands of Christian missionaries flocked into the country. The colonial administrators did not always aid them directly, and there were no forced conversions to Christianity. Many Muslims felt safer than before, because in some parts of India they had suffered oppression by Hindus and Sikhs. Under the British, Islamic practice was not hindered in any way. But Muslims were ill-prepared to meet the challenge of better educated missionaries, with the result that tens of thousands converted to Christianity. This caused deep resentment, comparable to the resentment of Greeks and Bulgarians who "lost" masses of their coreligionists to Islam after the establishment of Ottoman rule.

The same resentment is felt by many Hindus with regard to the so-called voluntary conversion of millions of Indians to Islam after Muslims triumphed militarily. Few Muslims are prepared to acknowledge the parallels. Admittedly the issue is complex, but Muslims have yet to muster the courage to look at this history self-critically. Professor Badawi, an Islamic scholar from Egypt who is teaching in Britain, has suggested a lecture tour of India to apologize to Hindus for the misdeeds of Muslim conquerors in the past. Hopefully such initiatives will multiply.

Recognizing the Prophethood of Muhammad (p)

Dialogue, as defined by Leonard Swidler in his path-breaking *Dialogue Decalogue* (see Chapter Two: The Dialogue Decalogue), does not aim at leveling differences or forging unity among religions by way of syncretism. The aim is to understand the other and to respect his or her position. This is comparatively easy where belief systems are concerned that are very different from ours, such as Buddhism and Hinduism. Should we discover that a certain tribe of American Indians held beliefs similar to those of Islam, we still would have no problem with the differences because there is no historical dispute at the root of our religions.

Things are different with Jews, and especially with Christians. As Muslims, we recognize the biblical prophets; they are our own. Jesus (p) is recognized as one of those prophets. His mother, Mary, is honored by Islam like no other woman; an entire chapter of Al-Qur'an is devoted to her (Sura 19—Maryam). As Muslims we understand that our recognition of Jesus as a prophet is a far cry from believing in Jesus as God incarnate. But we do recognize Judaism and Christianity in a very special way. Al-Qur'an treats them almost at par with ourselves.

For this reason it has always saddened Muslims to see that this is a unilateral recognition, that there is no reciprocity. Muhammad (p) and Al-Qur'an have no place in Jewish or Christian theology. Logically speaking they cannot have one, because Islam as a religious community—is roughly six hundred years younger than Christianity. Jewish and Christian scriptures contain no reference to Islam. Muslims, though, love to understand some cryptic allusions in the Bible as prophecies foretelling the advent of Muhammad (p).

This is undoubtedly an imbalance. One among three persons tells the other two, "I know you, you are my predecessors." But those two do not regard themselves as out of office. They see themselves still in charge. To them, the successor is an impostor. Number three, however, has no reason to regard himself as an impostor; he sees himself confirmed in his role as a successor, confirmed in so many ways. To him, the lack of recognition on the part of his predecessors is nothing but grudge.

Since the 1970s, serious efforts have been expended, especially by the Catholic Church, to come to terms with this issue. Muhammad (p), it has been said, can be recognized as a prophet standing in the tradition of the Hebrew Bible prophets among whom there were non-Jews such as Hiob (Ayyub). This position has not been ratified by the Vatican, but it is openly subscribed to by several leading dignitaries of the Church and by many Catholics actively engaged in interreligious dialogue.

Some Jewish theologians, too, subscribe to this vision of Muhammad (p). In fact, the position has its origin with the medieval Jewish theologian Maimonides of Cordova. In other words, Muhammad (p) is recognized not the way Muslims view him, that is, as the "Seal of the Prophets," but as a prophet among others, which is a revolutionary step away from the traditional Christian position that he was a "false prophet."

Also regarding the recognition of Muhammad's prophethood, most Muslims fail to see that Christians do not make as much of prophethood as we Muslims do. For us the position of a prophet (*nabi*) is the highest a human being can attain to. From our point of view Jesus (p) could not be honored more than he is in Al-Qur'an where he has a rank equal to that of Muhammad (p). To many Christians this does not mean much. First of all, they regard Jesus as totally exceptional, as an incarnation of the divine. Second, even those Christians who regard Jesus as more human than divine, still do not regard prophethood as so exceptional as Muslims do. We ostracize a sect that claims its founder was a prophet in the metaphorical sense only, in the shadow of Muhammad.[9]

Many Christians fail to understand what the fuss is about. In a metaphorical sense all kinds of people are called prophet all the time. Non-Muslims have difficulties understanding our sensitivities in this matter. One has to be familiar with the very special sanctity the term prophet (*nabi*) acquired in Islam. In our theology the word *nabi* has become a highly technical term.

This notwithstanding, through the ages there have been Christian scholars of Islam who understood our sensitivities—and felt that they, as faithful Christians, could recognize Muhammad as a prophet. Among those were Timothy, a Patriarch of the Nestorian Church in Syria, Bede the Venerable, Abelard, Nicolas Cusanus, one of the first translators of Al-Qur'an into Latin, Juan de Segovia, Louis Massignon, a twentieth century French Arabist and clergyman, Roger Arnaldez, a renowned professor of Islamic Studies, and many other learned men of the Church.[10]

This revision, if made public and official, would relieve an ancient Muslim grievance to a large extent. But what about similar grievances Jews and Christians have with regard to Islam? Christians, especially Catholics, are offended by Muslims doubting their monotheism. They believe in Jesus (p) as the Son of God, forming the Holy Trinity together with God the Father and the Holy Spirit, but they do not conceive of the Trinity as a belief in three Gods. They insist that their God is one, though he has three major aspects of manifesting Godself.

One should think that this issue could be resolved by Muslims, because Trinity, as explained above, is not essentially different from the Muslim belief in the attributes of God, his "beautiful names." We speak of the ninety-nine names or attributes of God; why should others not reduce those to three major ones? We feel that the large number helps us understand that we are dealing with attributes of one and the same being, not with several different beings. But in principle we should have no difficulty in accepting that with Christians the belief in the Trinity is not polytheism, but a particular form of trying to understand the One God and of being near to him. Besides, the way Al-Qur'an speaks of Christians as "People of the Book" makes it plain enough that our revelation accepts them as monotheists, otherwise there would not be that clear distinction between the "People of the Book" and the idol-worshiper. Al-Qur'an could not be more explicit on this point:

> Yet they are not all alike: some of the People of the Book stand for the right, they recite God's signs in the watches of the night, bowing themselves, believing in God and in the Last Day. They enjoin what is right and forbid what is wrong, vying with one another in good works: those are righteous. Of the good that they do, nothing will be rejected. God knows the godfearing (3:109).

The Challenge of Supersessionism and Ethical Competition

More difficult is the grievance Christians, and especially Jews, have with regard to our notion of religious evolution. Darwinism or no Darwinism, Al-Qur'an teaches us a history of religions with an upward development from Adam via Noah and Abraham to Moses and Jesus, and finally to Muhammad. The notion seems to be in tune with biblical statements such as "the light of the just shineth forth and forth until the perfect day."

Implicitly, and sometimes explicitly, this tells Jews and Christians that they are out of date. They feel looked down upon as belonging to a bygone age, as fossils of religious history. Can we free them of this feeling? Not easily, because we believe that their revelations have been handed down incomplete and that those establishments, the Jewish and the Christian religions, have been superseded by a new enterprise, all-comprehensive and well preserved. This is basic to our self-understanding as Muslims. They feel offended by our supersessionist attitude.

One way to overcome such Jewish or Christian misgivings is to rely on passages in Al-Qur'an that speak of a pious competition between the three of us: *fastabiqu l-khairat*—"compete with one another in good deeds!"[11] As long as the ethical test remains the ultimate criterion, Jews and Christians will feel accepted as partners and not just as old-fashioned models that ought to be discarded. Most Jews would expect their Christian partners in dialogue to avoid supersessionist language. Can we Muslims do the same? Or does our religious identity depend on the supersessionist argument?

Taken to its logical conclusion, the concept of a moral test assigns a role to Jews and Christians even after the coming of Jesus. God has not disqualified them, and religious history has not overtaken them. The moral test requires us Muslims to attempt understanding the other without triumphalism. The moral imperative makes it incumbent upon us to recognize other believers as persons of God.

For Reflection and Discussion

1. Muslims view Jesus as: a mouthpiece (*nabi*) for God; a messenger (*rasul*) from God; son of the virgin Mary; someone who followed in a line of prophets including Adam, Moses, and David; Messiah of the Jews; the one who will come again at the final Day of Judgment. Are these beliefs compatible with Christianity?
2. Can Jesus be a means of commonality between Christians and Muslims, or are differing views about him a stumbling block to Christian-Muslim dialogue? Explain your answers.
3. Is there any window by which Christians might view Muhammad as a prophet?
4. Do you think that Christians are more likely to accept Buddha as an "enlightened being" than Muhammad as a prophet? Explain.

CHAPTER SIXTEEN

Defining Ourselves Favorably and Others Unfavorably

The development from *islam* into Islam, from a principle of faith into a social reality, entailed distinctions based on comparisons, comparisons that had to be favorable to Muslims and unfavorable to Jews and Christians. Based on the Prophet's experience with the Jews of Medina, Jews came to be seen as self-conceited. They felt special and had no desire to share this specialness with others, except when those others joined them by giving up their own identity. Al-Qur'an picks up the thread of biblical history and concedes to Jews a very special position in God's plan of salvation. Muhammad (p) is neither taken out of context nor is he placed in a historical tradition separate from that of the biblical prophets. His mission is inextricably linked to those of Moses and Jesus, who are venerated as his colleagues and predecessors.

The Jews of Medina scoffed at Muhammad (p) as a Prophet of the Goyim—*ummiyin* in Arabic. The term *ummi* has the connotation of "illiterate" and became a term of pride with the rejected ones, so much so that Muslims venerate Muhammad (p) as *an-nabi al-ummi*, "the prophet who could neither read nor write" but enunciated the literary masterpiece of all times, Al-Qur'an. Many are not aware that the term *ummiyin* (*qoyim*) has a history of its own, but they are aware that the Prophet (p) was ridiculed because he was supposedly illiterate. Muhammad's reading capacity was certainly rudimentary and he was able to write hardly more than his name, but that only enhances his prestige in Muslim eyes, because it makes Al-Qur'an a miracle all the more: such a masterpiece cannot come from an illiterate, therefore it is divine.

Muslims see Muhammad's advent foretold by Moses who spoke of "a prophet from amongst your brethren," which Muslims understand as a reference to the Ishmaelites (Arabs) as the brethren of the Israelites (Jews). The

Jews of Medina disputed this, causing Muslims to believe that Jews distorted their own scriptures in order to maintain a monopolistic claim on revelation. Hence the conviction that whereas Al-Qur'an is authentic, the Bible is not, that it has been interpolated.

The Two Extremes—Must They Be Jews and Christians?

Jews in particular take offense at the interpretation of our prayer—*Suratu l-Fatiha* (The Opening Chapter)—according to which the phrase "those upon whom is your wrath" refers to them. The text of the prayer is: "Lead us the straight path, the path of those upon whom You have bestowed Your bounty, not those upon whom is Your wrath, nor those who go astray."

The Jews of Medina do not seem to have been given to spirituality, with the resultant image of Jews as overly this-worldly and materialistic. Muhammad (p) experienced them as deviators from the path of God, as having transgressed from the right course prescribed by the Almighty. Later commentators saw them as "those on whom there is the wrath of God" (*al-maghdub 'alaihim*).

By contrast, Christians were experienced as almost the opposite, as overly otherworldly, as off track in what was regarded as their exaggerated veneration for Prophet Jesus (p), going to such an extreme as to take the honorific title "Son of God" literally as meaning that Jesus (p) was part of God, God incarnate in human flesh and blood. Later commentators wrote that it is the Christians whom Al-Qur'an rebukes for having gone astray (*ad-dalin*) in their love of Jesus (p), compromising the very principle of monotheism, the strict belief in One God with whom nothing is to be associated.[1]

In the Prophet's time some Christians thought of Trinity as consisting not of the Father, Son, and Holy Spirit, but as Father, Mother (Mary), and Son, making it appear as if Christians did not believe in One God but in a divine family.

Seventh-century Arabia was the favorite refuge for Christian hermits of various denominations. Many of them were spiritualists who found repugnant the Christian societies of Syria and Byzantium, of Egypt and Ethiopia. One might call them dropouts of imperial Christianity with its endless doctrinal feuds and theological squabbles.

Muhammad (p) met and discussed with quite a few of them and was favorably impressed by their piety but felt that they had fallen into another extreme. He thus had two disparate images of Christians: one was the imperial one, the aggressive Christianity of the Roman Empire that insisted upon everybody's subscribing to the doctrines of the Church. The other was that of Christian dissidents who were kind to the Arab in search of truth and encouraged him when he had his call to prophethood. When persecution of the early community in Mecca became unbearable, the Prophet (p) sent a number of his followers to Christian Ethiopia, where the ruler (*Negus*) received them warmly, as spiritual kin.

Muhammad (p) envisioned his new community as one treading the *via media*, the Aristotelian middle path, which he expressed in Arabic as *khairu l-umuri ausatuha*—"the best course is the middle course." Al-Qur'an speaks of Muslims as a community in the middle, one between the extremes of Judaism and Christianity as perceived in the days of the Prophet, neither too this-worldly nor too otherworldly: "Thus have We made of you a community justly balanced, that you might be witnesses over the nations" (2:143).[2]

Muslims tend to absolutize these images as if they were eternal and everlasting. Not many of us show an awareness of the fact that a similar split—into this worldliness and other-worldliness—occurred in the Muslim community itself and continues to this very day.

After the rapid expansion of Muslim rule over a large part of the world, the Caliphate became exceedingly powerful, and imperial Muslim society immensely rich. Soon there arose a movement of social protest against the boisterous materialism of a new class of Muslims. This was a movement of asceticism, of people who shunned the Caliphal court and retreated to provincial towns in order to flee the sinfulness of the capital (Damascus, Baghdad, Cordova), and other imperial cities.

The Prophet (p) had ordered that silk and gold be reserved for women. Men should dress simpler in order to avoid class distinctions. But in the capital cities high society broke those rules. In protest against such indulgence the pious began to wear garments of coarse wool (*suf*), and this was the beginning of Sufism, often translated as Islamic mysticism. Later many Sufis provoked the authorities by concentrating their veneration on Jesus (p), till one of them, Mansur Al-Hallaj, claimed to be identical with the divine truth and had himself crucified in Baghdad in 922. Others began venerating Muhammad (p) in a way indistinguishable from the Christian worship of Jesus (p), except for the formulation of doctrine. Muhammad (p) was not made part of the Godhead, but some Sufis endowed him with all kinds of divine qualities. The pendulum swings back and forth. What were once considered characteristics of Jews and Christians have long since become characteristics of Muslims themselves.

To sum up, there is no compelling reason to narrow the contents of our prayer—*Suratu l-Fatiha*—down in such a way that it be understood as a negative reference to Jews and Christians. Generally we follow the opposite tendency by taking passages out of Al-Qur'an that have a clear point of historical reference, detach them from those narrow confines and endow them with much more general applicability. In the present case of our prayer—*Suratu l-Fatiha*—some commentators have done the opposite. They have taken a passage with a very broad and general applicability and unduly restricted it to Jews and Christians.

The vast majority of Muslims who learn this prayer are not taught about any particular reference to Jews and Christians. Most are unaware of such an interpretation, to the extent that they find it hard to believe if told about such commentaries. There are more than enough human beings, Muslims and others, who incur the wrath of God or who go astray. And we ask God to keep us away from the path of those.

Of all the verses of Al-Qur'an, the opening Chapter is the least time-bound and the most general in applicability. The historical context knew all kinds of people who had incurred the wrath of God or gone astray, both in the lifetime of the Prophet (p) and before. There were, first and foremost, the idolatrous clansmen of Muhammad (p) who had incurred the wrath of God, and there were Companions of his who had gone astray.

To take those two categories as references primarily to Jews and Christians is a notion born out of the historical antagonisms subsequent to the revelation. We can dispense with this one-sided interpretation without compunction. Certainly, there are Jews who incur the wrath of God and there are Christians who go astray, but so are there Muslims.

Muslim Supremacism versus Western Imperialism

Muslims reject the Jewish notion of chosenness without giving themselves account of how strong this notion is among ourselves. Al-Qur'an speaks of Muslims as "the best community ever brought forth for the benefit of humankind" (3:110). True, this is not meant in any ethnic sense, but it has long since acquired a communal connotation, as if any Muslim were better than a non-Muslim simply because he is a Muslim.

Such a non-superior view vis-a-vis non-Muslims is unacceptable to Islamists who insist that adherents of Islam are automatically superior to others, demanding that Jews and Christians be put in their place as was done during certain periods in the Ottoman Empire. 'Abdullah 'Azzam, an Islamist who led an Arab Legion into battle in Afghanistan, never tired of extolling those glorious days when any Britisher, Bulgarian, Frenchman, Greek, or Russian would be referred to as *kafir* (infidel). Some Ottoman officials would not admit any other classification but that of Muslim and *kafir*.[3] It is not enough for us to debunk such *jihadism*[4] as deviant. We need to challenge it as un-Islamic, openly and ceaselessly.

Some Islamists make the cause of any Muslim anywhere in the world their own, no matter whether those Muslims are the aggressors or the aggressed. Sometimes they espouse the cause of Muslims who do not want them to espouse their cause. For example, most Bosnian Muslims did not want the cause of Bosnia to be turned into an issue of Christian-Muslim conflict, because that only served the purpose of their tormentors. Serb militarists sought to camouflage their land-grabbing in Bosnia by claiming that they were defending Europe against Islam. But many Christians have fought all along on the side of the Bosnian government. General Jovan Zivjak, the heroic defender of Sarajevo, is an Orthodox Christian (a Serb, according to the Serbs). Bosnians, Muslims, and Christians alike, fought for a pluralist society against Serb expansionism which used a religion without faith as a shield for its rapacity.

All the same, Islamists championed the cause of Bosnia, just as they championed the cause of Northern Sudan, despite the fact that in Sudan the Arabized Muslim North is the aggressor, the Christianized African South the aggressed. Northern Sudan pursues a policy of "ethnic cleansing" against the indigenous population of southern Sudan and Darfur. In Bosnia Muslims were the victims of genocide; in Sudan and Darfur Muslims are the perpetrators of genocide. Conscientious Muslims have joined the Southerners in their defense against Northern supremacists, among them military officers and a former Foreign Minister of Sudan. They are the equivalent to the Christians in Bosnia who fight on the government side against Serb aggression. But Islamists do not distinguish. They mention Bosnia, Sudan, and Darfur in one breath, because for them Muslims are always right, others always wrong. (This *jihadism* of course was extended in its extreme form in Iraq where al Zaqari and his al-

Qaida and Baathist cohorts delight in blowing up not so much American military as other Muslim Iraqis who do not agree with their ideology.)

This attitude is strangely contradictory, because the same Islamists are also the first to declare other Muslims as unbelievers simply because they differ with them on one or the other score. One of the major characteristics of Islamism is the recourse to *takfir*, that is, to declare a Muslim opponent a *kafir*. A somewhat rough but helpful translation of *takfir* would be "excommunication." This is noteworthy in view of the fact that according to Islamic tenets *takfir* is a major sin.[5] Muslims are prohibited from declaring other Muslims as unbelievers because it is next to impossible to prove that somebody is not a Muslim as long as he insists on being one.

Important in the present context is that despite their proclivity for *takfir*, Islamists postulate a near-automatic superiority of Muslims over non-Muslims. They derive this notion from a rigid interpretation of Islamic law, the *Shari'a*, but the underlying consideration is that of moral excellence over depravity.

Today most Muslims find it hard to believe that such discrimination as idealized by the ardent Islamist 'Abdullah 'Azzam in his ruminations about the Ottoman Empire ever existed. We tend to cherish a highly romantic notion of the equality enunciated by Islam. In part this is our strength, for as long as we subscribe to this ideal, there is hope for reality. Islamists such as 'Azzam subscribe to a different ideal, one that eventuates in self-defeat.

For the majority of Muslims the difficult task is to hold on to the ideal while at the same time being self-critical as far as our reality is concerned. The phenomenon of 'Azzam's *jihadism* illustrates that residues of our historical supremacist attitude persist and surface every now and then. In the case of 'Azzam and his Islamists, this is strident and easily detectable. More often our supremacist past surges within us imperceptibly.

Overall, most Muslims sincerely believe that we are more accommodating, peaceful, and tolerant than Jews and Christians, that our record compares favorably with theirs. A basic fallacy is that we tend to hold our ideals against their reality. The fact that many of them do the same should not deter us from being more self-critical.

Western Licentiousness

A major issue is that of sexual mores. There is a widespread tendency to regard "the West" as morally corrupt, and to allege that moral corruption spreading in the Muslim world is due to the Western impact. More or less fifty percent of Islamist literature is devoted to this subject, but non-Islamist Muslims are not immune to such thinking. In fact, this is the one issue where Islamists do not stand outside the mainstream of Muslim thought. A majority of Muslims reject Islamist stringency, often vehemently, and doubt whether Islamists are any better than others. All the same, the notion that "the West" is morally depraved is shared by many.

In 1973 a film was produced in Pakistan that became the prototype for an entire new genre in the film industry. The film was titled *Tahdhib*, which in Urdu stands for "civilization." The reference is not to civilization as such, but to morally corrupt Western civilization. A young couple from Pakistan spends some time in England where they begin to drink and commit adultery. Fed up with such a life of sinfulness they return home to start again in purity, not without passing via Arabia where they shed tears of repentance at the Hallowed Places.

The essential point is the near-inevitability of sinfulness in the utterly depraved West. And the West is so bad because Christians do not uphold the same lofty moral standards as Muslims do, Jews even less. Islam uncompromisingly rejects premarital sex, extramarital sex, and homosexuality. But what about Muslims? When Arabs rape their domestic servants from South Asia, the blame is put on the oil wealth and its corrupting Western influences. History, however, tells us that this is an old story. Moral depravity existed long before the oil wealth, not more and not less than in other societies. Most religions are grappling with the same universal issues of human nature.

Many Muslims live in the West without going into the depth of Western societies. There is no dearth of Muslims who live in "the West" and have a profound understanding of "the West," but they tend to disregard the others as irrelevant fanatics. The larger the Muslim presence in the West becomes and the more interaction takes place, the more superficial this interaction seems to become. This, at least, is the impression one gets in Islamist circles. A closer look reveals that the situation is much more promising than might appear at first sight. Still, a fairly large segment of Muslims takes recourse to stereotypes and chooses to insulate itself against the Western environment.

As far as business and politics are concerned, people from the Muslim world have penetrated right to the core of "the West" and become compatible with any other segment of American society. But has their sociological understanding kept pace?

The first Muslim intellectuals who spent some years in European countries had the knack of making in-depth studies of Western societies, such as Sayyid Ahmad Khan of India, and Rifa'a At-Tahtawi of Egypt, both in the nineteenth century. Tahtawi, an Islamic scholar, spent four years in France, during which he learned more about Western societies and cultures than others had learned in thirty years or more. His opposite was an Egyptian too, the playwright Sayyid Qutb, who spent three years in the United States in the early 1950s. His vituperations make pathetic reading. He leaves no doubt that his stay in America mainly served the purpose of seeking confirmation for his prejudices and lending credibility to fantasies he was bent on spreading anyhow.[6]

Muslims need to take stock of the moral decrepitude that has become a common feature of many Muslim societies. We need to analyze the local causes that lie at the root of such developments. In some countries, Muslim scholars and the media make admirable contributions in this regard. What needs to be intensified is the sociological study of "the West" in order to rid Muslim imagery of the stereotype of Jews and Christians as nothing but depraved, as scapegoats on which to blame all ills of society. This two-pronged approach is a necessity not only for interreligious dialogue, but is also of extreme importance for social reform in many Muslim societies currently in a deep moral crisis.

Dehumanizing Technology

Muslims love to accuse the Jewish-Christian West of a lack of humanity, saying we want the progress based on technology but without sacrificing humanity, we want technology with a human face. And yet, there is nothing anywhere in the Muslim world even remotely resembling such endeavors as the Rosenstock-Huessy Society in Europe, a society unknown in the Muslim world. Rosenstock-Huessy was a Christian, born a Jew. As a sociologist he devoted his life to giving technology a human face. He was lucky in finding much cooperation at Daimler-Benz, the company that produces Mercedes cars. Rosenstock-Huessy and his disciples experimented for many years with the aim of ameliorating the lot of factory workers, with considerable success. Their efforts centered on improving conditions at the place of work by humanizing the process of production. Early on they recognized the dehumanizing effect of technology on workers who are forced to become like cogs in a machine.

Rosenstock-Huessy and others made great strides in giving technology a human face long before this became an issue in the Muslim world. In other words, Muslims often treat Jews and Christians unjustly by contrasting a "spiritual East" with a "materialist West." The fallacy of such comparisons, favorable to Muslims and unfavorable to Jews and Christians, was pointed out by Ahmad Amin, an Islamic scholar in Egypt back in 1948 when he published a treatise devoted to this subject entitled *Ash-Sharq wa l-Gharb* ("East and West"). Lesser minds have published hundreds of books perpetuating the stereotype of a "materialist West" versus a "spiritual East," and of Jewish-Christian immorality versus Muslim sexual purity.

The Imam of an African-American mosque in Louisiana, himself a convert to Islam, has understood much better that the essential divisions in a pluralist society are no longer those of Jews, Christians, and Muslims, but those between people with a religious vision and a moral commitment and those who do not share that vision. He sends his daughter to a Catholic school. He takes care of her instruction in matters of religious doctrine; for the rest, the Catholic school is what he wishes an Islamic school to be.

As mentioned earlier, Al-Qur'an calls us "the best community ever brought forth for the benefit of humankind." This extraordinary distinction is not to be understood as a positive appraisal. It is not as if the Almighty had given us an "A" grade. We had better understand this verse as a moral *imperative.* We have been granted the potential to be the best, and God tells us that this is what God wants us to strive for. We Muslims should aspire to this role and make this distinction a reality. For Al-Qur'an also tells us that should we not be up to the mark, God would replace us with another people. Jews will easily recognize this teaching as biblical.

Irving Greenberg, an Orthodox rabbi from New York, explains the Jewish concept of chosenness very much along these lines. To him, as to many other teachers of the Mosaic religion, chosenness is not so much a privilege as it is an obligation. God has assigned believers a difficult task. Some ask, not without reason, "why us?"

To sum up, we might say that both Jews and Muslims are assigned by their holy Scriptures an honorable position, a charge with great moral responsibility, at the risk of being sacked if we do not meet those high expectations.

For Reflection and Discussion

1. What are some examples of the historical legacy that creates roadblocks to interreligious dialogue among the Abrahamic faiths?
2. All members of a particular religion do not speak with one voice. For example, are the Christian Bible, the Torah, or Al-Qur'an literally true? Disagreement exists on these questions within religious communities themselves. Frequently, internal disagreements on religious matters are the most heated and contentious. What is your opinion on this question?
3. Do liberal-minded Muslims have more in common with fundamentalist-leaning fellow Muslims or with liberals in other religious communities? Apply this same question to Jews, Catholics, and Protestants.
4. Explore this question in regard to specific issues. For instance, would liberal-minded women feel more at home among liberal-minded women from other traditions than with fundamentalist women in their own religious community? Would the same be true for gay men and lesbian women? Advocates of capital punishment, abortion rights, and pre-marital sex?

CHAPTER SEVENTEEN

Attitude of the Churches toward Muslims

Some years ago, when Pope John Paul II visited France, *Le Monde*, the country's leading daily newspaper, requested the Moroccan writer Tahar Benjelloun to comment upon the visit. Aside from being an illustrious novelist, Benjelloun also is a prominent spokesman for the Muslim diaspora. Delighted to welcome the Holy Father, Benjelloun pointed out the fact that in Western Europe the Church has become a sign of hope for Muslims. Church buildings have even been turned into sanctuaries in the literal sense, since as a number of times Muslim immigrants had to take refuge in a church to escape being expelled from the country. The case of several hundred Moroccans finding shelter in a Dutch church, a case that made headlines in 1985, was only the most publicized example. Various church bodies grant scholarships to Muslim students and many hostels are run by the Churches who perform countless other charitable deeds.

In his welcome to the pope, Benjelloun highlighted a fact that seems to be common to most countries in the West: While political parties and trade unions failed the new workforce from the Muslim world, the Churches proved their mettle, buried the hatchet of ancient Christian-Muslim rivalry, and came to the rescue of the "stranger in the land."

All the same, there is as yet little awareness among the broader masses of Muslims of the profound changes Church attitudes have undergone with regard to Islam. The 1975 Assembly of the World Council of Churches in Nairobi emphasized "dialogue in community," defining it as:

> dialogue with our neighbors of other faiths in the communities we as Christians share with them, exploring such issues as peace, justice, and humanity's relation to nature. We have found repeatedly that

> Christians may not behave as if we were the only people of faith as we face common problems of an interdependent world. It is evident that the various religious traditions of the world have much to contribute in wisdom and inspiration toward solving these problems.[1]

This "dialogue in community" was reaffirmed in the *Guidelines to Dialogue*, published in 1979, that speak of a "common adventure" of believers:

> Today our greater awareness and appreciation of religious plurality leads us to move toward a more adequate theology of religions. There is widely felt need for such a theology, for without it Christians remain ill-equipped to understand the profound religious experiences which they witness in the lives of people of other faiths or to articulate their own experience in a way that will be understood by people of other faiths.... We see the plurality of religious traditions as both the result of the manifold ways in which God has related to peoples and nations as well as a manifestation of the richness and diversity of humankind. We affirm that God has been present in their seeking and finding, that where there is truth and wisdom in their teachings, and love and holiness in their living, this like any wisdom, insight, knowledge, understanding, love, and holiness that is found among us is the gift of the Holy Spirit.[2]

This position is reminiscent of the history of many a Muslim theologian on becoming acquainted with other religious traditions. Many of the early Muslims thought of all religions other than Judaism and Christianity as idol worship. In the sixth century, Zoroastrianism, the ancient religion of Iran, had lost much of its original dynamism and had become distorted by a decadent society. Its priesthood served the interests of an oppressive landed gentry. To Muslims it all looked like fire-worship and black magic. After becoming familiar with centers of Zoroastrian learning and studying this prophetic religion more closely, Islamic scholars discovered many an affinity between the teachings of Zoroaster and those of Muhammad (p). They realized that Zoroastrianism originated with a prophet of God who received revelations. Accordingly, those Islamic scholars began to count Zoroastrians as "People of the Book" at par with Jews and Christians. It was a belated decision, and it never found unanimous approval. Nonetheless, it shows Islam's potential for dialogue and Muslims' recognition of wisdom and piety in other religious traditions.

Al-Qur'an speaks repeatedly of the equality of believers in the One God, mentioning monotheists outside the Jewish/Christian/Muslim purview, such as the Sabeans,[3] and expressly states that God sent a messenger to every nation (10:47; 16:36). Some of these messengers are mentioned in Al-Qur'an by name (those with whom the people of the area were familiar), but it is also pointed out that there were others not mentioned by name: "We sent messengers before you. There are some whose story We have related to you, and some whose story We have not related" (Al-Qur'an 40:78).

Proceeding from these Qur'anic teachings, Islamic scholars in India repeated what others had done earlier in Iran—they recognized sections of the Hindus as "People of the Book" on the basis of their belief in Krishna, whom those scholars came to recognize as a prophet, and his book, the *Bhagavad Gita*, as a revelation from God.

To be sure, the attitude of the Churches toward Muslims are not uniform. Positions are different not only from Church to Church, but within each denomination itself the attitudes of individual clergymen can differ starkly. Some of this has to do with local conditions and developments. In some places the attitude is extraordinarily positive, for example in Scandinavia and Spain. By contrast, in Croatia the attitude of some Catholic clergy toward Muslims has been outright criminal recently, displaying hatred without any tangible provocation on the part of the Muslims—historical myths apart.

In like manner, the attitude of Muslims toward the Churches tends to differ starkly, from place to place and occasion to occasion. Turkish laborers in Germany were furious on discovering that the government withheld Church taxes from their wages, following the law in some European countries where every citizen pays taxes to his or her respective Church. Factory managers often did not know what religion their new Turkish laborers were and registered them simply as Catholics or Protestants. It was not difficult to correct this mistake and have the Turks exempted from the Church tax. Once it was explained to them what positive work the Churches are doing on behalf of many Muslims, they no longer minded the loss incurred.

Such instances illustrate the necessity of trust that needs to be built up patiently, a trust that cannot come about by means of information only. Just as many Christians are full of prejudices regarding Muslims, many Muslims are haunted by a memory of bitter experiences with Christians, though mostly those were not their own experiences but experiences of their forebears and other Muslims.

Oddbjørn Leirvik, a clergyman in Oslo, was deeply touched on discovering that the immigrant family sweeping his large church building always did so by taking off their shoes. Without giving it a thought he had employed Muslims from Morocco. He tried to make them understand that there was no need to take off their shoes in a church, but they insisted that a house of God was a house of God. If his parishioners did not take off their shoes, bad enough; they, as Muslims, would not commit such a sacrilege. "Idolaters—God shall distinguish between them on the Day of Resurrection; assuredly God is witness over everything."

In countries of Western Europe, it is not uncommon to hear clergymen admonish their parishioners to take Muslim immigrants as an example of piety. "Forget about differences of ritual," they say, "your Turkish neighbors may appear strange to you, but they can serve as a reminder of what faith is, of what religion is all about." Some have gone so far as to say "let us borrow the Islam-car to recharge the battery of our car."

Some Muslims are filled with pride on hearing such comments. Others reflect and ask if it is not the other way around sometimes. Can our charitable institutions compare with those of Jews and Christians? There are more than a hundred Muslim millionaires in Chicago alone. Some of them help finance extremist groups, hoping to remain in the good books of the tough guys should those rise to power in one country or another. But what about educational institutions? What academic foundations can Muslim students rely on? On the positive side, recently (after 9/11/2001!) A group of wealthy Turkish Muslims in Chicago, inspired by the Turkish Sufi Muslim Fetullah Gülen, launched the Niagara Foundation, which is devoted to fostering interreligious dialogue.

Oddbjørn Leirvik studied Islam and is today in charge of relations between Norway's Lutheran Church and the country's Muslim community. Like many of his colleagues in other countries, clergy in charge of public relations with local Muslim communities, he complains about a lack of interest among Church leaders. Of late, many Churches have apparently become more inward looking and see less urgency in interaction with people of other faiths. In addition, an increasing number of Church leaders complain about a lack of Muslim reciprocity and point to restrictions on the practice of Christian rites in Arabia, or increasing oppression of Christians in Egypt and Sudan.

Such "seasonal" lows, however, should not discourage and divert attention from the important fact that, overall, the general attitude of the Churches toward Muslims has undergone a tremendous change for the better. (See Appendices 4, 5, 6.)

For Reflection and Discussion

1. What are some of the significant changes in the attitude of the Churches to Islam?
2. How does the attitude of the Churches toward immigrant Muslims compare with often that of political parties and the unions?
3. What possibilities exist to reciprocate openness of the Churches toward Muslims?
4. What do we Muslims make of the model character Christian clergy sometimes ascribe to Muslim communities? Do you have any experience of this personally?

CHAPTER EIGHTEEN

Understanding Al-Qur'an

Many of us mistakenly surmise that every Muslim looks at Al-Qur'an in the same way, all over the world. In reality there is a fairly wide range of understanding revelation, not just in different countries, but even in one and the same place, from person to person. And if we look at it historically, the variety becomes even larger, because in different ages people have looked at Al-Qur'an in multiple ways. To many of us, some of those viewpoints sound unbelievable today, and yet they are part of our intellectual history, part of our religious heritage.

An "orthodox" dogma states that Al-Qur'an is nothing but the word of God, from A-Z. It is not Muhammad's book, but the book of God, from cover to cover. It is a divine text brought to the Prophet (p) by the Archangel Gabriel who ordered him to read it out to men. This is what the name Al-Qur'an implies: "that what is recited, what is read out." Somewhat freely, one might translate it as a "proclamation."

One of the great controversies in the history of Islamic theology arose in the ninth century over the question as of whether the text as such, the words, are from God, or only the meaning. Rational theologians reasoned that the Arabic language is a product of human development, like any other language. It evolved over thousands of years, slightly changing with each generation. The Arabic we have in Al-Qur'an is the particular Arabic spoken by the tribe of Quraish in seventh century Mecca. In other parts of Arabia people spoke a different Arabic even then, and a century earlier the Arabic of the Quraish was not the same as it was when Muhammad (p) was born. Today, there are many different types of Arabic spoken in a wide geographic range, and the people of Mecca no longer speak exactly the same Arabic as we have in Al-Qur'an. Therefore, Gabriel can only have passed on to Muhammad (p) the ideas or the meanings of the words. The Prophet then uttered them in the language he knew.

In other words, Al-Qur'an was created by God Almighty at that moment, and Muhammad (p) was his coworker because on the human level it was he who created the text. This is why the Mu'tazila, a school of rational theologians in ninth-century Baghdad, held that Al-Qur'an was divine in spirit, eternal in meaning, but time-bound in expression, a seventh-century Arab testimony to the will of God.

In this century many an Islamic thinker has picked up the Mu'tazila thread, such as Professor Fadlu-r-Rahman of Islamabad/Chicago (d. 1988) who wrote that Al-Qur'an is the word both of God and Muhammad (p). He did not mean to imply that part of Al-Qur'an is from God and part from the Prophet. He said quite clearly that the meaning is divine but the articulation is human.[1]

There was strong opposition to such rational theology right from the start, analogous to later controversies in Christianity. Some theologians, such as Ahmad Ibn Hambal (d. 845) took up a position comparable to some American Protestants in the early twentieth century who called themselves Fundamentalists. Ibn Hambal rejected the idea of Al-Qur'an having been created by God in time. He taught that it was part of God, a divine attribute, and as such Al-Qur'an has always been there.

Some Mu'tazila and other theologians believed that this was a way of Christianizing Islam, because if Al-Qur'an is considered uncreated, as part of divinity, then it becomes equivalent to Christ in Christianity. In the concept of Trinity, Jesus is the Son and he is the *Logos*, a Greek word meaning "word," like *kalima* in Arabic. We call Al-Qur'an *kalimatu-llah* or *kalamu-llah*—"the word of God." According to Christian belief, God manifested Himself as a human being in the shape of Jesus Christ. According to the belief of Muslim "fundamentalist" theologians such as Ibn Hambal, God manifested Himself in the form of a text, Al-Qur'an. He did not assume the characteristics of a human being but of a book.

Along with this theology went a popular belief that the Arabic of Al-Qur'an was not a historical language evolved out of earlier languages, but was the original language of humanity, the language of God, the angels, and of paradise. It was the language taught the first humans when they were created.

This "fundamentalist" understanding of Al-Qur'an won the approval of the Caliphate in ninth-century Baghdad and became official dogma, largely by force of arms. Earlier the Mu'tazila had tried to enforce their point of view by using coercive measures.

Today most Muslims are more or less free to choose between these different understandings of the Holy Book. Apparently a majority of the educated class is more inclined toward the rational theology of the Mu'tazila. Many know nothing or only very little about these theological controversies and their history, but their own reflection leads them to believe that the divine element in Al-Qur'an cannot possibly be anything but the concepts behind the words, ageless meanings articulated in the language of seventh-century Arabs.

Al-Qur'an was translated very early on into a number of languages. The first probably was Persian. There are hundreds of millions of Muslims who know their Holy Book through translation only. In fact, this applies to the vast majority of the more than one billion Muslims in the world. There are instances of translations that have become revered as masterpieces of literature in those respective languages, for example the Urdu translation of Al-Qur'an by former Indian Minister of Education, Maulana Abu-Kalam Azad, who was one of the greatest Islamic scholars of his day. People say it gives them the feeling of reading the original and they love this translation so much that Sayyid 'Abdu-l-Latif, another outstanding Islamic scholar, produced an English translation of Azad's Urdu translation, and many believe that this is the best translation of Al-Qur'an into English.

Today voices are heard demanding that Islam's Holy Book be translated from seventh-century Arabic into present-day Arabic. The proposal that all Muslims learn the language of Al-Qur'an and use it in order to keep the original understanding alive is certainly an appealing ideal. But its practicality is more than doubtful. Should a miracle happen and tomorrow all of us use nothing but the language of Al-Qur'an, the next generation would deviate from it again, because language is an ongoing process that cannot be arrested. Future generations will have no choice but to produce specialists who then seek to capture the spirit underlying the revelation and to reproduce it for us in the language we speak which, in the twenty-first century, might be Japanese or Spanish.

The big issue is how to understand what Al-Qur'an tells us in detail. The book was revealed over a span of twenty-three years, and invariably the revelations occurred as responses to challenges in the Prophet's life. In the case of many verses, the time-bound character is not apparent, the wording being such that the text provides everlasting moral guidance, applicable to any situation no matter where and when. However, there also is much that appears time-bound. Muslims have always found eternal meanings in that too, but not without an extra effort at interpretation. Besides, turning those particular life-situations, some of which were unique, into de-historicized maxims is fraught with the pitfalls of arbitrariness.

In the course of such efforts, our theologians very early on developed a special science. It is called *'ilm asbabi n-nuzul*, meaning the probing into the special circumstances surrounding a revelation: How and why did this or that verse descend upon the Prophet? This science can be fairly neutral, leaving it to us to draw our conclusions. But it is very helpful in explaining such passages as the one that warns us against befriending Jews and Christians, for example. An American convert to Islam reading Al-Qur'an in 1995, without any knowledge of the Prophet's life and the story of revelation, might be inclined to regard this as a categorical injunction: no friendship with any Jew or any Christian under any circumstances.

By contrast, a Muslim trained in the discipline of *asbabu n-nuzul* will take that passage as a reference to a certain type of Jew and a certain type of Christian only. He may even regard this verse as restricted to particular events in the Prophet's life, outbalancing it by other passages that speak of Jews and Christians in a more general sense, which happens to be positive.[2] He will clearly see that the appellation of Jews and Christians in Al-Qur'an as "People of the Book" is an overriding principle, teaching us to regard Jews and Christians as spiritual kinfolk, as religious relatives. The theological discipline of *asbabu n-nuzul* helps us to read Al-Qur'an in its original Meccan/Medinese context and to recapture a level of meaning that lies otherwise buried under seventh-century debris.

Another discipline in Islamic theology is that of "Abrogation," more precisely, the science of *an-nasikh wa l-mansukh* ("the abrogator and the abrogated"). Some early verses of Al-Qur'an are said to have been abrogated by later ones. This is important in the context of militancy. In Mecca the Prophet (p) was a pacifist preacher who endured all kinds of indignities and whose community was subjected to inhuman tribulations. In the second phase of his career as a prophet, Muhammad (p) was the head of a polity in what became the city state of Medina. Arab tribal alliances waged war against this polity, forcing Muslims to take up arms to defend themselves and those in town whom they had pledged to defend.

In this way the nonviolent resistance of Mecca gave way to the armed resistance of Medina. This process was initiated with the famous verse in Al-Qur'an stating that permission to fight is given those who have been expelled from their homes because of their belief in God.[3]

According to some theologians, this verse became an abrogator (*nasikh*) allowing for *jihad*, a strictly defensive war to safeguard the faith. Earlier revelations enunciating nonviolence were now abrogated (*mansukh*). Later theologians preferred to have both options coexist side by side, nonviolent resistance as the general rule, armed resistance as a rare exception under very special circumstances only. For this reason they tended to limit the number of abrogated verses to a minimum, or to explain away the notion of abrogation altogether. Again others reached the conclusion that the abrogation was a temporary affair, limited to the special circumstances of Medina. What was abrogated is to be the rule again, and the abrogating verses are now to be regarded as abrogated: in other words, no more permission to fight.

In our days, this issue has become important in the context of women's rights. The early revelations in Mecca were very emphatic on the equality of men and women, while later revelations in Medina conceded to men the right of control over women. The complete equality of women was abrogated in favor of conditional equality. Women's rights, and human rights in general, stand to gain if the theological viewpoint is accepted that the abrogation of verses in Medina is regarded as a one-time act of time-bound validity, and if the abrogated verses of Mecca are no longer considered as abrogated, but become the overriding principle once again.

The vast majority of Muslims has never heard of these theological disputes over *an-nasikh wa l-mansukh*. This explains the variety of viewpoints on a number of issues. Is Islam more pacifist or more militant? Does it afford full equality to women, or do women stand under the tutelage (*wisaya*) of men as the law (*shari'a*) stipulates? The law is based on the doctrine of abrogation and, therefore, declares the assumption of political power by women to be illegal. In 1994-95, three Muslim-majority countries—Bangladesh, Pakistan, and Turkey—had female prime ministers. According to the "fundamentalist" understanding of Al-Qur'an, this was a violation of *shari'a* norms.

The Muslim masses who voted those women into office did so on the basis of their belief in God's justice as enshrined in Al-Qur'an. But they did so without a knowledge of Islamic law and theology, simply assuming that their common sense decision could not be but in accordance with the revered revelation. From the viewpoint of our "fundamentalists," the masses acted out of ignorance.

As it is at present, everybody understands Al-Qur'an their own way; there is unrestrained selectivity and little consensus. We Muslims need a clear and simple overview explaining the phenomenon of understanding revelation in its historical context with all its consequences. Most of all we need to realize that there is a history to understanding Al-Qur'an. Secondly, we need to shed the fear that Qur'anic studies on the pattern of biblical studies will denaturalize our Islamic relationship to revelation.

Historically speaking, scriptural critique among Muslims preceded that among Christians. Some Christian fundamentalists with a knowledge of history have indeed held this against Islam, accusing Muslims of being precursors of the Marxists!

The analytical study of Al-Qur'an should not be held up because we might be imitating Christian Bible critique, or that we are paying homage to the former colonial master. At the time of the great controversies in Islamic theology, we were intellectually far more daring and far ahead of religious studies in Europe. Not that this matters much, but it is patently wrong to think that today critical Islamic scholars are slavishly emulating "foreigners." This is not a question of *gharbzadegi* ("West-intoxication") as some Iranian clerics say. The Mu'tazila in ninth-century Baghdad were not smitten with admiration for things Western. In those days Non-Muslims suffered from Baghdad-intoxication or Córdova-intoxication.

Because Muslim theologians in those ages of splendor were free of complexes, they were able to decipher many an ancient symbolism and to give new meanings to key concepts such as the angels, the jinn, miracles, prophesy—and revelation *per se.* They excelled in the comparative study of religion and established the groundwork for a methodology that came to be called historicism in the West. By making "doubt" a matter of principle in their investigations, they created the scientific method of research.

Hermeneutics, as a methodology of Scripture study, was familiar to the Mu'tazila. We might even say that it started with them. This is important, not because we were first, the others second and third, but because it is wrong to reject hermeneutics as an un-Islamic approach Westerners want to talk us into.

The issue reminds us of the controversy about the discovery of America. Some of us blame Christian Europe for such a devilish deed, others claim that we Muslims reached America before them. We Muslims have to make up our mind: was the idea of going West good or bad? If it was bad, then we should put the blame on ourselves, because we definitely had the idea, and almost certainly earlier than Christians. If it was good, then we should give them the credit for having completed what we started.

Those of us who reject hermeneutics in the study of Al-Qur'an would be better advised to tell Jewish and Christian partners in dialogue: "We have been through it long ago. We know what it leads to and we do not want it." There is no point in rejecting something as "foreign" while actually it is not.

This is primarily a question of inner-Islamic dialogue. Unfortunately, such dialogue among Muslims is rare, trapped as we are in a quagmire of mutual recriminations. As long as Muslims representing different schools of thought speak at cross-purposes in an undisciplined manner there is not much hope for clarity.

For Reflection and Discussion

1. What are different ways of understanding the contents of Al-Qur'an?
2. What are different ways of looking at revelation as such?
3. Within Judaism, Christianity, and Islam we have controversies regarding the way we read and interpret our Sacred Texts. What are the similarities and the differences in those controversies?
4. Is the historicist study of sacred texts a Muslim or a Western invention? How might you exlpore this further?

CHAPTER NINETEEN

A Variety of Positions

Traditionally Muslims have been divided into Sunnis and Shi'is as two major denominations. Sunni Muslims know a further division into the four "Schools of Law" (Hanafi, Hambali, Maliki, Shafi'i), although this division is a minor one, and many of us regard it as irrelevant. Some do not even know about it, or not more than the names. Other divisions are more decisive, such as the one between Sufis and "Wahhabis" ("fundamentalists").

Due to the largeness of the traditional Muslim realm, from Morocco to Indonesia, the practice of Islam acquired many a local tinge. Some countries came under the sway of the *shari'a*, the law that evolved in the early phase of the Caliphate. Others have never known the *shari'a*, without being less fervently Islamic. The only difference it made is one of outlook, with each group thinking of itself as the better Muslims.

Most Muslim cultures witnessed the emergence of popular religion—Islamic cults impregnated with religious practices of earlier times. Much of that goes by the name of Sufism, though strictly speaking Sufism is the name for Islamic mysticism, which originally meant asceticism, abstinence from many of the pleasures of the world, a life of simplicity and humility—and a protest against un-Islamic indulgence by the privileged class of Muslims.

For the above reasons, there are many different forms of practicing Islam. In traditional Muslim societies people holding different views on religion have their own mechanisms of avoiding one another. We have separate mosques for Sunnis and Shi'is, but we do not usually designate our mosques as such and such. Exceptions confirm the rule.

In diaspora communities, as for example in the United States, Muslims of very disparate cultural background come together, which often means a coming to terms with ways of understanding or practicing Islam that are a little foreign to us. People from the Indian subcontinent (Bangladesh, India,

Pakistan) are distinct from Arab communities, not only in language but also in some religious practices. Sunnis from West Africa sometimes have difficulties in recognizing their religion while observing Shi'is from Iran, especially when it comes to *Muharram*, the Shi'i month of mourning.

Apart from such differences of tradition, there are the differences of interpretation and position. At present a very noticeable difference can be observed in the position of women, which differs from mosque to mosque, sometimes radically. Women play a different role in each one of four mosques in the Los Angeles area, for instance. There is a mosque where the separation of the sexes is extreme, with different entrances for male and female. Women sit in their own hall and listen to the preacher on a video screen. The atmosphere is more relaxed in another mosque, though the congregation is very conservative. In another Islamic Center it is much freer, and in the fourth mosque the atmosphere is scarcely different from a church. Men and women sit separately, but in the same room. Women are in the majority and participate fully and freely in all social activities. The fatherly Imam treats non-Muslim female visitors with the kindness of a spiritual guide. In 2005 in New York, one mosque even had services for men and women together led by a woman!

Only one of the four Los Angeles mosques is marked as being either Sunni or Shi'i. There are no such labels as Orthodox, Reformist, or Liberal, not to speak of Fundamentalist. And yet, these differences exist, they are very real, and occasionally they have led to brawls. In England police had to intervene in a mosque to separate fighting Sunnis and Shi'is, in Germany to separate battling Kurds and Turks, in New York to separate radicals from moderates.

These are extreme cases that may be regarded as marginal. In general, though, the community at large would benefit from a more realistic attitude, that is, by openly admitting these divisions common to all sections of humanity. Oneness is an ideal that should be maintained. Admitting the realities might help attaining the ideal. Other differences are central and are found everywhere, especially differences with regard to the position we Muslims adopt to our social environment. Are we to cooperate closely with Jews and Christians, or do we keep a distance? Do we want to be an alternative in a competition, or should we become partners in a joint effort to save humanity and to improve life for coming generations? Without a certain degree of closeness between Jews, Christians, and Muslims, the prospects for humanity's future seem bleak.

In the United States there are many indications of an increasing competition between Jews and Muslims, two dynamic communities with more or less the same numerical strength. If they could put their energies and talents together instead of using them against one another, prospects would be much brighter for all of us. That such joint action is possible has been demonstrated in Bosnia where Jews mustered stronger support than Muslims themselves.

The mainstream of the African-American Muslim community has long abandoned its erstwhile isolationist attitude (understandable in view of its special situation) and become particularly supportive of interfaith dialogue. The reason is partly pragmatic, partly theological. Benjamin Hoag of Detroit stated that there are social ills such as drugs and teenage pregnancy that Muslims have difficulties coping with alone. To overcome these problems, various forces of society have to cooperate, especially religious Jews, Christians, and Muslims.

Growing acquaintance with the Islamic sources, especially a profound study of Al-Qur'an, has created a greater awareness among African-American Muslims of their spiritual kinship with Jews and Christians. By actively participating in interfaith activities they will hopefully set the pace for some of the immigrant Muslims whose attitudes are still conditioned by the communalist (confrontational) atmosphere in their place of origin.

Most religious communities would love to overcome the divisive factors in their own ranks. Dialogue provides encouragement by making us aware how similar the situation is from community to community—from Jews to Christians to Muslims. Getting closer together as Jews, Christians, and Muslims is sometimes a stimulus to getting closer together as Muslims—charity should "begin at home," but sometimes it can be helped from the outside.

For Reflection and Discussion

1. From what you've read, do you believe that the ideals and basic principles of each of these religions are similar?
2. One way to look upon interreligious dialogue is to see it as *an exchange of gifts*. Can each religion learn from the other two? If so, what does each religion offer the others?
3. Would you prefer that in fifty years there would no longer be Jews, Christians, and/or Muslims? Why or why not?
4. What would you like the world's religious landscape to be like in fifty years?

APPENDIX 1

Populations of Religions of the World (Mid-1997)

	Population	%	Number of Countries
Christians	**1,929,987,000**	**33.0**	**244**
Unaffiliated Christians	104,939,000	1.8	201
Affiliated Christians	1,825,048,000	31.2	243
Catholics	1,040,354,000	17.8	240
Protestants	360,913,000	6.2	237
Orthodox	223,204,000	3.8	137
Anglicans	54,785,000	.9	167
Other Christians	287,857,000	4.9	213
Non-Christians	**3,918,752,000**	**67.0**	**244**
Atheists	146,615,000	2.5	163
Baha'is	7,666,000	0.1	213
Buddhists	353,141,000	6.0	123
Chinese folk religionists	363,334,000	6.2	88
Confucianists	6,112,000	0.1	14
Ethnic religionists	231,694,000	4.0	141
Hindus	746,797,000	12.8	109
Jains	4,016,000	0.1	10
Jews	14,890,000	0.3	137
Mandeans	40,000	0.0	2
Muslims	1,147,494,000	19.6	204
New-Religionists	98,699,000	1.7	57
Nonreligious	760,280,000	3.0	238
Shintoists	2,672,000	0.0	8
Sikhs	22,518,000	0.4	32
Spiritists	11,467,000	0.2	54
Zoroastrians	272,000	0.0	16
Other religionists	1,045,000	0.0	78
Total population	**5,848,739,000**	**100**	**244**

APPENDIX 2

Vatican Council II

Declaration on the Relation of the Church to Non-Christian Religions[1]

1. In our time, when day by day mankind is being drawn closer together, and the ties between different peoples are becoming stronger, the Church examines more closely her relationship to non-Christian religions. In her tasks of promoting unity and love among men, indeed among nations, she considers above all in this declaration what men have in common and what draws them to fellowship.

One is the community of all peoples, one in their origin, for God made the whole human race to live over the face of the earth.[2] One also is their final goal, God. His providence, his manifestations of goodness, his saving design extend to all people,[3] until that time when the elect will be united in the Holy City, the city ablaze with the glory of God, where the nations will walk in his light.[4]

People expect from the various religions answers to the unsolved riddles of the human condition, which today, even as in former times, deeply stir the hearts of humanity: What is humanity? What is the meaning, the aim of our life? What is moral good, what sin? Whence suffering and what purpose does it serve? Which is the road to true happiness? What are death, judgment, and retribution after death? What, finally is the ultimate inexpressible mystery which encompasses our existence: whence do we come, and where are we going?

2. From ancient times down to the present, there is found among various peoples a certain perception of that hidden power which hovers over the course of things and over the events of human history; at times some indeed have come to the recognition of a Supreme Being, or even of a Father. This perception and recognition penetrates their lives with a profound religious sense.

Religions, however, that are bound up with an advanced culture have struggled to answer the same questions by means of more refined concepts and a more developed language. Thus in Hinduism, men contemplate the divine mystery and express it through an inexhaustible abundance of myths and through searching philosophical inquiry. They seek freedom from the anguish of our human condition either through ascetical practices or profound meditation or a flight to God with love and trust. Again, Buddhism, in its various forms, realizes the radical insufficiency of this changeable world; it teaches a way by which men, in a devout and confident spirit, may be able either to acquire the state of perfect liberation, or attain, by their own efforts or through higher help, supreme illumination. Likewise, other religions found everywhere try to counter the restlessness of the human heart, each in its own manner, by proposing "ways," comprising teachings, rules of life, and sacred rites.

The Catholic Church rejects nothing that is true and holy in these religions. She regards with sincere reverence those ways of conduct and of life, those precepts and teachings which, though differing in many aspects from the ones she holds and sets forth, nonetheless often reflect a ray of that Truth which enlightens all men. Indeed, she proclaims, and ever must proclaim Christ, "the way, the truth, and the life" (John 14: 6), in whom men may find the fullness of religious life, in whom God has reconciled all things to himself.[5]

The Church therefore, exhorts her sons, that through dialogue and collaboration with the followers of other religions, carried out with prudence and love and in witness to the Christian faith and life, they recognize, preserve, and promote the good things, spiritual and moral, as well as the socio-cultural values found among these men.

3. The Church regards with esteem also the Moslems. They adore the one God, living and subsisting in himself, merciful and all-powerful, the Creator of heaven and earth,[6] who has spoken to men; they take pains to submit wholeheartedly to even his inscrutable decrees, just as Abraham, with whom the faith of Islam takes great pleasure in linking itself, submitted to God. Though they do not acknowledge Jesus as God, they revere him as a prophet. They also honor Mary, his virgin mother; at times they even call on her with devotion. In addition, they await the day of judgment when God will render their deserts to all those who have been raised up from the dead. Finally, they value the moral life and worship God especially through prayer, almsgiving, and fasting.

Since in the course of centuries not a few quarrels and hostilities have arisen between Christians and Moslems, this Sacred Synod urges all to forget the past and to work sincerely for mutual understanding and to preserve as well as to promote together for the benefit of all mankind social justice and moral welfare, as well as peace and freedom.

4. As the Sacred Synod searches into the mystery of the Church, it remembers the bond that spiritually ties the people of the New Covenant to Abraham's stock.

Thus the Church of Christ acknowledges that, according to God's saving design, the beginnings of her faith and her election are found already among the patriarchs, Moses, and the prophets. She professes that all who believe in Christ—Abraham's sons according to faith[7]—are included in the same patriarch's call, and likewise that the salvation of the Church is mysteriously foreshadowed by the chosen people's exodus from the land of bondage. The Church, therefore, cannot forget that she received the revelation of the Old Testament through the people with whom God in his inexpressible mercy concluded the Ancient Covenant. Nor can she forget that she draws sustenance from the root of that well-cultivated olive tree onto which have been grafted the wild shoots, the Gentiles.[8] Indeed, the Church believes that by his Cross Christ Our Peace reconciled Jews and Gentiles, making both one in Himself.[9]

The Church keeps ever in mind the words of the Apostle about his kinsmen: "There is the sonship and the glory and the covenants and the law and the worship and the promises; theirs are the fathers and from them is the Christ according to the flesh" (Rom 8, 4–5), the Son of the Virgin Mary. She also recalls that the Apostles, the Church's mainstay and pillars, as well as most of the early disciples who proclaimed Christ's gospel to the world, sprang from the Jewish people.

As Holy Scripture testifies, Jerusalem did not recognize the time of her visitation,[10] nor did the Jews in large number accept the gospel; indeed not a few opposed its spreading.[11] Nevertheless God holds the Jews most dear for the sake of their Fathers; He does not repent of the gifts He makes or of the calls He issues—such is the witness of the Apostle.[12] In company with the prophets and the same Apostle, the Church awaits that day, known to God alone, on which all peoples will address the Lord in a single voice and "serve him shoulder to shoulder" (Zeph 3:9).[13]

Since the spiritual patrimony common to Christians and Jews is thus so great, this Sacred Synod wants to foster and recommend that mutual understanding and respect which is the fruit, above all, of biblical and theological studies as well as fraternal dialogues.

True, the Jewish authorities and those who followed their lead pressed for the death of Christ;[14] still, what happened in his passion cannot be charged against all the Jews, without distinction, then alive, nor against the Jews of today. Although the Church is the new People of God, the Jews should not be presented as rejected or accursed by God, as if this followed from the Holy Scriptures. All should see to it, then, that in catechetical work or in the preaching of the Word of God they do not teach anything that does not conform to the truth of the gospel and the spirit of Christ.

Furthermore, in her rejection of every persecution against any man, the Church, mindful of the patrimony she shares with the Jews and moved not by political reasons but by the gospel's spiritual love, decries hatred, persecutions, displays of anti-Semitism, directed against Jews at any time and by anyone.

Besides, as the Church has always held and holds now, Christ underwent His passion and death freely, because of the sins of men and out of infinite love, in order that all may reach salvation. It is, therefore, the burden of the Church's preaching to proclaim the cross of Christ as the sign of God's all-embracing love and as the fountain from which every grace flows.

5. We cannot truly call on God, the Father of all, if we refuse to treat in a brotherly way any man, created as he is in the image of God. Man's relation to God the Father and his relation to men his brothers are so linked together that Scripture says: "He who does not love does not know God" (1 John 4:8).

No foundation therefore remains for any theory or practice that leads to discrimination between man and man or people and people, so far as their human dignity and the rights flowing from it are concerned.

The Church reproves, as foreign to the mind of Christ, any discrimination against men or harassment of them because of their race, color, condition of life, or religion. On the contrary, following in the footsteps of the holy Apostles Peter and Paul, this Sacred Synod ardently implores the Christian faithful to "maintain good fellowship among the nations" (1 Peter 2:12), and, if possible to live for their part in peace with all men,[15] so that they may truly be sons of the Father who is in heaven.[16]

The entire text and all the individual elements which have been set forth in this Declaration have pleased the Fathers. And by the apostolic power conferred on us by Christ, we, together with the Venerable Fathers, in the Holy Spirit, approve, decree, and enact them; and we order that what has been thus enacted in Council be promulgated, to the glory of God.

Rome, at St. Peter's, 28 October, 1965.
I, PAUL, Bishop of the Catholic Church
There follow the signatures of the Fathers.

APPENDIX 3

World Council of Churches[1]

Striving Together in Dialogue (A Muslim-Christian Call to Reflection and Action)

This document has been published by the World Council of Churches and other partners, including Islamic organizations and specialized journals. Hopefully, it will be widely circulated and used in discussions and educational programs.

It is the fruit of a Muslim-Christian meeting held in Amersfoort, Netherlands in November 2000. Convened by the World Council of Churches, it took stock of the various Christian-Muslim dialogue initiatives of this organization since 1991.

During the last nine years, Christian and Muslim religious leaders, educators, and activists have discussed the thorny and sometimes divisive issues of religion, law and society, human rights, religious freedom, community rights, mission and *da'wa*, and communal tensions. This document draws largely on their questions, reflections, and conclusions.

The History of Dialogue: Taking Stock

Among the many objections to and reservations toward dialogue, five particular ones are worth being underlined. There are those who insist that the local context of communal relations in a given society often makes broader dialogue irrelevant. Others suggest that dialogue may function as a cover for unequal power relations or as an ornament, concealing purposes different from those stated. There are also those who are weary of controversy and tend to be apprehensive of any mutual inquiry and questioning. Fourthly, one finds those who see dialogue as compromising the truth and a betrayal of the divine call to mission or *da'wa*. A fifth position argues that dialogue is, on the contrary, a more sophisticated form of mission or, even if that is not the intention of its initiators, leading to mission.

It is needless to repeat that current developments, political and otherwise, may be threatening to build up new attitudes of distrust and hostility. This imposes a new urgency in the consideration of Christian-Muslim relations and priorities on dialogue and cooperation. The patient work of recent decades is a reliable resource. Its value cannot be quantified but this does not mean that it bears no fruits. Countless local, national, and international experiences confirm this. Participants have discovered that interreligious dialogue is informed by, and informs, the internal dialogue within each religion. What was learned in the last decades lays the foundation for a continuing dialogue which is both hopeful and takes account of the contemporary realities.

The Current Situation: Threats and Opportunities

Muslim and Christian leaders and activists in dialogue are intensifying their efforts to "de-globalize Christian-Muslim tensions." They constantly warn against essentialism and sensationalism and draw attention to the specific local causes of conflicts, whose solutions can be found, first and foremost, in addressing those local causes. They refuse to be drawn into others' conflicts on the basis of uncritical responses to calls for solidarity and instead help to apply common principles of peace, justice, and reconciliation. They can thus help parties to local conflicts to release Islam and Christianity from the burden of sectional interests and self-serving interpretations of beliefs and convictions. Christian and Islamic beliefs and convictions can then constitute a basis for critical engagement with human weakness and defective social and economic orders, in a common search for human well-being, dignity, social justice, and civil peace.

It is needless to repeat that a culture of peace among religious communities is grounded in the culture of dialogue. The decades of dialogue between Muslims and Christians at all levels have strengthened relationships between the two religions, both individually and institutionally. Extensive personal networks of friendship and trust have been created through dialogue in the midst of conflicts labeled Christian-Muslim, making joint efforts for peace and justice both imperative and realistic. Growing mutual knowledge and interest in a greater understanding are replacing simplistic and uninformed stereotypes. Theological training and religious studies are beginning to include the other in their searching. Although there is clearly a long way to go, the fact of such beginnings gives reason for hope. It is a significant resource for future action.

Renewing Common Affirmations

In a world where Christians and Muslims live as neighbors and co-citizens, dialogue is not only an activity of meetings and conferences. It is a way of living out our faith commitment in relation to each other, sharing as partners common concerns and aspirations and striving together in response to the problems and challenges of our time. Widely accepted guidelines for genuine dialogue need to be reemphasized and reaffirmed. A number of common affirmations are to be renewed taking stock of the previous experience and in the light of a Christian-Muslim appraisal of the current situation.

Differences are inherent in the human condition and a manifestation of divine wisdom. In recognition of such differences, interreligious dialogue is based on mutual respect and understanding. It should not be used for a theological debate in which adherents of each religion try to prove religious truth at the expense of the other.

Partners involved in interreligious work are not required to compromise on any of their basic religious beliefs in order to engage in a constructive dialogue. Much of the significance of dialogue between Muslims and Christians depends on its ability to engage those who are faithful to their respective religions and rooted in their communities. Dialogue is motivated by a religious vocation and is founded on religious values.

In dialogue, the deepest meaning of what our scriptures say to us is opened up and speaks anew. Christians are motivated by the teaching that God wills love of neighbor inseparably from the love of God, which is shown in human action through love of others (Luke 10:27; Romans 13:9–10; Galatians 5:15; John 4:20–21). Christ's teaching of love includes all those we view as friends and those with whom we may feel enmity for any reason. Such love is not a mere sentimental emotion but an impetus to action (1 John 3:18) and the basis of trust (1 John 4:18). Christians also recall that they are not to bear false witness against their neighbor (Exodus 20:16). In dialogue, they come to know their neighbors of other religions in ways that enable them to keep this commandment in fact, not simply through vague intention. "What does the Lord require of you," the prophet Micah asks, "but to do justice, and to love kindness, and to walk humbly with your God?" (Micah 6:8).

As Muslims enter dialogue, they recognise the Qur'anic texts concerning diversity and God's purpose which say: "O people: we created you from a single (pair) of male and female, and made you into nations and tribes, that you may know each other" (49:13) and "We sent you solely as a mercy for all creatures" (21:07). Plurality is inscribed in God's design: "To each among you have we prescribed a law and open way. If God has so willed, He would have made you a single people but (His plan) is to test you in what He has given you: so excel each other in good deeds; it is He that will show you the truth of the matters in which you dispute" (5:48). Muslims are called to seek justice through their dialogue activities. The Al-Qur'an teaches "Give just measures and weight; do not deprive others of their due" (7:85), and "O you who believe! Stand out firmly for God as witnesses for fair dealing, and let not the hatred of others turn you away from justice, be just: that is nearer to piety" (5:8).

Therefore dialogue is not a negotiation between parties who have conflicting interests and claims. It should not be bound by the constraints of power relations. Rather, it needs to be a process of mutual empowerment of both Christians and Muslims toward their joint engagement in public concerns and their common pursuit of justice, peace, and constructive action on behalf of the common good of all people. In this process, Muslims and Christians will draw on their spiritual resources.

With this perspective in mind, genuine dialogue implies a recognition of and respect for differences. At the same time, it seeks to discover and appreciate common values of Christianity and Islam. A fruitful mutual understanding can not be enhanced unless both convergences and recognized differences are held in a creative relationship. This is equally true of debates within each religious community. Intrareligious and interreligious dialogue depend on and feed into each other.

Appreciation of both diversity and commonalities can be achieved in dialogue as an educational process that enables each community to come to know better both the other and itself. Muslims and Christians are thus helped to be critical of and overcome the many mutual stereotypes, prejudices, and misconceptions that serve to propagate suspicions and fear and justify exclusion.

But dialogue is not confined to communication or exchange of knowledge. It offers opportunities for interaction and practical engagement in matters of common concern at the grassroots level and in everyday life. Dialogue brings intellectual pursuits and life engagement into an integrated whole. The persuasiveness of the moral messages and the credibility of the intellectual pursuit necessarily depend on inclusive action on behalf of the common good.

In a context where religions are finding renewed public vigor, issues of freedom of conscience and human rights generally have reemerged in the last few years as sensitive and even divisive. In this respect, Christian-Muslim dialogue has an indispensable contribution to make in affirming that the principles of human rights and religious freedom are indivisible. It is called to direct the forces of religiosity toward common good, instead of allowing them to breed intrareligious and interreligious hatred and conflicts. Muslims and Christians agree that freedom of conscience is essential to their respective faiths. But religious freedom does not only imply freedom of conscience but also the right to live in accord with religious values and the recognition of cultural and religious diversity as basic to human reality. More broadly, Christians and Muslims can contribute, through dialogue, to a discourse on human rights that can help reconcile truly universal principles and culturally specific claims. Such a discourse needs to be grounded in the respective religions to be genuinely inclusive and universal.

While recognizing that mission and *da'wa* are essential religious duties in both Christianity and Islam, Muslims and Christians need to uphold the spiritual and the material well-being of all. Many missionary activities, and the methods they use, arouse legitimate suspicions. There are situations where humanitarian service is undertaken for ulterior motives and takes advantage of the vulnerability of people. Thus the clear distinction between witness and proselytism become crucial. It is the basis for the recognition that people of faith can enjoy the liberty to convince and be convinced and, at the same time, respect each other's religious integrity, faithfulness to tradition, and loyalty to community.

APPENDIX 4

Dialogue and Jihad—Jihad as Dialogue[1]

In view of extremist virulence, the issue of *jihad* is of utmost concern to Jews and Christians. A section of the Islamist minority among Muslims insists that *jihad* should never be understood as anything else but warfare against infidels. The vast majority of Muslims disagree, but do we have a clear vision of the *jihad* concept? What does it mean to us and how do we make it meaningful to our partners in dialogue? Muhammad Talibi, an Islamic scholar from Tunis, has spent a lifetime in intense dialogue with Jews and Christians. In recognition of his efforts he was awarded a special distinction by the University of Tübingen in Germany. A devout Muslim, retired Professor Talibi is eminently qualified to formulate a dialogical definition of *jihad* that may serve as a guideline.

> The apostolate becomes essentially an attentive openness toward our neighbor, an incessant seeking for truth through a continuous deepening and assimilation of the values of faith, and, in the final analysis, pure witness. This sort of apostolate is called, in Arabic, *jihad.*
>
> This statement may well surprise all those for whom this word recalls the clash of holy wars past and present. Let me explain to them that *jihad*, both etymologically and fundamentally, has nothing to do with war. Arabic has no lack of words to describe all kinds of warfare. If Al-Qur'an had really wanted to talk of war there would have been an embarrassing choice of words to be found in the rich and colorful vocabulary of pre-Islamic poetry, which is entirely given over to exalting the "great days" of the Arab race (*ayyamu l-'arab*) when this people engaged in their favorite pastime of disemboweling one another. *Jihad* must therefore be something different. Essentially and radically it is an extreme, total effort in the Way of God (*fi sabili llah*).

Tradition makes it clear that the purest, most dramatic, and most fruitful form of it is *al-jihadu l-akbar*, the combat which takes place in the secrecy of one's conscience. This means that the finest form of apostolate is the witness of a life in which the struggle for moral perfection has succeeded. This form of apostolate through witness is the only one which gives results and is, moreover, in agreement with modern thought. It has no need of proselytism. Did not Al-Qur'an itself remind the Prophet personally that he could not guide men toward God just as he liked it, but that it is really God who guides toward himself those whom he chooses? "You do not guide whom you like, but God guides whom he will" (28:56).

APPENDIX 5

Shari'a and Muslims in Europe

In 1985, the *Islam Working Group* (four Christians and two Muslims) of the *Conference of European Churches*' "Committee on Migrant Workers in Europe" issued these recommendations.[1]

To All Concerned

1. All public and private institutions and structures need to take seriously the increasingly multireligious and multicultural nature of European society.
2. The training of all professions potentially concerned, such as lawyers, teachers, clergy, and social workers, should include an awareness of Islam and Muslim concerns, which should not be restricted to one particular national or cultural expression of Islam.
3. Institutions, like schools, hospitals, and prisons, and employers and government authorities should meet Muslim needs and sensitivities by the provision, for example, of room and time for prayer, correct food, respect for dress, extension to Muslims of chaplaincy facilities, etc.
4. Educators should make efforts to identify ways in which they may more fully take account of the religious identity of Muslim children.

To Public Authorities

To Legislators

5. The legal rights enjoyed by longstanding European religious communities should be extended as appropriate also to Muslims, and affirmative action should be taken to redress the disadvantages experienced by newly arrived religious communities.

To the Legal Profession

6. Judicial institutions should take account of the *shari'a* as a genuine source of law with impact on the present situation in Europe through the Muslim communities, separately from the national legal systems of the countries of origin.

To the Courts

7. The courts should take a more understanding attitude to cases before them involving Muslims; this can be achieved through appropriate training, a greater readiness to seek advice, and a more flexible application of the law.

To Social and Welfare Agencies

8. Special care should be taken when Muslim children are in children's homes, or are fostered or adopted, that provision is made for their cultural and religious identity to be respected.

APPENDIX 6

Muslim-Christian Seminar Declaration

Valetta, Malta 1991[1]

In an unprecedented effort, representatives of Christian and Islamic organizations attempted to confront together the critical issue of refugees, migrants, and internally displaced persons in today's world. Forty persons met in Malta (April 22-24, 1991) to reflect upon, from their respective faith traditions, their responsibility in addressing the problem faced by no less than thirty million people.

Both communities have witnessed massive emigration and immigration trends. We have seen hundreds of thousands of Christians recruited to work temporarily, or for extended periods, in the oil-producing Muslim countries of the Middle East. At the same time, we have seen hundreds of thousands of Muslims compelled by circumstances to leave their homelands. Many have sought to resettle—often permanently—in the secularized but predominantly Christian countries of Europe and North America.

In both Christian and Muslims societies, socio-economic and political dynamics are intertwined with differences in tradition, cultural behavior, and religious practices. At times, these dynamics play off against the differences to provoke friction and conflict. Some Christians in predominantly Muslim countries still face the experience of being treated as strangers, although Christian communities have been present in them for nearly two thousand years. At the same time, even second- and third-generation Muslim residents are viewed as foreigners in European and other countries. Unfortunately, despite signs of acceptance and understanding by many toward the strangers, manifestations of visible hostility and rejection of immigrants are increasing in many countries.

The deliberations of the seminar identified commonalities but also explored a thorny difference in examining the relationship between religion and public policy. Information was exchanged to help build trust between Christians and Muslims facing the same difficulties and suffering, yet often found working in parallel and sometimes misunderstanding each other.

The following declaration highlights their agreement on the urgency of a new beginning. It sets an agenda for exchange and cooperation and proposes the establishment of a joint working group:

1. We have come together, as Muslims and Christians, as representatives of organizations related to our faiths, and as concerned persons of goodwill, on 22-24 April 1991, 8-10 Shawwal 1400, in Malta, to address a problem of major importance to our world: the plight of refugees, internally displaced persons, and migrants.

2. This seminar was built on past interfaith discussions. It is the first such international Muslim-Christian encounter to focus specifically on establishing practical cooperation on the global humanitarian problem of refugees and migrants.

3. During this period of discussion, analysis, and sharing, we have strengthened our understanding of the imperative within both of our faith traditions to protect and assist those who must leave their homelands to seek hospitality elsewhere.

4. Since we are both people who believe and trust in God, we have indeed been able to identify a number of commonalities in our respective holy writings and traditions. These include the following:

a. The earth belongs to God; its resources being entrusted to humanity to be accessible to all with justice and compassion.

b. We are called upon by God to love one another as ourselves and hence to serve all peoples, without any self-interest and irrespective of their race or ethnicity, of their social or economic class, of their political opinion, or of their religion. Our aid should be given for truly humanitarian purposes and without any intention to proselytize.

c. Both Christianity and Islam were born in the midst of persecution; and many of their faithful have directly experienced the plight of being refugees.

5. Out of these faith traditions, we have seen the common challenge to protect and assist the victims of natural and human-made disasters, such as war, civil unrest, persecution, inhumanity, and injustice.

6. We have acknowledged that the circumstances of refugees, displaced persons, and migrants differ and require sometimes distinct responses. Nonetheless, we affirm that we must work together to ensure that the rights

and dignity of all persons on the move, and their families if separated, are respected and upheld, no matter who these people are or wherever they may be found.

7. We have recognized that the situation of people forced to leave their homes and lands is a worsening problem. We have concluded that we, as Muslims and Christians, as well as our respective organizations, must go beyond aiding the ever growing numbers of victims to address and ultimately prevent the root causes of such mass movements of peoples.

Endnotes

Chapter One

1. Thomas Aquinas, *Summa Theologiae*, II/II, Q. 1, a. 2.

2. For a more detailed discussion, see Leonard Swidler, *After the Absolute: The Dialogical Future of Religious Reflection*. Minneapolis: Fortress Press, 1990. For the full text see: http://globaldialogue.com/swidlerbooks/.

3. For a description of the *Una Sancta* Movement and the early development of intra- and interreligious dialogue, see Leonard Swidler, *The Ecumenical Vanguard* (Pittsburgh: Duquesne University Press, 1965). For the full text see: http://global-dialogue.com/swidlerbooks/.

4. Secretariatus pro Non-credenti, *Humanae personae dignitatem*, August 28, 1968. Secretariat for Unbelievers, quoted in full in Austin Flannery, *Vatican Council II* (Collegeville, MN: Liturgical Press, 1975), p. 1010.

5. Johannes Schwartländer, ed., *Modernes Freiheitsethos und christlicher Glaube* (Munich/Mainz: Kaiser/Grünewald, 1981), p. 11.

6. Thomas Aquinas, *Summa Theologiae*, I-II, Q. 91, a. 2: "Among other things, however, the rational creature submits to divine providence in a more excellent manner in so far as it participates itself in providence by acting as providence both for itself and for others." "*Inter cetera autem rationalis creature excellentiori quondam modo divinae providentiae subiacet, inquantum et ipsa fit providentiae particeps, sibi ipsi et aliis providens.*"

7. See Leonard Swidler, *For All Life. Toward a Universal Declaration of a Global Ethic: An Interreligious Dialogue*. Ashland: White Cloud Press, 1999, and http://globalethic.org/.

Chapter Two

1. The *Dialogue Decalogue* was first published by Leonard Swidler in the *Journal of Ecumenical Studies* in 1983. It has been republished in more than forty other places and translated into ten foreign languages. See http://global-dialogue.com/course/.

Chapter Three

1. The structure of these stages was developed by Ashok Gangadean and Leonard Swidler. See *Global Dialogue Institute: The Technology of Deep-Dialogue/Critical-Thinking* (Philadelphia: 2000).

Chapter Four

1. *Ecclesiam suam*, no. 78, quoted in Austin Flannery, *Vatican Council II* (Collegeville, MN: Liturgical Press, 1975), p. 1003.

2. See the detailed report by Eugene Fisher, "Kennedy Institute Jewish-Christian-Muslim Trialogue," *Journal of Ecumenical Studies*, 19, 1 (Winter 1982), pp. 197-200.

3. For a history of this several-decades-long movement, see Leonard Swidler, *The Ecumenical Vanguard* (Pittsburgh: Duquesne University Press, 1965).

4. For more detail see, Leonard Swidler, *Yeshua: A Model for Moderns.* (Kansas City: Sheed/Ward, 1988; 2nd expanded edition, 1993).

Chapter Five

1. This differentiation between an organized and benign universe under the One God in contrast to a fractious and chaotic universe of "the Gods" is actually a presumptive construct that monotheists can agree upon without argument, but it is an *a priori* assumption. The Hebrew Bible, New Testament, and Al-Qur'an, all of which assume the rule of the One God, also include important passages describing a universe that is on the verge of chaos and destruction.

2. This belief is also known as "monolatry." Standard English convention is to capitalize only designations for the monotheistic deity while referring to deities in polytheistic systems in lower case. I prefer to refer to the deity or deities in the same manner.

3. Donald Redford, "The Monotheism of Akhenaten," in Hershel Shanks and Jack Meinhardt, *Aspects of Monotheism* (Washington: Biblical Archaeology Society, 1996), pp. 11-26. For a fuller discussion, see Erik Horning, *Akhenaten and the Religion of Light* (transl. David Lorton, Ithica, NY: Cornell University Press, 1999), pp. 87-94.

4. Polymnia Athanassiadi and Michael Frede, *Pagan Monotheism in Late Antiquity* (Oxford: Oxford University Press, 1991).

5. Most references are to Abraham the *hanif.* Some note how his monotheism is prior to those of Judaism or Christianity, and Muhammad himself is referred to as a *hanif* on at least one occasion (Q.2:135, 3:67, 95, 4:125, 6:79, 10:105, 30:30). See Uri Rubin, "*Hanifiyya* and Ka'ba: An Inquiry into the pre-Islamic Background of *din ibrahim*," in *Jerusalem Studies in Arabic and Islam* 13 (1990), 85, 112; Andrew Rippin, "*Rhmnn* and the *hanifs*," in Hallaq and Little, *Islamic Studies Presented to Charles J. Adams* (Leiden: Brill, 1991), 153-168; Dale Eickelman, "Musaylima: An Approach to the Social Anthropology of Seventh Century Arabia," in *Journal of the Economic and Social History of the Orient* 10 (1967), 17-52; Ella Landau-Tasseron, "Unearthing a Pre-Islamic Arabian Prophet," in JSAI 21 (1997), 42-61, and G. R. Hawting, *The Idea of*

Idolatry and the Emergence of Islam: From Polemic to History (Cambridge: Cambridge University Press, 1999).

6. See, for example, Exodus 20:1–4, Leviticus 19:1–4, Deuteronomy 12:6–14, Psalm 96:4–5. Many other verses could be cited.

7. The "People of the Book" is a recurring reference in the Al-Qur'an to members of the established scriptural religions of Judaism and Christianity.

8. The word is *munafiqun*, which is often translated as hypocrites.

Chapter Six

1. Today it is much more accepted to refer to what Christians traditionally called the "Old Testament" as the Hebrew Bible. "Old Testament" conveys a certain theology that was current until recently, that the old testament or covenant between God and the Jews is no longer valid, and that the only real or true expression of divine relationship with humanity is through the Church. The term Hebrew Bible ascribes more respect and also reflects that its language is, for the most part, in Hebrew (there is some Aramaic as well in the books of Ezra, Nehemiah, and Daniel).

2. It is becoming conventional to use BCE and CE rather than BC and AD because use of the Christian designations suggests a universal acceptance of Christian theologies. There are other valid ways to count the passage of time as well, such as the Islamic use of the "Hijri" calendar marking the date of Muhammad's emigration from Mecca to Medina, or the Jewish biblical accounting from the Bible's estimate of the date of the creation of the world. Muslims often use the Hijri calendar and Jews the Biblical calendar, but the international community must use a common system. Because of the international economic and political power of the West, which uses the Gregorian calendar, it became customary to use it for international reckoning of time, but its theological assumptions have been removed so that all who use it may feel the same comfort.

3. For a more contemporary perception of Paul understood as a Jew, which he was, rather than as a Greek philosopher, which he was not, see, e.g., the Protestant scholar E. P. Sanders, *Jesus and Judaism* (Philadelphia: Fortress Press, 1985), and Catholic scholar Gerard Sloyan in Leonard Swidler, Lewis John Eron, Gerard Sloyan, Lester Dean, *Bursting the Bonds: A Jewish-Christian Dialogue on Jesus and Paul* (Maryknoll, NY: Orbis Books, 1990).

4. Maimonides, *Guide for the Perplexed* [1190 CE], 3:29.

5. See also Galatians 4:21–32, Hebrews 8:6–13, 1 Peter 2:7–8.

6. Al-Qur'an 3:110, 3:65–67, 22:77–78.

7. Tractate *Shabbat* 87a.

Chapter Seven

1. Tractate *Sanhedrin* 44a.

2. Arthur Hertzberg, *The Zionist Idea* (NY: Atheneum, 1959 and reprinted many times), p. 121.

3. Hertzberg, pp. 416-431.

4. Tosefta, *Sanhedrin* 13:2, Talmud *Megillah* 13a.

Chapter Ten

1. Pope Paul VI, cited in *Charter of the Rights of Catholics in the Church*, in Leonard Swidler and Herbert O'Brien, eds., *A Catholic Bill of Rights* (Kansas City, MO: Sheed & Ward, 1988), p. 2.

2. See my article "Jesus Was a Feminist," *The Catholic World*, January, 1971, reproduced dozens of times and in seven languages, and an expanded version in my *Biblical Affirmations of Woman* (Philadelphia: Westminster Press, 1979), *Yeshua: A Model For Moderns* (Kansas City, MO: Sheed & Ward, 1988, 2nd expanded edition, 1993), and *Jesus Was a Feminist. Why Aren't We?!* (Lanham, MD: Sheed & Ward, 2007).

3. See, for example, my *Yeshua: A Model for Moderns*; and *After the Absolute* (St. Paul, MN: Fortress Press, 1990).

4. For my attempt at a contemporary explanation, see my book *Yeshua: A Model for Moderns.*

5. For further information on *Aufklärung* Catholicism see Leonard Swidler, *Aufklärung Catholicism 1780-1850. Liturgical and Other Reforms in the Catholic Aufklärung* (Missoula, MT: Scholars Press, 1978); and on later Catholic democratic reforms, see Leonard Swidler, *Toward a Catholic Constitution* (New York: Crossroad Press, 1996); Leonard Swidler, *Making the Church Our Own* (Lanham, MD: Sheed & Ward, 2007).

6. See Leonard Swidler, *The Ecumenical Vanguard* (Pittsburgh: Duquesne University Press, 1965), p. 4.

7. See Leonard Swidler, *Aufklärung Catholicism.*

8. See his *Wesen des Christentums* (Leipzig, 1901); English: *What is Christianity* (New York, 1957).

9. See, e.g., Leonard Swidler and Hans Küng, eds., *The Church in Anguish: Has the Vatican Betrayed Vatican II?* (San Francisco: Harper & Row, 1987); Bernard Häring, *My Witness For the Church*, Translation and Introduction by Leonard Swidler (Mahwah, NJ: Paulist Press, 1992).

10. For a detailed discussion of this document and its implications, see Leonard Swidler, *Freedom in the Church.* (Dayton, OH: Pflaum Press, 1969), chapter V.

11. For a discussion of "salvation" and other key terms about the ultimate goal of life, see Leonard Swidler, *The Meaning of Life? Some Answers at the Edge of the Third Millennium*, (Mahwah, NJ: Paulist, 1992).

12. See, e.g., Leonard Swidler, *Freedom in the Church*, Leonard Swidler, *Aufklärung Catholicism*; and Leonard and Arlene Swidler, *Bishops and People* (Philadelphia: Westminster Press, 1970).

13. For a detailed history of the Catholic resistance to and then embrace of ecumenism, see, Leonard Swidler, *The Ecumenical Vanguard.*

Chapter Eleven

1. See Margaret Smith, *Rabi'a the Mystic* (Cambridge: Cambridge University Press, 1928, reprint 1984), pp. 98f.

2. See Khalid Duran, *Children of Abraham: An Introduction to Islam for Jews* (Hoboken, NJ: KTAV, 2001), pp. 49-88, which was extraordinarily prescient, sadly. See also his book with Michael Pohly, *Osama bin Laden und der internationale Terroismus* (Munich: Ullstein, 2001) published immediately in the wake of the 9/11 attack.

Chapter Twelve

1. *Ad scapulam*, Migne, ed., *Patrologia Latina*, I, p. 699.

2. From the Edict of Milan as contained in *De mortibus persecutorum*, in Migne, ed., *Patrologia Latina*, VII, pp. 267f.

3. *Codex Theodosianus*, XVI, I, 2, in, Coleman J. Barry, ed., *Readings in Church History* (Westminster, MD: Newman Press, 1960), vol. I, p. 142.

4. *Summa Theol.*, IIa IIae, q. 11, art. 3. "Circa haereticos....meruerunt non solum ab Ecclesia per excommunicationem separari, sed etiam per mortem a mundo excludi. Multo enim gravius est corumpere fidem, per quam est animae vita, quam falsare pecuniam, per quam temporali vitae subvenitur....relinquit eum iudicio saeculari a mundo exterminandum per mortem. Dicit enim Hieronymus: Resecandae sint putridae carnes" (*Comm. sup. Ep. ad Gal.*, Commentary on the Epistle to the Galatians)

5. A. Yusuf Ali, *The Holy Qur'an The Text, Translation, and Commentary* (Washington, D.C. The Islamic Center, 1978—original in Lahore, 1934), p. 510, n. 1480.

6. Mohammed Talbi, "Religious Liberty: A Muslim Perspective," in Leonard Swidler, ed., *Religious Liberty and Human Rights in Nations and in Religions* (Philadelphia/New York: Ecumenical Press/Hippocrene Books, 1986), pp. 175-187; and Leonard Swidler,

Muslims in Dialogue: The Evolution of a Dialogue (Lewiston, NY: Edwin Mellen Press, 1992), p. 328.

7. Quoted in Roger Aubert, "Religious Liberty from 'Mirari vos' to the 'Syllabus.'" in *Historical Problems of Church Renewal, Concilium*, VII (Glen Rock, NJ, 1965), pp. 91f.

8. Ibid., pp. 143f.

9. Ibid., pp. 145f.

10. See: General Assembly Res. 217A (III), U.N. Doc. A/180, at 71 (1948).

11. See: U.N. GAOR Supp. (51), U.N. Doc. A/RES/36/55 (1982).

12. See: GA. Res. 2200 (XXI), U.N. Doc. A/6316 (1966), respectively.

13. See Leonard Swidler, *The Ecumenical Vanguard* for a detailed documentation and discussion of largely foiled pre-Vatican II Catholic attempts at intra-Christian—to say nothing of interreligious—dialogue.

14. Abdullahi, Ahmed An-Na'im, "Mahmud Muhammad Taha and the Crisis in Islamic Law Reform: Implications for Interreligious Relations," *Journal of Ecumenical Studies*, 25:1 (Winter, 1988), and in Swidler, *Muslims in Dialogue*, p. 39.

15. Apion, II, 201. See also Leonard Swidler, *Women in Judaism: Status of Women in Formative Judaism* (Metuchen, NJ: Scarecrow Press, 1976).

16. 1 Tim 2:11ff. This letter is probably not written by Paul, but later by some of his followers. For the proportionately minor, but nevertheless important, percentage of positive statements about women in the biblical materials, see Leonard Swidler, *Biblical Affirmation of Women.* Philadelphia: Westminster Press, 1979 (8th printing, 1993).

17. See Leonard Swidler, "Jesus Was a Feminist," *Catholic World*, January, 1971, pp. 171-183—reproduced dozens of times in many languages. When I did this simple research in 1970, no book contained more than a paragraph or a short page on Jesus' attitude toward women, although many entire books on Paul and women had been published. See also, Swidler, *Jesus Was a Feminist. Why Aren't We?*

18. Khalid Duran, *Children of Abraham*, p. 232.

19. For up-to-date efforts to prevent this constant killing of Muslim women in Pakistan by their own relatives, see the Web site of Professor Riffat Hassan: http:/inrfvvp.org/.

Chapter Thirteen

1. Quotes from Al-Qur'an are based on translations by 'Abdullah Yusuf 'Ali, *The Meaning of the Holy Qur'an*; new edition with revised translation and commentary (Brentwood, MD: Amana Publications, 1991). Arthur J. Arberry, *The Koran Interpreted.* The World's Classics. Oxford University Press, 1982.

2. Muhammad Lutfi (Mohamed Lotfi), star among Morocco's filmmakers, has produced a film featuring the *hilula*, with a delegation of American Jews participating in the rituals.

3. A note for non-Muslim readers: P stands for "peace be upon him" and is said whenever prophets are mentioned, for instance, Abraham (p), Moses (p), Jesus (p).

4. Cairo edition, 1319/1901, pp. 75-78.

5. See Muhammad 'Abduh, *Tafsiru l-Manar*, 1st ed., 1346/1927-28; vol. 1, pp. 333-5. A Syrian disciple of 'Abduh' s, the conservative Rashid Rida (d. 1935), who edited the commentary, stressed that "faith in the prophecy of Muhammad (p) is not a precondition...salvation is not the automatic result of belonging sociologically to any given religion, rather it depends on the sincerity of one's faith and on pious deeds" p. 336.

6. Muhammad Talibi (Talbi), "Islam and Dialogue: Some Reflections On A Current Topic," *Islam and the Modern Age*; vol. 9, no. 2 (New Delhi: Islam and the Modern Age Society, May 1978), p. 16.

Chapter Fourteen

1. Kuwait gave more aid than any other Muslim nation. It is an irony of fate that a few years later Kuwait was betrayed by many with the argument that Kuwaitis did not share their wealth with others, not even with their brethren-in-faith.

2. Quoted by Peter Steinfels, "Beliefs—Two World Conferences and Two Very Different Roles for Religion," *The New York Times*, March 18, 1995.

3. There is no relationship whatsoever between the Spanish association *Crislam* and the Argentinean army coterie by the same name. The similarity of the name is purely coincidental.

4. "To Him we surrender" in Arabic is "we are *muslimun* to Him."

Chapter Fifteen

1. A frequent theme of lectures by the Jordanian Shaikh Ahmad Naufal during visits to the United States. The speeches are available on audio cassettes and video tapes.

2. This the title of a book by 'Abdu-s-Sattar Fathullah Sa'id: *Ma'rakatu l-wudud baina l-qur'an wa t-talmud.* (Plainfield, IN: MAYA [Muslim Arab Youth Association] RPI, 1980), p. 412.

3. Martin Kramer, "The Salience of Islamic Antisemitism," *Reports* (London: Institute of Jewish Affairs, October 1995), No. 2; also found at http://www.ict.org.il/articles/articledet.cfm?articleid'32 .

4. Among those aware of this new trend toward an anti-Jewish theology is Professor Rashid Ahmad Jallandhari, head of the Institute of Islamic Culture in Lahore, Pakistan, and a former director of the Pakistan government's Islamic Research Institute. He has condemned such misinterpretation of Islam in numerous lectures. The same holds true of Professor Smail Balic from Bosnia who is a retired chairman of the Muslim community of Austria and editor of the journal *Islam and the West.* These are just two examples out of many.

5. Bassam Al-'Ammush, an Islamist deputy in Jordan's parliament, delivered a lecture at the 1994 Jerusalem Day in Chicago, ruminating in a way that could be described as "pathological archeology of religion": "Our brothers in Saudi Arabia, those who live in Medina or close by, know the fortress of Ka'b Ibn Ashraf (a Jewish leader in the time of the Prophet). It is still there, as it was, unchanged. According to what I have heard, I am not sure if this is correct, but I suppose it is correct, this is because of the Zionist lobby in the world which has imposed this condition upon Saudi Arabia that no changes should be effected in those areas. Everything should remain as it is until they come to claim it because it belonged to their ancestors. In 1967, what did Golda Meir say, or at least has been attributed to her that she said 'I smell the fragrance of my ancestors, my ancestors in Khaibar.'" (Khaibar was a Jewish village in Arabia during the time of the Prophet. Muslims evicted the Jews from Khaibar. Islamists never tire of claiming that Israelis plan the conquest of much of Arabia in order to get Khaibar back. In reality very few Israelis have ever heard of Khaibar.)

6. The principle of "ethnic cleansing," as devised in Croatia in 1941, stated that "one third of the enemy population should be killed, another third expelled, and the remaining third converted." In the "ethnic cleansing" carried out by Serbs, forced conversions of Muslims to the Orthodox Church may be less than 1,000, as against some 750,000 people expelled, and double that number killed. In other words, what happened in Bosnia is closer to genocide than to "ethnic cleansing."

7. S. Muhammad Asad, *The Message of the Qur'an* (Gibraltar: Dar al-Andalus, 1980).

8. Hamid Marcus was a Sufi-type person who shunned fame. The translation was published in prewar Germany under the name of Maulana Sadruddint, a Pakistani preacher whose knowledge of German never advanced beyond the elementary stage. The translation is so excellent that it has several times been reprinted in recent years.

9. The Ahmadiya sect calls its founder, Mirza Ghulam Ahmad (d. 1908), a shadow prophet—*nabi zilli.* He wrote "I was named a prophet by way of metaphor, not in the real sense." For the majority of Muslims this is unacceptable nonetheless.

10. See Gregorio Ruiz, "En que sentido puede ser Mahoma considerado profeta por los cristianos?" (In What Sense Can Muhammad Be Considered a Prophet by

Christians?), *Encuentro—Documentos para el entendimiento islamo-cristiano.* Serie C: *Islam y Cristianismo.* No. 81. Madrid, January 1979.

11. Al-Qur'an 2:148: "To each is a goal to which God turns him; Then strive together (as in a race) toward all that is good. Wherever you may be, God will bring you together."

Chapter Sixteen

1. Some Christian missionaries were fond of alleging that Muhammad (p) misunderstood the Trinity, but the fact is that Al-Qur'an is not primarily a book of scholarly dispute. First and foremost it addresses popular belief. Apart from that, historical research tells us that among the many Christian sects represented in Arabia there were also those who took Mary to be part of the Trinity.

2. A more literal translation runs: "Thus We appointed you a midmost nation that you might be witnesses to the people" *The Koran Interpreted*, trans. Arthur J. Arberry. *World's Classics* (Oxford: Oxford University Press, 1982), p. 18.

3. Abdullah 'Azzam preached the recreation of those conditions during lectures in the United States, full of contempt for the pluralistic society that allowed him to preach what he could not preach elsewhere. He praised the days when a Jew or Christian had to move to the other side of the street to make way for an approaching Muslim. In actual fact this was rarely the case. 'Azzam molded history to fit his triumphalist vision of Islamist supremacy.

4. Abdullah 'Azzam interpreted *jihad* precisely the way anti-Islamic propaganda explains it—as Holy War. *Jihad*, according to 'Abdullah 'Azzam, Shaikh 'Umar 'Abdu-r-Rahman, and others from their school of thought, never means anything else but to take up a weapon and fight the infidels. They totally reject the mainstream understanding of *jihad* as primarily a moral concept. According to them, the Hadith about the Greater and the Lesser Jihad is not just a "weak" Hadith (of doubtful authenticity), it just is no Hadith. It is simply concocted. The Prophet (p), they aver, never said such a thing.

Apart from this one-sided interpretation, 'Abdullah 'Azzam preached *jihad* the way others preach Islam. A listener, or reader, could not help getting the impression that here *jihad* was not called for as a method of liberation, but as an end in itself. *Jihad* for self-fulfillment, *jihad* for *jihad's* sake. At stake is no longer Islam, not even Islamism but *jihadism.*

5. This was made strikingly clear by one of the most influential conservative Muslim writer of the twentieth century, Maulana Sayyid Abul Ala Maudoodi (d. 1979), who wrote: "Takfir is violation of the rights of an individual...a crime against society...an

act of injustice against entire Islamic society...does immense harm to the Muslim community." http://www.muslim.org/light/96-6.htm.

6. See his treatise *Ma'rakatuna ma'a l-yahud* (Our Battle with the Jews) where he relates that while hospitalized he was surprised by the festivities that kept the entire country in their grip. He then learned from a nurse that all America was celebrating the assassination of Hasan Al-Banna, the founder of the Muslim Brotherhood Party in Egypt. That was in 1949 when barely a dozen Americans had ever heard the name of Hasan Al-Banna and his movement.

Chapter Seventeen

1. Quoted by S. Wesley Ariarajah in "Theological Perspectives on Plurality," *Current Dialogue* (Geneva: World Council of Churches), no. 18, June 1980. p. 2.

2. Ibid., p. 3. Muhammad Talibi reacts perhaps too strongly, but his self-critical reflections are shared by many, and they are surely helpful for a meaningful dialogue: "And what is Islam doing in face of such an unprecedented effort by the Church? It offers us a theology whose evolution practically came to an end in the 12th century.... If we wish to overcome this difficulty, which gives birth to mental reservations and distrust, we must expose it in public in all frankness and serenity." "Islam and Dialogue: Some Reflections On A Current Topic," *Islam and the Modern Age* (New Delhi: Islam and the Modern Age Society), vol. 9, no. 2, May, 1978, pp. 5-6.

3. 22:17—"Surely they that believe, and those of Jewry, the Sabeans, the Christians, the Magians (Zoroastrians) and the idolators—God shall distinguish between them on the Day of Resurrection; assuredly God is witness over everything."

Chapter Eighteen

1. See Fazlur Rahman, *Islam.* (Chicago: University of Chicago Press, 1979, 2nd ed.), and, *Major Themes of the Qur'an* (Minneapolis and Chicago: Bibliotheca Islamica, 1980).

2. Al-Qur'an 3:75 "Among the People of the Book are some, if you trust them with a hundredweight of gold, will pay it back; and among them are others who, if you trust them with a single silver coin, will not repay it to you."

3. Al-Qur'an 22:39—"Permission to fight is given to those against whom war is made, because they are wronged. Surely God is able to help them. Those who have been expelled from their homes in defiance of right except that they say, 'Our Lord is God.' Had God not driven back one set of people by means of another there would surely have been pulled down monasteries, churches, synagogues, and mosques wherein God's name is much mentioned."

Appendix 2

1. See Austin Flannery, ed., *Vatican Council II* (Collegeville, MN, 1975).

2. Cf. Acts 17, 26.

3. Cf. Wis 8, 1; Acts 14, 17; Rom 2, 6–7; 1 Tim 2, 4.

4. Cf. Apoc 21, 23f.

5. Cf 2 Cor 5, 18–19.

6. Cf St. Gregory VII, Letter XXI to Anzir (Nacir), King of Mauritania (PL 148, col 450f.)

7. Cf. Gal 3, 7.

8. Cf. Rom 11, 17–24.

9. Cf. Eph 2, 14–16

10. Cf. Lk 19, 44.

11. Cf. Rom 11, 28.

12. Cf. Rom 11, 28–29; cf. Dogmatic Constitution, *Lumen gentium* (Light of Nations), AAS, 55 (1965), p. 20.

13. Cf. Is 66, 23; Ps 65, 4: Rom 11, 11–32.

14. Cf. Jn 19, 6.

15. Cf. Rom 12, 18.

16. Cf. Mt 5, 45.

Appendix 3

1. See: http://www.wcccoe.org/wcc/what/interreligious/strivinge.html.

Appendix 4

1. Muhammad Talibi (Mohamed Talbi), "Islam and Dialogue: Some Reflections on a Current Topic," *Islam and the Modern Age* (New Delhi: Islam and the Modern Age Society), vol. IX, no. 2, May, 1978, pp. 11-12.

Appendix 5

1. *Current Dialogue* (Geneva: World Council of Churches), no. 12, June, 1987, p. 14.

Appendix 6

1. Abridged from *Current Dialogue* (Geneva: World Council of Churches), no. 21, December 1991, pp. 6-8.

Index